"The trunk of the ʻulu, or breadfruit tree, was used to make parts of canoes, surfboards, and huts. The fiber of its inner bark could be used to make kapa, a Hawaiian cloth. The fruit was cooked in an underground oven, and was also made into a type of poi. The white sap of the ʻulu was used as a glue, chewing gum for children, and caulk for canoe seams. The bird catchers would use the glue to catch birds and pluck their feathers to make ceremonial capes and helmets worn by the aliʻi, or chiefs. After plucking the feathers, they would use the oil from the kukui nut to clean the bird's feet and then set it free."

—Kahanu National Tropical Botanical Garden

MAUI TRAILBLAZER
Where to Hike, Snorkel, Paddle, Surf, Drive
first edition
text by Jerry Sprout
photographs, design, production by Janine Sprout

For Thomas Mobius Sagues and Lea Alexandra Butler

ISBN 0-9670072-4-0
Library of Congress Catalog Card Number:2001127203

Diamond Valley Company, Publisher
89 Lower Manzanita Drive
Markleeville, CA 96120
www.trailblazertravelbooks.com
trailblazer@gbis.com

Printed in the United States of America
Copyright © 2002 by Jerry and Janine Sprout

Mahalo Nui:

The Hyde family, Mark, Vicki, Blair and Spencer; Paula Pennington and Jim Dunn; John and Patty Brissenden; John and Suzanne Barr; Gail and Brian Butler; Deanne Hawkins; Brian and Sue Kanegai; Matthew and Amy Sagues; Georgia Sagues; Michael and Cynthia Sagues; Jack and Sandy Lewin; Carol Mallory and Jim Rowley; Rich and Kate Harvey; Greg Hayes and Joan Wright; John Manzolati and Linda Kearney; Ellen Scott and Joe Stroud; Margaret, Mina and Chris, Markleeville Post Office.

Charlene Kauhane, Marsha Wienert, and Marissa, Maui Visitors Bureau; Lucienne de Naie, Maui Tomorrow; Amy Kastens, Reel Maui Film Commission; Dr. Jonathan London; Larry Rodrigues and friends, Baldwin Beach; Dana, Tedeschi Winery; Mike Jones, Matthew Chilcott and the folks at Wilderness Press; Marian Feenstra, Department of Parks and Recreation; Steve Knight, Captains Roger and Andy, Island Marine; Bob Chambers, Dave Castles, and Captain Rae, Maui Dive Shop; Stacey, Wailuku Main Street Association; Buffalo Bill Wittman, Kaupo Store; Diney and the Boys, Kanaha Beach; Lahaina Restoration Foundation; Maui Historical Society; Waveslider from Princeville; Robert at Hotel Lanai; Dexter Tom, Carol Sh'e, Hattie, and Chris, Department of Land and Natural Resources; Becky and others at Haleakala National Park; Sarah from Kai Pali Place; Hannah Bernard and Steve Still, Maui Ocean Center; Jerry and Claire, Hawaiian Islands National Humpback Whale Sanctuary; Melissa Kirkendall, State Historic Preservation Division; Rosalyn Baker, Leanne, Office of Economic Development; Russell Sparks, Division of Aquatic Resources; Brittney Dinson, Anuhea Rodrigues Auld, Debi and Dan Strick, Tim Wertheimer, Bill Price, Tim Switzer.

Proofreaders: Cynthia Sprout, Greg Hayes

Keanae

MAUI TRAILBLAZER is an offering to these islands, to all their plants and animals and living things in the sea, and to all persons who dedicate their lives to fulfilling the promise of Aloha.

Iao Needle

MAUI

Trailblazer

WHERE TO
HIKE, SNORKEL, PADDLE, SURF, DRIVE

JERRY AND JANINE SPROUT

DIAMOND VALLEY COMPANY

MARKLEEVILLE, CALIFORNIA

PUBLISHERS

TABLE OF CONTENTS

Aficionados of Hawaii debate which is the favorite among the islands, a discussion akin to picking the most charming rock star in a universally beloved band. People on this island have an expression meant to cut the friendly rivalry short—*Maui No Ka Oi,* Maui Is The Best.

With some eighty beaches, more than any other island, Maui will make converts of those whose primary quest is for sand, sun, and surf. The entire west coast—from Kapalua, Ka'anapali and Lahaina in the north to Kihei, Wailea and Makena in the south—is a run of beaches and coves, all with usually safe swimming. As an added bonus, offshore are enticing views of the sister islands that make up Maui County—Molokai, Lanai, Molokini, and Kahoolawe.

West Maui beaches (the island is hour-glass shaped, connected by an isthmus) will fulfill most people's fantasy of a Polynesian vacation: Coco palms shading white sand and warm aquamarine waters, while inland loom dark green valleys and ridges 5,000-feet high. This side of Maui is about two-million years old, twice the age of East Maui, giving nature time to add shape and nuance.

The beaches of Kihei and Wailea, sometimes called the Gold Coast, lie at the foot of Haleakala, a 10,000-foot high active volcano that rises into another dimension on East Maui. In the lee of the volcano, this coast is more arid and sunnier, although gardens and parks add greenery to the coastline. South of the resorts, Makena State Park and the Ahihi-Kinau Reserve are natural areas, with beaches and lava peninsulas that serve up pristine snorkeling and coastal hiking.

Having explored these areas, beachcombers will just be beginning. Maui's windward east coast has rain forests, an arid wilderness coast, and more coco palms and white sand beaches—along with red, black, and yellow sand beaches. Add in as well, remote boulder bays, pastoral bluffs, and lava reefs fringed by forests.

Along this windward side is Paia, the world capital of windsurfing, and just south of that is Jaws, where some of the biggest waves draw surfers from all over the world. And if surf's not up here, try Honolua Bay just north of Kapalua, another five-star wave ride. For tamer water sports like snorkeling and scuba, Maui offers dozens of coral reefs, including several Marine Life Conservation Districts. Molokini Island, just offshore, is considered one of the best dive spots in the world.

For all these reasons—the mind reels at the scope—beach lovers may well agree that *Maui No Ka Oi.* But beaches are only part of the

Olowalu Landing

story. Hikers will be drawn to West Maui's tropical mountains and streams, like Iao Valley and Waiheʻe Ridge. The north coast is an undeveloped series of bluffs and bays, made for whale-and-wave watching, or hiking grasslands toward the jungly interior.

The road to Hana zigzags over fifty-plus one-lane bridges, penetrating rain forest that is one of the wettest spots on earth. The highway is a world-class attraction, and driving it sets heads gamboling and eyes popping. The coast is wild, where waves meet cliffs. A new waterfall appears at every turn, punctuated by tropical flora literally too copious to comprehend. Visitors can pause at several arboretum and garden hikes, and take side trips to villages where Old Hawaii lives on.

It's a tall order not to be an anticlimax after such a highway, but Hana has the charm to pull it off. History and pastoral scenery overlay the town, set beside a pleasantly diverse coast that ranges from sculpted lava bluffs, to red-cinder coves, to a white-sand beach at Hamoa.

The pilgrimage to Hana ends down the road, at the Pools of Oheo, which are the lower section of Haleakala National Park. Nature's bathtubs await in a stream, while a trail inland ascends to towering waterfalls in a subtropical forest and bamboo grove.

The upper part of Haleakala National Park bears no resemblance to the lower—or to anywhere else. The crater at the summit, some 19 square miles, draws millions of visitors each year—Maui's main event in an all-star array of attractions. Bike down it, hike within it on miles of trails past cinder cones and mysterious lava caves, or stroll from roadside turnouts to sky-high overlooks. The drive to the top is the steepest in the world, and along Haleakala's slopes are eight biological zones, designated as an International Biosphere Reserve.

Keawakapu Beach

Silversword at Haleakala, Baldwin Beach

All these charms have made readers of national travel magazines tout Maui as the "World's Best Island" for several years running. Visitors can choose from a range of accommodations—rustic beach cottages, wilderness camping, country bed-and-breakfast cottages, beachside condos, and the destination resort strips at Ka'anapali and Wailea. Maui's fine restaurants and art galleries are numerous.

Even considering all these glitzy superlatives, the most surprising aspect of the island is its wealth of cultural sites and archeological ruins. Some are well preserved, like the Haleki'i-Pihana Heiaus State Historical Monument in Kahului and the Pi'ilanihale Heiau near Hana. Others are overgrown and uncharted, like many along the Kaupo coast, Kipahulu, and the interior valleys of West Maui. Here are reminders of the Hawaiian culture and geographical wonders. For many visitors, these intrigues will overshadow the island's allure as a vacation wonderland.

GETTING TO AND AROUND ON MAUI

AIRLINES

Most flights to Kahului Airport in Maui include a stopover and change of terminals in Honolulu. Most international airlines service Honolulu. Some airlines have non-stop flights to Maui: From Los Angeles, check with American, Delta, and United. From San Francisco try United, and from Seattle, give Hawaiian a call. Aloha Airlines flies nonstop to Maui from Oakland and Orange County. Hawaiian has fewer length-of-stay restrictions and the most flights.

Hawaiian and Aloha airlines are the major inter-island carriers. Several small airlines travel to Lanai and Molokai, as do passenger ferries. See *Resource Links* for all telephone numbers.

CAR RENTAL

All the major companies, plus a few local companies, service Maui. Book early and phone around to get the best deals. Some companies, such as Avis, offer mini-leases, if you're planning to stay longer. Numbers are in *Resource Links*.

Most highways and streets have bike lanes, and it's possible to navigate by bicycle as a means of transportation. But most roadways also have traffic, and dedicated bike paths and quiet rural thoroughfares are uncommon. There is no public transportation system, other than hitchhiking. Tour companies and shuttle taxis are widely available. For independent travelers, a car is essential.

WHEN TO COME

High season is when school's out during the summer, and also briefly around Christmas and New Year's. Maui visitation doesn't drop off much during any month. But if you'd like a slack time, early autumn and mid-to-late winter are the best bets. Room occupancy rates vary from 60 to 80 percent.

See *Driving Tours* at the start of each trailhead section for specific road descriptions. Also see *Free Advice & Opinion* for driving conditions and tips.

KAHULUI AIRPORT TO:
Hana 55 mi., 2.5 hr.
Wailuku, 5 mi., 10 min.
Maʻalaea 14 mi., 30 min.
Lahaina 28 mi., 40 min.
Kaʻanapali 32 mi., 50 min.
Kapalua 39 mi., 1 hr.
Kihei, 10 mi., 20 min.
Wailea, 15 mi., 30 min.
Makena, 20 mi., 45 min.

KAʻANAPALI TO:
Lahaina 4 mi., 10 min.
Kihei 25 mi., 50 min.
Haleakala summit 65 mi., 2.5 hr.
Hana 83 mi., 3.5 hr.

KIHEI TO:
Haleakala summit 45 mi., 2 hr.
Hana 62 mi., 3 hr.
Lahaina 25 mi., 50 min.

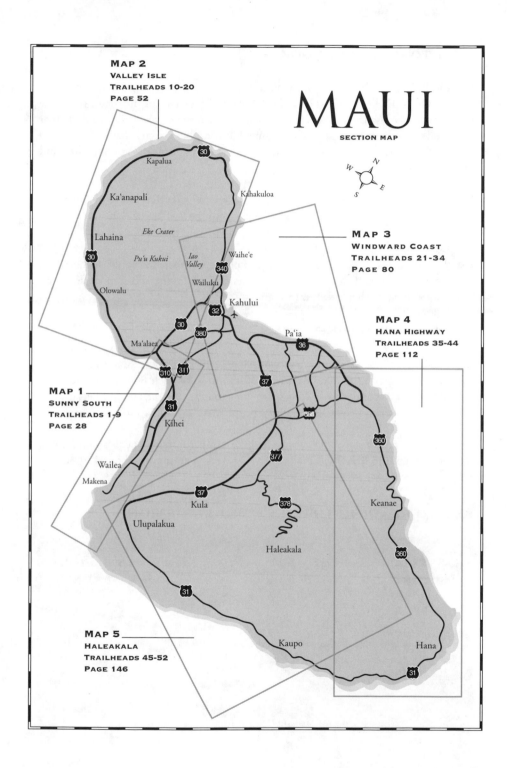

MAP 2
VALLEY ISLE
TRAILHEADS 10-20
PAGE 52

MAUI
SECTION MAP

Kapalua

Ka'anapali

Kahakuloa

MAP 3
WINDWARD COAST
TRAILHEADS 21-34
PAGE 80

Lahaina

Eke Crater

Pu'u Kukui

Iao
Valley

Waihe'e

Wailuku

Olowalu

Kahului

MAP 4
HANA HIGHWAY
TRAILHEADS 35-44
PAGE 112

Ma'alaea

Pa'ia

MAP 1
SUNNY SOUTH
TRAILHEADS 1-9
PAGE 28

Kihei

Wailea

Makena

Kula

Haleakala

Keanae

Ulupalakua

MAP 5
HALEAKALA
TRAILHEADS 45-52
PAGE 146

Kaupo

Hana

HOW TO USE THIS BOOK

Use the INDEX to locate a trail or place that you've already heard about. Use the TABLE OF CONTENTS and MASTER MAP to find a part of the island you'd like to explore. Then use the TRAILHEAD MAP for each region to focus on a particular spot, and go to the descriptions to pick out a hike or other activity that looks good to you. Each trailhead contains hikes of varying lengths, and most have snorkeling and other water sports.

Use the Activities Banner in the TRAILHEAD DIRECTORY to see which recreational opportunities are available and where. Go to the BEST OF section to locate a hike or other activity that suits your interests, mood, and the day.

Use RESOURCE LINKS to find listings and phone numbers for public agencies and organizations, museums and attractions, tours and outfitters, accommodations and restaurants, and all other visitor information.

CALCULATING HIKE TIMES

Hikers in average condition will cover about 2 mph, including stops. Groups and slower-movers will make about 1.5 mph, or less. Well-conditioned hikers can cover 3-to-3.5 mph. Everyone should add about 30 minutes for each 800 feet of elevation gain. Also add 60 minutes to daylong hikes, for a margin of error, and just because this is Maui—trails are not generally easy, and people tend to look around more.

To check your rate of speed: 65 average-length steps per minute, equals about 2 mph; 80 steps per minute, about 2.5 mph; 95 average steps per minute, about 3 mph.

KEY TO READING TRAILHEAD DESCRIPTIONS

> **23. TRAILHEAD NAME**   **ACTIVITIES BANNER**
>
> Best For:
> Parking:
>
> *(SAMPLE)*
>
> **H:**   Hike Destination (distance, elevation)
>   Hike descriptions.
>   *Be Aware:*
>   *More Stuff:*
>   **SN:**   **P:**   **SF:**
>   Snorkeling, Paddling, Surfing descriptions.

"23." Trailhead Number: These correspond to the numbers shown on the five Trailhead Maps, plus the three outer islands. Numbers begin with Map 1, Sunny South, continue to Map 5, Haleakala, and conclude with the three outer islands. In most cases, trailhead numbers that are close together numerically will be close geographically. There are 55 trailheads, listed sequentially in the text of the book. When looking for a particular trailhead, "TH23" for example, you may find it easier to flip through the text rather than look up the page number in the Trailhead Directory.

Trailhead Name: Each trailhead offers one or more of the activities—hiking, snorkeling, paddling, and surfing. Some trailheads have one parking place and a single activity. Other trailheads have several parking places, all close together, and several recreational activities. Some trailheads take a whole day, or more, to explore, while others can be combined with other nearby trailheads to fill out a day of adventuring.

Activities Banner: This shows which of the four recreational activities are available at this trailhead. Activities include one or more of the following, always listed in the same order.

> **H:** Hikes, ranging from long treks to easy strolls.
> **SN:** Snorkeling and swimming, including freshwater pools.
> **P:** Paddling, in kayaks and canoes.
> **SF:** Surfing, with boards, boogie boards, and bodies. Also includes windsurfing.

Best For: A thumbnail description of what to expect when visiting this trailhead.

Parking: Gives specific directions from the nearest highway to the parking spot for the trailhead's primary hike destination, which will be listed first in the descriptions that follow. Secondary parking directions are also given for nearby hikes that follow in order. Additional parking directions are always *noted*, in italics.

H: The first paragraph after the **H:** symbol lists each Hike Destination available at the trailhead, followed by the (distance, and elevation gain) for each hike, in parentheses. Distances are given to the nearest .25-mile. Only elevation gains of 100 feet or greater are noted. All hiking distances in parentheses are ROUND TRIP.

The second paragraph after the **H:** symbol often gives background and history for the trailhead. Following paragraphs give trail descriptions. The first reference to a **Hike Destination** is boldfaced. Trail descriptions include junctions with other trails, the type of terrain and walking surface, as well as elevation changes and landmarks along the way. **Second Destinations** follow in subsequent paragraphs, boldfaced and described in the order they are listed in the first **H:** paragraph.

Be Aware: Notes special precautions and difficulties associated with a hike or other activity. Also read *Free Advice & Opinion* for listings of rules and hazards that apply to adventuring on Maui.

More Stuff: Gives other hikes and activities available at this trailhead that are not among the primary listings. Normally these are out-of-the-way spots, sometimes with difficult access and terrain. Fewer visitors will be at these places. A hike for "trailblazers" means, in general, you're on your own.

SN: P: SF: Descriptions for snorkeling, paddling, and surfing follow, in order, after the hike paragraphs. Descriptions include where to go for these water sports, as well as notations for precautions. Parking directions for these activities will be included in the descriptions—unless they have already been listed in the parking directions or hike descriptions above. For example, parking directions for a snorkel or surf spot will most often be among those already given for a beach walk. **Snorkel** and **Surf** locations are boldfaced. One trailhead may have several locations for each activity.

Wailea Coast

WHAT DO YOU WANT TO DO TODAY?

*Pick out a hike or activity that suits your mood
and the day. Lists are in ascending order of
trailhead numbers.*   TH = trailhead

HIKES
Includes coastal and beaches

RAIN FOREST,
STREAM VALLEYS, WATERFALLS

GARDENS, ARBORETUMS, FOREST

RIDGES WITH A VIEW

SHORT WALKS TO EXQUISITE PLACES

BEACH WALKS, WHERE
THE ACTION IS

BEACH WALK, NATURAL SETTING

SURFING

Ho'okipa

OFFSHORE BREAKS
Olowalu Landing, TH12, page 58
Lahaina Seawall, TH13, page 63
Hana Wharf, TH41, page 129

WHERE THE BIG BOYS GO
Ma'alaea Bay, TH9, page 45
Slaughterhouse, TH16, page 70
Lipoa Point, TH16, page 70
Ho'okipa, TH32, page 101
Jaws, TH33, page 103

TIERS, LEFT AND RIGHT
Ironwoods, TH15, page 69
Windmills, TH16, page 70
Honomanu Bay, TH37, page 120

PLACES TO WATCH SURFERS AND WINDSURFERS
Ma'alaea Breakwater, TH9, page 45
Lahaina Seawall, TH13, page 63
Lipoa Point, TH16, page 70
Kahului Breakwater, TH28, page 94
Kanaha Beach Park, TH29, page 96
Ho'okipa Lookout, TH32, page 101
Hana Wharf, TH41, page 129

WINDSURFING

Mai Poina 'Oe Iau Beach, TH8, page 44
Ma'alaea Beach, TH9, page 45
Kanaha Beach Park, TH29, page 96
Ho'okipa, TH32, page 101

KAYAKING

La Perouse Bay, TH1, page 30
Makena Landing, TH4, page 36
Pu'unoa Beach, TH13, page 63
Kahekili Beach Park, TH14, page 66
Hoaloha Park, TH28, page 94
Maliko Bay, TH33, page 102
Keanae Landing, TH37, page 120
Hana Bay, TH41, page 129

PICNIC SPOTS

OUT OF THE WAY BEACH PARKS
Waipuilani, TH8, page 42
Haycraft, TH9, page 45
Honokowai, TH15, page 68
Koki, TH42, page 130
Kipahulu Point (bluff), TH44, page 134

PRIME LOCATIONS
Kamaole I and II, TH7, page 7
Launiupoko Beach Park, TH12, page 57
Kahekili Beach Park, TH14, page 64
Waihe'e Beach Park, TH24, page 86
Kepaniwai Heritage Gardens,
    TH25, page 87
Kanaha Beach Park, TH29, page 94
Hana Beach Park, TH41, page 126
Rice Park, Kula Driving Tour, page 144

Waikomo Ridge Nature Trail

TRAILHEAD DIRECTORY

H: HIKING
SN: SNORKELING, SWIMMING
P: KAYAKS, CANOES
SF: SURFING, BOOGIE BOARDING, WIND SPORTS

Sundown at Kahekili Beach

Sunny South

Big Beach, Makena State Park

SUNNY SOUTH

You'll need fingers and toes to count all the different beaches along the twenty-plus mile coast from La Perouse Bay to Ma'alaea. Take a survey on this snorkeling safari. Although sun, sand, and surf remain constants, the settings range from the rugged lava wilderness of the King's Trail, to swank destination resorts with poolside gardens, to neighborhood beach parks with lawns and coco palms, and finally to a harbor where the tour boats return and nearby cliffs are perches to watch whales.

DRIVING TOUR
PICKING THE RIGHT DAY

This is called the Sunny South—and also Maui's Gold Coast—for a reason: In the lee of the trade winds and the rain-shadow of Haleakala, the southwest coast has reliable beach-going weather—320 days a year of sunshine. The isthmus, a land bridge between West and East Maui, moderates ocean currents. You may want to save this tour for a day when weather is inclement elsewhere. Beach parks and local's beaches, in the middle section of the tour, will see more action on the weekends. For a quieter time, pick a weekday.

THE ROADS

From Makena State Park to La Perouse, the road is narrow and bumpy in places, but easily navigated. From Makena north, the roads are all good, but traffic can be a problem. By starting in the south in the morning, you will avoid the slow going on Highway 31 that occurs in the afternoons. South Kihei Road, fronted by condos and small malls, has pedestrians and cross traffic. But a slow pace is compatible with sightseeing—you could miss things even going the speed limit.

THE COURSE

Follow along on the Sunny South map, page 28. Refer to trailhead descriptions beginning on page 29 for more details.

EARLY MORNING. BEGIN LA PEROUSE BAY. Kayak tours and snorkelers hit the water early at La Perouse Bay. But the morning is the best time to venture on the sun-baked lava fields for a look at the King's Trail, which is a walk back to ancient times. Then return to the present with a refreshing a dip in the bay, or move up the road a short distance and get in the water at Ahihi Cove.

MID-MORNING. Move north to the main parking area for Makena State Park. A short beach walk leads to the point separating Big Beach from Little Beach. You can also take the scamper up Pu'u Olai for a great view, beginning here, or from the trail at Black Sand Beach. Then get back in the car, and, past the Maui Prince Hotel, head to Makena Landing. Meander the shade and gardens of Keawalai Church, and then take the road north, hugging the coast past Chang's Point, as well as Po'olenalena and Palauea beaches. Locals will be here as soon as it warms up on the weekends.

NOON. North of Palauea Beach, you'll come to the parking for Polo Beach Park. Here is the south end of the Wailea Coast Walk, a promenade past several beaches and opulent resorts. You can opt for an out-and-back on part of this paved path—or a driver can drop off walkers and then drive north around the resorts to pick up the walkers at Keawakapu Beach. For lunch, choose a plate lunch or deli sandwich from among the many choices in Kihei, and hang around the Kamaole Beach Parks. If you want beverages and snacks for sunset, pick them up here also.

Kealia Pond, Kihei, Maluaka Beach

AFTERNOON. Continue north on Kihei Road. On weekends you might find some big doings at Kalama Park, or a race finale at the Kihei Canoe Club. You'll want to stop in at the Humpback Whale National Marine Sanctuary, where you can also visit the ancient fishpond. Birdwatchers can stop off at the Kealia Pond National Wildlife Sanctuary, either by taking a side-trip inland or strolling the boardwalk on the north end near the beach. Save the late afternoon for a visit to the Maui Ocean Center in Ma'alaea Bay.

SUNSET. Head out to the wharf at Ma'alaea Bay and watch the tour boats and fishermen returning from a day at the ocean. You can also go to McGregor Point, on the west end of the bay, or Papawai Point, and watch the sun take a dive from a higher elevation.

Kamaole III, Kings Trail, Wailea

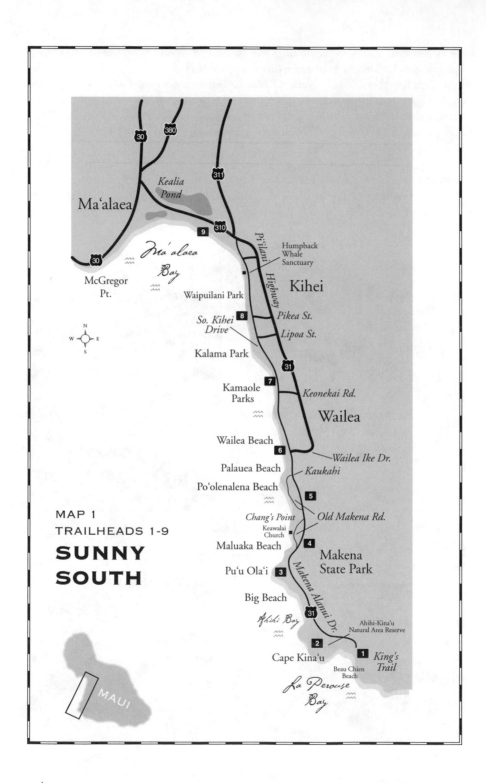

30 **380**

311

Kealia
Pond

Ma'alaea

310

9

Piʻilani

Ma'alaea
Bay

Humpback
Whale
Sanctuary

McGregor
Pt.

30

Waipuilani Park

Kihei

Highway

8

So. Kihei
Drive

Pikea St.

Lipoa St.

N
W   E
S

Kalama Park

31

Kamaole
Parks

7

Keonekai Rd.

Wailea

Wailea Beach

6

Wailea Ike Dr.

Palauea Beach

Kaukahi

Po'olenalena Beach

5

MAP 1
TRAILHEADS 1-9

Chang's Point

Old Makena Rd.

Keawalai
Church

**SUNNY
SOUTH**

Maluaka Beach

4

Makena
State Park

Pu'u Ola'i

3

Big Beach

Makena Alanui Dr.

Ahihi Bay

31

Ahihi-Kina'u
Natural Area Reserve

2

Cape Kina'u

Beau Chien
Beach

1 King's
Trail

La Perouse
Bay

MAUI

SUNNY SOUTH

T R A I L H E A D S

1 - 9

H   HIKING
SN   SNORKELING
P   KAYAKING, CANOEING
SF   SURFING, BOOGIE BOARDING, WIND SPORTS

TH = Trailhead
mm = mile marker; corresponds to highway signs
All hiking distances in parentheses are ROUND TRIP.
Elevation gains of 100 feet or more are noted.

1.   LA PEROUSE BAY   H, SN, P

Best For: The ancient King's Trail that runs through historic ruins and jumbled lava fields to a remote bay. Then return to snorkel or paddle in one of Maui's more pristine locales.

Parking: Take Hwy. 31, the Pi'ilani Hwy., south to Wailea. Continue south on Wailea Alanui for about 8 mi., as route becomes Makena Alanui and then So. Makena Rd. Road narrows. Continue to the end at La Perouse monument. Park on right in unimproved lot at the shore.

H: King's Trail to Kanaio Beach (6.5 mi., 200 ft.); Cape Hanamanioa (3.25 mi.)

The parking area is within Keoneoio Village, a 65-acre historic district. Some of the lava-rock ruins and walls you will see along the hikes date back about 500 years. The bay is named for French Admiral Compte de la Perouse, who thought this a "dismal coast" when he laid anchor in 1786, the first documented landing by Europeans on Maui. Four years after La Perouse's departure, a wave of lava three-miles wide, some 40-million cubic yards, swept down from above—the most recent flow of Maui's million years of volcanic activity. New charcoal dating by volcanologists suggest this eruption may have occurred 300 years earlier—and La Perouse simply had not included the flow on his map. Captain George Vancouver mapped Cape Kinau in 1793, leading historians to believe the flow had take place between the two visits.

For the **King's Trail to Kanaio Beach** hike, head south on the road that continues straight at the right turn to the parking lot. You'll come to shaded camping spots along the bay shore, and then reach an open area with a small sandy shore, called Beau Chien

(Pretty Dog) Beach. Here, about .5-mile from the parking, go left, departing the shore road. You'll see an opening in the wire fence. Turn right on the wide, lava-stone trail. You'll soon come to a large trailhead sign, noting the Hoapili Trail—named for Maui's governor in the early 1800s who improved the roads built by King Pi'ilani and his son, Kiha, in the early 1500s. It's also called the King's Highway, the alaloa, literally "long road" that encircled Maui—metaphorically, the path of life that we all travel from birth to death.

Much of the road has deteriorated or been destroyed, but on this intact segment you can relive the experience of walking as in times gone by. The 8-foot-wide paved trail leads gradually upward for a mile from the trailhead sign, until reaching a rise from which you can see southward toward Hana. You then descend for almost a mile before reaching the welcome shade of kiawe trees at Kanaio Beach. White sand and coral among the black rocks will interest beachcombers. Water entry is rough, and swimming here is most often not advisable. *More Stuff:* The King's (Hoapili) Trail continues for another 10 miles across no-man's-land, although the footing is rougher and trail less defined after Kanaio Beach. See Manwainui, TH49, for access from other side.

To reach **Cape Hanamanioa**, the light beacon at the southern end of La Perouse Bay, follow the trail at water's edge to Beau Chien Beach. You'll pass through the shaded campsites and keep right on the road closest to the water—passing two short connector trails that lead to the King's Trail. Follow the rough road to your right as it climbs briefly onto the cape. You'll get views of the bay and also inland toward the lava flow. The beacon is at the tip of the cape.

Be Aware: Once you see the King's Trail, you're going to want to continue. Sturdy shoes and hiking poles are recommended for both hikes. Don't leave the car without plenty of water, sun block, and a hat.

SN: The **north side of the La Perouse Bay** is one of Maui's four marine preserves. From the parking area, head to your right, passing the haggard, barbed-wire fence. You'll find a few smooth spots to sit down, but this rocky area is tough for tenderfoots. Booties will help. Swim across the sandy-bottomed bay, and then out the lava fingers of Cape Kinau, which forms the northern border of the bay. More adventurous snorkelers can try the **Beau Chien Beach**. Follow the directions for the Cape Hanamanioa hike, but veer out to the lava-and-sand beach with kiawe trees at the shore, instead of taking the road up to the cape.

P: Tour groups put in at the La Perouse parking area. Wave action can make entry tricky, but not dangerous. Paddle out and head north, up the lava coast of the Ahihi-Kinau Natural Reserve. This coastline features excellent snorkeling and is difficult to reach on foot, consisting of sharp piles of lava.

Beau Chien Beach, Halua Pond

2. AHIHI-KINAU NATURAL AREA RESERVE   H, SN, P

Best For: Several excellent snorkeling pools, and a hike across the lava to sacred fishponds and a hidden beach.

Parking: Take Hwy. 31, the Pi'ilani Hwy., south to Wailea. Continue south on Wailea Alanui for about 4 mi., as route becomes Makena Alanui and then So. Makena Rd. The Ahihi-Kinau boundary is about .75-mi. past last entry to Makena State Park, after the road narrows.

H: Halua Pond (1.5 mi.)

Halua Pond sits close to the sea, one of several brackish ponds in the lava fields where ancient Hawaiians raised large mullet from the small fry caught in sea ponds. To get to the trailhead, drive across the barren lava of Cape Kinau—about 1.5 miles from the reserve boundary—to where the road dips into a grove of trees. A large Ahihi-Kinau sign is on the right; several roadside parking spots are on your left. This interesting hike is the easiest footing across terrain that would stop a rhinoceros—Maui's most recent lava flow.

From the parking spot, take the trail along the fence line, under the shade of kiawe trees. After a few hundred feet you break into the open on a sandy trail. Keep right, following the direction of the fence, avoiding options that lead left toward La Perouse Bay. Keep spotting the meandering trail ahead over broken tabletops of lava. You'll come to the first pond, Kauhioaiakini, with greenery at its banks. (Some of the green ery is the rare Makaloa sedge, coveted by ancient chiefs for the supple weavings it can make.) Go right—avoiding another left-bearing option—keeping the pond on your left. You'll reach a black-cinder trail above the pond that continues due west toward the ocean. Halua Pond will be visible from the low ridge. Stay to the left of the Pond and make your way down to the small bay that lies just beyond. This bay is marked by a good-sized kiawe tree, casting precious shade upon a rare patch of sand to plant the fanny.

Be Aware: Spur trails lead to nowhere on Cape Kinau, as lost souls go out and back, trying to find hospitable passage. Hikers are like ants on heaps of broken glass. Wear sturdy shoes, bring lots of water, and avoid cross-country jaunts. Gloves are helpful to avoid nicking fingers when grabbing rocks for balance.

More Stuff: About .5-mile from the reserve boundary, just beyond where the road comes close to houses and the shore of Ahihi Cove, you'll see a large trailhead parking on your right. A well-used trail leads from a sign to the rocky bay, .25-mile distant. Tide-pool lovers can follow a ragged trail along the coast to Kalaemamane Point, the south boundary of Ahihi Bay. Additionally, as you drive the 1.5 miles across Cape Kinau, you will see a number of turnouts. Hidden lava tubes are the reward for trailblazers willing to venture into the jagged lands.

SN: **Ahihi Cove** offers excellent snorkeling with easy access. After entering the reserve, park at the small inlet that is very close to the road. You'll see a few parking spots to the right just before the cove, and a few just after. The best entry is on the north side of the cove, via a smooth submerged rock. Swim out to the point on your right, and then double back. You can also snorkel the **southern boundary of Ahihi Bay** by taking the trailhead described above in *More Stuff.*

Another excellent snorkeling area involves a pesky, 1.5-mile round-trip hike. For **Kalaeloa Point cove**, also known as the **Aquarium**, follow the directions to the Halua Pond trailhead above. From trailhead parking, follow the fence line through the grove of kiawe trees. After leaving the trees take a left-bearing trail, which leads toward La Perouse Bay. As you descend to the bay, avoid spur trails that go to the water and select options that lead toward the point that is the northern boundary of the bay. As you reach the point, veer to your right to the cove, which is directly to the north of the point. Near the end, on treacherous lava, you'll see several options, as everyone gets semi-lost during the last part. Once at the cove, select from several entry points, all of which are from sharp lava perches. Low surf and clean lava make for great visibility, and the fish are bountiful. You may have company at this popular spot, in spite of the hassle getting here.

P: Put in from roadside parking areas, just after the first sign marking the natural area reserve. Paddlers go south from here, exploring the pocketed lava shores of Cape Kinau. You'll find snorkeling spots not accessible by foot.

3. MAKENA STATE PARK

H, SN, P, SF

Best For: Three beautiful beaches that offer surf strolls, wave skipping, sunning, and snorkeling. And a short hike to a Maui landmark ends with a knock-out view of geographical significance.

Parking: Take Hwy. 31, the Pi'ilani Hwy., south to Wailea. Continue south on Wailea Alanui, which becomes Makena Alanui. Pass the entrance to Maui Prince Hotel and a jct. with a spur of Makena Rd. *Note:* Three access points: *Oneuli Beach,* or Black Sand Beach, is .25-mi. past Makena Rd. jct.; look for pipe gate and dirt road. *Big Beach* has two parking lots; the first is .5-mi. past the Makena Rd. jct., and the second parking lot is .25-mi. beyond the first.

H: **Pu'u Olai (1 mi., 350 ft.); Big and Little Beach (up to 1.5 mi.)**

Known variously as Hill of Earthquakes, Round Mountain, and Red Hill, **Pu'u Olai** is the volcanic hillock that is prominent from many viewpoints on the west side of Maui. To get the classic view from its summit, turn toward Oneuli Beach, the first access described above. A rutted, .25-mile dirt road leads to an unimproved lot. From the lot you can head up a steep, red-cinder trail near the beach; or backtrack a short distance from the beach and head up through the trees, near a signpost that holds multiple messages. Either way, after a short burst upward, you'll reach a trail that heads directly to the top of the north side of the pu'u. Once there you'll see that the top is a crater, overgrown with greenery. Head to your left along the rim. Once at the south side of the crater, the trail circumnavigates the rim, and you'll wind up making a loop.

According to local lore, Pu'u Olai was near the epicenter of an earthquake in the last century. A fishing shrine, or heiau, once adorned its summit. On a clear day you'll see Mauna Loa and Mauna Kea on the Big Island to the south, as well as Maui's outer islands. *Notes:* Makena was made a state park, rather than resort development, due to the efforts in the 1980s of Jack Lewin, Rick Sands and others. Efforts to preserve this coast continue.

Skimboarding along the Makena Coast

For the **Big and Little Beach** stroll, turn in at the first Big Beach access described above. A short path leads through trees from the lot to the northern end of the beach. *Note:* This parking lot tends to fill up first; if arriving late on a weekend, try the second lot, or continue past the second lot and use roadside parking where the road narrows. From the first lot access, the wide sand beach extends about .5-mile to the left, or south. Big Beach is officially called Oneloa Beach, and is also known as Makena Beach. To walk to Little Beach, head to your right along a path that skirts the sand, toward the point that marks the north end of Big Beach. You'll reach a short sand-and-rock connector trail that takes you up and over to Little Beach. You'll also want to walk out through trees to the point, a lava terrace with sunset views and tide pools. Also, to your right as you reach the terrace between the beaches, you'll see a trail heading steeply inland, leading to the top of Pu'u Olai. *Be Aware:* Although nudity is unlawful and not part of Hawaiian culture, Little Beach has become known as a clothing optional beach.

SN: The south end of **Oneuli Beach**, or **Black Sand Beach**—see first access parking—attracts snorkeling and scuba tours. Swim out along the base of Pu'u Olai. Lack of freshwater runoff creates clear waters here when the surf is low. You can also walk north along the black sand to **Maluaka Point**, which separates this beach from Maluaka Beach to the north; see TH4. The reef has good snorkeling, with occasional turtle sightings, although wave action and rocky entry makes this area less than ideal.

P: Pass all the entrances to Makena State Park. As the road narrows, look for a Shoreline Access opening in an eight-foot lava wall. A short path leads to a lava cove with entry for paddlers wishing to explore both Ahihi Bay to the south and Makena Landing to the north.

SF: Bodysurfers are drawn to **Little Beach**, although the shore break can sometimes be hazardous. While at Little Beach, keep a lookout for spinner dolphin, who like to play offshore of Pu'u Olai. Surfers and boogie boarders like the south end of **Big Beach**, particularly in the summer when the Kona surf is up. Pass all park entrances, and park along the road for the easiest board access.

Makena Landing

4.   MAKENA LANDING

Best For: Snorkeling, beachcombing, and historical sites which combine for a full day at this less visited coastline.

Parking: Hwy. 31, the Pi'ilani Hwy., south to Wailea. Continue south on Wailea Alanui, about 2 mi. Road becomes Makena Alanui past Kaukahi St. Pass first Makena Rd. and turn right on second Makena Rd.

H: **Chang's Point (.25-mi); Maluaka Beach loop (up to 1.25 mi.)**

For the short **Chang's Point** hike, continue on Makena Road for less than .5-mile amid high-end homes, and look for a Shoreline Access on right, just before ascending a hill. Walk out a low lava wall and look for graves to your left—remnants from the 1800s when Chinese emigrants had a settlement on this coast below their larger villages in Kula. This point is also called Five Graves—though they are not all together. Continue out to water's edge and make your way a short distance to the end—its formal name is Nahuna Point.

For the **Maluaka Beach loop**, continue over the hill from the Chang's Point access, and pass Makena Landing County Park and Honoiki Street. Park at lot with rest rooms on left, across from Keawalai Church. Start by exploring the pleasant gardens and Hawaiiana around the church, built in 1832 using coral rocks. Then continue walking a short distance down the road, to near its end, where a parking turnout provides access to the beach. Walk the tree-fringed swath of sand, which is sometimes confusingly called Makena Beach Park. At the end of the beach, you can skirt the golf course to Maluaka Point, with its view of Pu'u Olai. Then backtrack, cutting inland at the south end of the beach toward the Maui Prince Hotel. A paved path runs through gardens, between the hotel and the beach, leading back to Makena Road and your parking spot. *More Stuff:* You can also access Maluaka Beach, and the south end of the paved path, by driving past the Maui Prince entrance on Makena Alanui and making a hairpin right on Makena Road. This short spur of the old road leads to a big parking lot, less frequented by beach goers.

SN: **Five Graves**, also known as **Turtle Town** and **Five Caves**, is a popular spot among snorkeling tour boats. You can swim here from the shore using two access points: The easiest entry is at Makena Landing County Park, just over the hill from Chang's Point, as described above. From 1850 to the early 1900s, Makena was Maui's busiest port, used to ship sugar and also to send cattle to a large ranch on Kahoolawe. Today, it's a popular dive spot. Swim from the sandy landing entry to your right, a few hundred yards, out to the point. After the swim, you'll find a small sunning beach just around the shore from the county park. The five caves, accessible only by experienced scuba divers, are underwater off the north side of the point.

You can also explore Turtle Town/Five Caves from Chang's Point, as per the hike description above. Look for a small lava cove set in from the point. You'll have to do less swimming from this entry. Sea turtles commonly swim just off the point. *Be Aware:* Surf and rocks can make entry at Chang's Point tricky. Also, if swimming a distance off the point, watch out for boat traffic. Some snorkelers swim attached to a boogie board or a floatation buoy to better mark their presence.

P: Makena Landing is an easy place to put in, provided you get there early enough to find parking at this popular dive spot. From the entry, make your way south, along small Makena and Keawalai bays, and on toward Pu'u Olai. Around the point from the pu'u—where you might be joined by dolphins—is Ahihi Bay, and Big Beach.

SF: **Maluaka Beach** has a good bodysurfing break during summer swells.

5. PO'OLENALENA BEACHES   H, SN, SF

Best For: Weekdays with solitude at these local's beaches, made for strolling, surfing, snorkeling, or just hanging out.

Parking: Take Hwy. 31, the Pi'ilani Hwy., south to Wailea. Continue south on Wailea Alanui. After 1 mi., turn right on Kaukahi St., just past the Fairmont Kea Lani Hotel. At the bottom of the hill, turn left on Makena Rd. Three access points: To *Palauea Beach,* continue .25-mi. to unimproved parking amid shade trees and across from new homes. To *Po'olenalena Beach,* continue on Makena Rd. another .5-mi. until it loops back out to Makena Alanui. Turn right and then turn right immediately on short access road to unimproved parking lot. To *Chang's Cove,* stay on Wailea Alanui, which becomes Makena Alanui past Kaukahi St. Pass the first Makena Rd. jct. Just before second Makena Rd. jct., turn right at Shoreline Access sign into Makena Surf condos into improved lot with 10 or 12 spaces.

H: **Palauea to Po'olenalena Beach walk (up to 2.25 mi.)**

Off the main road—between the Wailea resorts on the north and the Makena beaches on the south—this mile-long run of sandy beaches interrupted by lava points is a longtime local's favorite. New homes have put the Po'olenalena Beaches on the map, but not to the point of detracting from their serene nature. Shade trees, swaths of sand and safe swimming—along with views of Molokini and Kahoolawe—fill the bill for a day at the beach.

For the **Palauea to Po'olenalena Beach walk,** make your way to the beach through the large kiawe trees and head left, or south. You'll soon run out of sand and have to

North from Pu'u Olai, Turtle Town resident

climb up and around the low-lying Haloa Point. Look for a fishing shrine, or heiau, on the point. In ancient times, this coast sported saltwater ponds and was a fruitful net-fishing area. You drop down from Haloa Point and reach the north end of Po'olenalena Beach. After crossing the first stretch of sand, you top a small point and reach the south portion of the beach, which runs for nearly .5-mile before hitting the rugged point on which the Makena Surf condos are situated. *More Stuff:* For a shorter walk that avoids rock hopping, follow the directions in the parking section above to Po'olenalena. The beach runs mainly to the south from this access but—hot tip—you can also go right, or north, over a low point to reach the "hidden" portion of the beach.

SN: **Haloa Point**, which is at the south end of Palauea Beach, has a reef offshore, but it's known more as a scuba zone. Although local residents frequent **Chang's Cove**, you may find this to be an ideal little snorkeling stop on weekdays. From the lot described in parking directions above, walk the improved path down through buildings and steps to the small sandy cove. Surf can be an issue here, but on calm days you'll have plenty of fish habitat in which to float.

SF: **Po'olenalena** and **Palauea** draw wave riders in the summer. Board and bodysurfers gather, along with the occasional windsurfer.

6.   WAILEA RESORTS COAST   H, SN, SF

Best For: A paved path that runs along five beaches and through the gardens of as many luxury resorts.

Parking: Take Hwy. 31, the Piʻilani Hwy., south to Wailea. Continue to the end, turn right on Wailea Ike Dr., and then left on Wailea Alanui. After about 1 mi., turn right on Kaukahi St. and follow signs to Polo Beach, Shoreline Access. *Note:* These directions begin at the south end of the beaches; direct access to all five beaches is given below in snorkeling descriptions.

H: Wailea Coast Walk (up to 4 mi.)

The five beaches of the Wailea are all curves of golden sand, ranging from about .25-mile to .5-mile in length, separated by low lava fingers, and flanked inland by the lawns, gardens, and poolside paraphernalia of destination resorts. Offshore, Kahoolawe is the island view, although West Maui, to the north, appears to be the separate island it once was. Picking your favorite among the beaches is like trying to select the cutest among quintuplets. Why bother? You can snorkel and stride your way along the beachfront, and then duck in to check out the galleries, restaurants, and decor of the of the resorts.

Begin the **Wailea Coast Walk** on the lawn and picnic area of Polo Beach Park and head to your right on the paved path. Polo Beach now welcomes the guests of the Fairmont Kea Lani, although the names of hotels shift with the sands of time. After Polo, the path rounds Wailea Point, a lava shelf with a viewing area amid a native Hawaiian plants garden. Then you'll cross a bridge and come to Wailea Beach, which is shared by the Four Seasons and Grand Wailea resorts. After Wailea Beach, the path crosses the lawns above the lava at the Wailea Outrigger—again, the names may vary, but the waves shall remain the same—and then drops alongside sweet Ulua Beach. The path peters out as you reach the next beach north, Mokapu Beach, which fronts the Renaissance Wailea Beach Resort. Mokapu Beach blends with Keawakapu Beach. This is the longest run of sand on the walk and the segue from Wailea to Kihei. Keawakapu (the "w" is pronounced as a "v") fronts private homes rather than resorts.

SN: **For all the Wailea beaches, snorkeling waters are normally clearer in the morning hours, before afternoon wave action creates turbidity. However, this is not a hard-and-fast rule, and note that sunshine doesn't fully hit some of the beaches until later in the day. **Polo Beach, reached via the parking directions above, has two entry points: At the left, or south, end of the beach near the beach club, which is a shorter swim; and to the right, or north, at Wailea Point, where you need to swim out a little farther but are rewarded with more colorful coral. At **Wailea Beach**, you want to go to the left, or south, to Wailea Point and flipper out around the lava. Some of the best coral on this coast awaits. To Wailea Beach direct access, head south on Wailea Alanui, as per parking instructions. Pass the entrances to the Grand Wailea Resort and look for a Wailea Beach sign on your right; drive down a short distance to a large parking lot.

Another good snorkeling spot is the lava point at north end of **Ulua Beach**, which is also the south end of **Mokapu Beach**. For direct access to these beaches, turn north, or right, on Wailea Alanui from Wailea Ike Drive. Look for an access sign and road on your left, across from Hale Ali'i Place; the access is just south of the Renaissance Wailea Resort. Ulua Beach will be just left from the beach facilities, and Mokapu is just to the right. The point is a good spot for novice snorkelers. Although snorkeling is not as good at **Keawakapu Beach**, you may wish to access it directly to take the coast walk beginning at the north, or to access Mokapu and Ulua beaches from the north. Keawakapu, with its long run of resort-free sand, gentle surf, and offshore views, is also a prime choice for hanging out. To get there, turn right on Wailea Alanui from Wailea Ike Drive and then go left on Okolani Drive. Go left again at South Kihei Road, and follow it a short distance to parking at the end. To access the north end of Keawakapu, go right when you get to South Kihei Road and look for Shoreline Access lot near Sarento's, at 2980 South Kihei Road.

SF: Bodysurfers and boogie boarders head to **Polo Beach** and **Ulua Beach** to catch the shore break. Afternoons are the best bet, and surf is usually bigger in the summer. During the summer, **Wailea Beach** is the site for the windsurfer race to Molokai, a spectacle you'll want to behold.

Wailea Coast Walk

7. KAMAOLE BEACH PARKS   H, SN, P, SF

Best For: Four beach parks with excellent swimming, spacious lawns, and shaded picnic spot—Maui's best family beach scene.

Parking: *North-end access:* Take Hwy. 31, the Pi'ilani Hwy., south toward Kihei and Wailea. About 2.5 mi. south of jct. with Hwy 311, turn right on Lipoa St. Continue to South Kihei Rd. Turn left, continue for 2.5 mi., and veer right on Ili'ili Rd. Go to end and park at the corner of Ili'ili and Kaiau Pl. *South-end access:* Take Hwy. 31 about 5 mi. south of the jct. with Hwy 311. Turn right on Keonekai Rd. Continue and turn left at South Kihei Rd. Park at lot for Kamaole III Beach Park.

Note: Hiking description starts at north access. To access the beach parks, you could continue down South Kihei Rd. and park anywhere you see fit. The Kihei Boat Ramp, .25-mi. south of Kam III, is a sure thing on busy weekends premium.

H: **Kamaole Beach Walk (up to 2.75 mi.)**

These pleasant beach parks are across a busy street from oodles of mid-range hotel and condo resorts, local-style eateries, souvenir and sundries stores, kayak rentals, and dive shops. Kihei is abuzz with the sandy-footed and sunburned, playing hard and living the good life on their Maui vacation. On weekends, local families join the fray. While not quaint, Kihei exemplifies fun-in-the-sun Maui. Each beach has lifeguards on duty until late afternoon. At sunset, bring a picnic dinner and beverage to Kamaole III and thank yourself for having the good sense to be in Hawaii.

The **Kamaole Beach Walk** begins at tiny Charley Young Beach Park, set on a palmy terrace that affords a postcard look south toward Kamaole I. Head down to the sand and walk to your left. After less than .5-mile, you'll run out of beach and need to cross the broad grassy bench in front of a large hotel. Then descend again to the sands of Kamaole II. Stroll the palm-fringed shores before ascending once again, to the rocky point that is the north boundary of Kamaole III. The grassy bluff at the south end of Kam III, beyond the shaded tables of its main picnic area, is a good place to relax out of the sand. Above the lawn to the south is the parking area for the Kihei Boat Ramp, where you can check out the small and mid-sized vessels heading out for whale watching, fishing, and snorkeling jaunts. On your return leg, you can walk the beaches again, or saunter along the trees and lawns that flank them.

SN: The best snorkeling is off the rocky point that separates **Kamaole II** from **Kamaole III**. Park at Kam III. Begin either at the north end of the sand at Kam III and snorkel toward the point, or start at the south end of Kam II and stroke out the same point. At Kamaole III, you can also snorkel closer to the shore on the south end of the beach—heading toward the bluff at the Kihei Boat Ramp.

Kamaole Beach Walk

At **Kamaole I**, dip your mask on the south end of the sand, out and around the lava rocks in front of the Royal Mauian Hotel. Of course, you can also access this area from the north end of Kam II. Unless the surf is up, which is rare, the waters along the beach parks are safe for beginning snorkelers.

P: The Kihei Boat Ramp sees its share of commercial activity, mostly in the morning, but kayakers can put in here without fear of being swamped by large vessels. Parking will be easy and the entry is protected. Heading south, past Wailea to Makena, is the wilder and more popular paddle.

SF: Body surfers and boogie borders ride the shore break, mostly during summer, at all three **Kamaole beaches**, but this shore is not known for wave sports.

8.   NORTH KIHEI   H, P, SF

Best For: Beach parks and historic sites often missed by visitors to this section of the sunny coast. And for whale watchers, this trailhead is a must.

Parking: Take either the Hwy. 31., the Pi'ilani Hwy., or Hwy. 311, Mokulele Hwy., south toward Kihei. At traffic signal where these highways join, take South Kihei Road. *Note:* Further directions, starting north and proceeding south, are given below.

H: Vancouver Monument to Sugar Beach (2 mi.); Hawaiian Islands Humpback Whale Sanctuary (.25-mi.); Waipuilani Park (.75-mi.); Cove Park to Kalama Park (.75-mi.)

The 4-mile coastline of north Kihei—featuring narrow sand strips, shallow waters, and rocky embankments—was in ancient times home to many of Maui's saltwater fishponds. Today, this quieter coast is mostly a State Beach Reserve, much of it set off from main roads and unvisited by tourists.

For the **Vancouver Monument to Sugar Beach** walk, park at Mai Poina 'Oe Iau Beach Park, which is about 1 mile south of the junction with Highway 311. The modest monument is less than .5-mile down the beach, walking to your left as you face the water. Look for a patch of coco palms, within which you will find a totem pole erected in 1968 to commemorate Captain George Vancouver. The famed British explorer visited in 1793 and is credited with fostering peace among the warring Hawaiians. From the monument, double back northward, to walk the fine sands of Sugar Beach. Less than .5-mile north of the beach park, you'll pass the remnants of Kihei Wharf, where Henry Baldwin's men shipped sugar in the late 1800s, and today paddlers of the Kihei Canoe Club put in. North of here is the long sweep of Ma'alaea Bay.

The **Hawaiian Islands Humpback Whale National Marine Sanctuary** is at 726 South Kihei Road, about 2 miles south of the Highway 311 junction. The center is a living classroom, where interpretive displays and knowledgeable docents teach the history and ecology of the seagoing mammals. Nearby, on the water is the center's administrative office, set in a historic building with a whale-watching deck. And next door is small Kalepolepo Beach Park, home to the ancient Koieie Loko Ia Fishpond. Today, the nonprofit Association of Fishponds in Maui is restoring the large semicircle of lava stone at the shore, which, centuries ago, were handed down in a human chain of workers from the uplands miles away. *Note:* The pond at the beach park is a safe place for the keikis to take a dip.

Waipuilani Park, for some reason, is absent from most maps. To get there, turn right on Waipuilani Road, about a mile south of Kalepolepo Beach Park, and drive a short distance to the end. The park offers a wide expanse of lawn spreading to the north toward low-key resorts. This strip of sand with shallow waters is the most peaceful beach walk in Kihei. Ancient fishpond ruins are offshore. *More Stuff:* Duck into Kawililipoa Beach by turning right on Lipoa Street, just south of the Post Office. You're sure to find solitude.

For the stroll from **Cove Park to Kalama Park**, continue on South Kihei Road, about 2 miles south of the humpback sanctuary. Turn right into Kalama Park, just past Waimahaihai Street. On weekends, the grassy expanses of the park are often the site of community festivities. The north end of the park, near the library, features the Koai Kamaole Fishing Shrine. Continue southward, curving out to a roadway bridge, across which is cozy Cove Park, a safe swimming and surfing spot. *Note:* Cove Park is where quiet Ili'ili Road veers off the main road, leading to Charley Young Beach, TH7.

P: The Kihei Canoe Club puts in at the north end of South Kihei Road, as described in the first hike above. You can also park at Mai Poina 'Oe Iau Beach Park. Cove Park—see directions in above paragraph—sometimes called Canoe Beach, is also home to a paddling club. Launch at the quiet landing to stroke either north or south.

SF: **Cove Park**, with a modest break at the mouth of the cove, is a popular place for beginning board surfers. Just north, at **Kalama Park**, boarders ride the 4- to 9-foot summer swells, breaking both left and right. Body and board surfing is fairly good at

Kalepolepo Beach Park, Vancouver Monument, Humpback Whale National Marine Sanctuary, Ma'alaea Bay

Mai Poina 'Oe Iau Beach Park, but the real action there is for windsurfers in the summer when the Kona surf arrives. The sail surfers are also here in winter months, though in fewer numbers, when the trade winds whip across the isthmus.

9.   MA'ALAEA BAY   H, P, SF

> **Best For:** Birdwatchers, exercise walkers, and joggers, who can roam free at Maui's longest beach and largest wildlife ponds.
>
> **Parking:**   Take Hwy. 31, which is North Kihei Rd., north from Kihei; or take Hwy. 31 south from its jct. with Hwy. 30, the Honoapi'ilani Hwy. Park at the ocean-side turnout that is west of Kealia Pond, just west of mm2. *Note:* Additional directions to the wildlife refuge and to Ma'alaea Harbor are given below in hiking descriptions.

H: Ma'alaea Beach Walk (up to 5.5 mi.); Wetlands Boardwalk (1.25 mi.); Kealia Pond Wildlife Refuge (.75-mi); Ma'alaea Harbor (about .75-mi.)

After crossing the dunes at the parking area, you will be about in the middle of **Ma'alaea Beach**. To your left is a 1.5-mile run of sand, near the highway, that gets you to Sugar Beach; see TH8. Headed to your right, you can look forward to 1.75 miles of open sand, with coastal wetlands and a large cane field as an inland buffer. The beach ends at Haycraft Park, near the harbor; see Ma'alaea Harbor description below. The packed sand at the shoreline provides a high-speed surface for runners and fast-walkers. You cross the outflow stream for Kealia Pond shortly into the walk. At night, from July through December, beach goers include hawksbill turtles, who come ashore to lay eggs at the high-tide line; watch out for the egg pits in the sand of these endangered reptiles. In the late 1700s, King Kalaniopu'u of the Big Island used these shores to invade Maui, and 800 of his elite warriors were annihilated in the Battle of the Sand Hills. In 1944 the U.S. Marines came ashore here in preparation for the taking of Iwo Jima. *Be Aware:* Wind often rips across the isthmus at midday. Try the beach walk at sunrise or sunset.

For **Wetlands Boardwalk**, veer right from the parking area, staying on the landside of the dune. Coastal mudflats and a good-sized pond provide a gathering place for both shorebirds and waterfowl. Among the dozens of species to be seen here are Hawaiian ducks and stilts. Golden plovers, ruddy turnstones, and wandering tattlers—migrating here from more than 2,000 miles away in Alaska and Canada—will be among the shorebirds.

The **Kealia Pond National Wildlife Refuge** is not accessible from Highway 31. To get there, take Highway 311, the Mokulele Highway, north from Highway 31 in upper Kihei. At mm6—be alert—turn left at a gate marked by a U.S. Fish and Wildlife sign. About .5-mile in are the offices for the refuge, located on the inland shore of the pond. Levees between rectangular fishponds provide raised trails that lead onto the water. In the 1600s, villagers dug a channel through the dunes, creating a pond for shore-dwelling fish. Kealia Pond was also the island's salt source. A century or two from now, erosion from Haleakala will fill the pond, unless, of course, the polar ice caps have melted and West and East Maui once again are two islands. *Be Aware:* Visitors should check in at the office to find out which areas are open.

To visit **Ma'alaea Harbor**, take Highway 30 west from its junction with Highway 31. After about a mile, veer left at signs for Ma'alaea Village. Your first stop should be the Maui Ocean Center, featuring the largest tropical aquarium in North America. Whale life, ocean ecology, and Hawaiian culture exhibits are evocative as well as educational. The aquarium's sea tunnel makes you feel like you're snorkeling without getting wet, and the shark tank makes you glad you're not. Sea turtles and a living reef highlight outdoor exhibits. *Note:* An admission is charged.

Next door to the center is the Pacific Whale Foundation, where visitors are welcome. And below the complex is the harbor and old village store. Sailors, whale-watchers, and sport fishing vessels depart this active harbor. Check out the nautical comings and goings from the west breakwater. To reach Haycraft Beach Park, drive inland, away from the harbor, on Hauoli Street. Pass all the condos to the end, at the Ma'alaea Community Garden. Haycraft, a less-used starting point for beach walkers, has a shower, tables, and a pretty beach with a view toward the south coast, Molokini, and Kahoolawe. This park is not on many maps.

P: Before roads to Lahaina were constructed—the most recent was in the 1950s—the waters from Ma'alaea north, around McGregor Point, were an active paddling zone. Though commercial traffic is considerable, the high cliffs around the point to Coral Gardens—see TH11—are a good choice for experienced kayakers. *Be Aware:* Afternoon trade winds and high seas make this coast chancy at times. Inquire locally.

SF: During the summer, **Ma'alaea Bay** brings the board heads running. There are three spots: **Mud Flats**, offshore in the middle of the bay, is a right-breaking 3- to 10-foot swell; watch out for the reef at low tide. **Breakwater**, accessible from the harbor, features a larger right break with long rides. The breakwater is a good place to view surfers under the right conditions. You can also access this surf spot via a paved access at the Lauloa Ma'alaea condos. The third spot, **Kapoli Beach Park**, is tough to find: Head toward Lahaina from Ma'alaea Harbor, pass Ma'alaea Bay Place, and look for an unsigned left turn, leading down a rugged road. Sometimes called Little Cape St. Francis, this spot offers long right-breaking tubes in the summer.

Windsurfers, usually in the summer, can be seen offshore of **Haycraft Beach Park**, reachable using the hike description above for Ma'alaea Harbor. You'll also see windsurfers taking off from the middle of Ma'alaea Beach, and from points eastward across from Kealia Pond.

Valley Isle

Ukumehame Valley

VALLEY ISLE

West Maui is almost two million years old, twice the age of Haleakala, but the years have been kind. Nature—rain, wind, waves, erosion—has cleaved 3,000-foot deep valleys into the old volcano and adorned them with tropical greenery. From the west side, you view these classic green chasms opening inland, one after another, from a coast that is almost continuous beach. As you go north, the coast becomes a series of bays and bluffs, and the tropical forests encroach the road. Finally, on the north, the coast is mainly steep cliffs, more arid here, with grassy upslopes that give way to forested ridgelines.

Resort beaches and coves are plentiful, and Lahaina is Maui's best strolling town, for history buffs and window-shoppers alike. Take your pick from several wave-watcher's walks along sea-sculpted bluffs, hikes deep into the forest, and roadside turnouts with panoramic views. You can afford to be fickle in the Valley Isle trailhead section, since the distance between being a beach potato or hardcore eco-adventurist is not far, in terms of miles.

DRIVING TOUR
PICKING THE RIGHT DAY

Get an early start to the north shore, and you'll feel like you're discovering the place. But don't go during or just after big rains: You'll get a discomforting look at erosion in progress, as mud and rocks wash into the roadway. In the winter, weather hits from Kapalua north. As you go south, sun is more likely. From Ka'anapali down to Olowalu will often be in the sunny lee of minor storms, giving a view of the weather in the West Maui Mountains while you bask in the sun.

THE ROADS

From McGregor Point to Lahaina, traffic often flows in a steady stream from midmorning to nightfall. You move along fine, but merging and getting across the highway can be exasperating. This driving tour has you going south during that period to minimize the hassle. Traffic bogs down in Lahaina, and Ka'anapali, especially since several beach parks front the road. But then it's normally smooth sailing on Highway 30 going north, since this newer road bypasses the condo coast at Kahana.

North of Kapalua, the scenery shifts dramatically. The highway becomes a nicely swerving view road for the next dozen miles along the north shore—until the abyss at Kahakuloa. Here, the road takes a several-mile dive through the valley, and you might grip the steering wheel like the reins on a wayward steed. Traction and clearance are no problem—four-wheel drive is not needed—but a two-foot wide car would be helpful.

Cars tend to wait for others oncoming, and then drive through in small caravans. After Kahakuloa, where the route becomes Highway 340, you encounter more one-lane spots, but they are shorter in length. This tour takes you down to Kahakuloa and back again, without circumnavigating West Maui.

THE COURSE

Follow along on the Valley Isle map, page 52. Refer to trailhead descriptions beginning on page 53 for more details.

BEGIN EARLY MORNING. TAKE HIGHWAY 30 NORTH TO KAHAKULOA VILLAGE. Get a cup of java to go and breakfast in a bag, and drive in the morning light. This tour plans for stops on the way back. Make your first stop Kahakuloa Head, the "Tall Lord" of a mountain that anchors the north side of the bay. Then double back and stroll the town—probably joined by roosters and barnyard beasts. Being here early will lessen concerns about navigating the narrow roads. When you drive back out—the way you entered—you may want to hike the first ten minutes of the Waikalai Road, which affords a view of the bay.

Aloha Fruit Stand, Waikalai Road, Ululani's Shave Ice

MIDMORNING. DRIVE NORTH SHORE. Some of the best whale-watching bluffs are along the highway over the next several miles heading back toward Kapalua. You'll find many unmarked trails to roam hillocks or descend to cliffside decks. Also keep an eye inland for segments of the alaloa, the King's Trail, that is identifiable because the ancient road builders didn't contour gullies, but instead went straight across, dipping and rising. You have an option of taking the short walk to Maui's sea geyser, the Nakalele Blowhole. Sometimes on this drive you will follow a whale family as it swims around the island.

Then continue on Highway 30—snagging some fruit at the Aloha Fruit Stand in Honokahau Bay, if it's open. Down the road, stop in and catch the surf scene at Lipoa Point, where world-renowned waves roll in. From the overlook, you can also check out Honolua Bay to decide if this is a good morning to swim with the fishes in the marine preserve. Just as the road gets wider, you may want to swing in to check out D.T. Fleming Beach Park, a good place to let kids play.

Launiupoko Beach, Lipoa Point

NOON. CONTINUE BACK ON HIGHWAY 30 AND THEN TURN RIGHT ON OF-FICE ROAD TOWARD THE RITZ CARLTON AND KAPALUA. A tasty place to stop is the Honolua Store, where you can pick up treats to suit any yen. If you'd like to laze in luxury for a spell, check out the Ritz, one of Maui's best. Office Road connects with Lower Honoapiʻilani Road—turn left—and take your culinary prize to Ironwood Beach, to relax on the sand.

Continue south on Lower Honoapiʻilani. This is the Condo Coast that the highway bypasses. On the north end you'll pass Kapalua and Napili bays, which are snorkeling and strolling havens. Then continue south on the coast road, a drive-by sight-see.

AFTERNOON. If you feel like an unfettered beach walk, pull into Kahekili Beach Park. Or, to gawk at the resort scene, try Dig Me Beach on the coast path at Kaʻanapali. But save most of the afternoon for Lahaina. Visit the north end of town by veering right on Front Street, to see the Mala Pier and Jodo Mission. Then drive straight through the hoopla on Front to park at the south end of town at Shaw Street. Just follow your senses around Lahaina Harbor. If you wander around for a couple hours, you'll see everything. The Thomas Edison vintage film at the Wo Hing Museum is … you gotta see it.

Honolua Store, Olowalu Petroglyphs, Honolua Bay Trail

SUNSET. Many will want to finish the shift in Lahaina, letting afternoon slide into evening, perhaps enjoying a cool beverage while watching the various vessels returning to harbor, or holding down a bench at Banyan Tree Square as the craft's fair winds down. Thoughts of moving to Maui might enter your mind.

Others can savor the waning hours with a drive south on Highway 30. Over the next few miles you'll pass several beach parks, beginning with Puamana where the local canoe club may be putting in for a late-day paddle. Each beach park offers a quiet spot under coco palms to view Lanai, and Haleakala to the south, which looks like an island from this coast. Inland are the green crags that gave Maui its nickname as the Valley Isle. The hot ticket for this experience is Olowalu Landing. If you want to look for the green flash of sunset from a higher elevation, continue on Highway 30 through the Lahaina Tunnel, and use the unimproved turnouts on the right, before reaching the logjam of sightseers at well-marked Papawai Point.

Ka'anapali (Dig Me) Beach, Lahaina Harbor

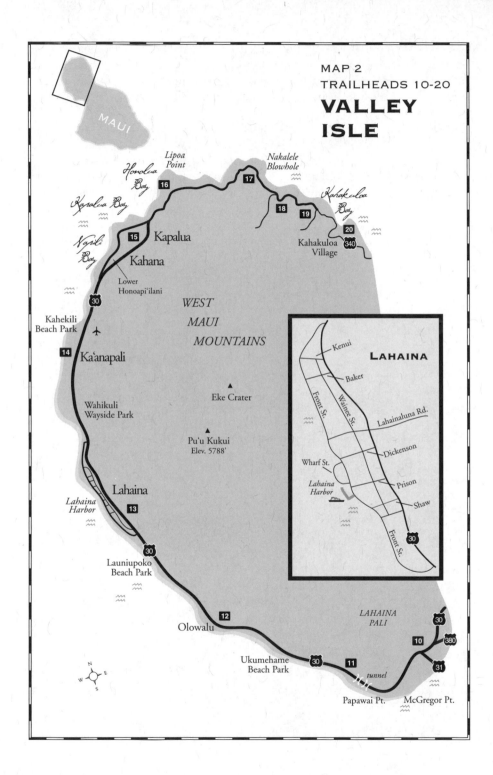

MAP 2
TRAILHEADS 10-20
VALLEY ISLE

MAUI

Lipoa Point

Nakalele Blowhole

Honolua Bay

16

17

Kapalua Bay

18

19

Kahakuloa Bay

15 Kapalua

20
340

Napili Bay

Kahana

Kahakuloa Village

Lower Honoapi'ilani

30

WEST MAUI MOUNTAINS

Kahekili Beach Park

14 Ka'anapali

Eke Crater

Wahikuli Wayside Park

Pu'u Kukui
Elev. 5788'

LAHAINA

Kenui

Baker

Front St.

Wainee St.

Lahainaluna Rd.

Dickenson

Wharf St.

Lahaina Harbor

Prison

Shaw

Front St.

30

Lahaina

Lahaina Harbor

13

30

Launiupoko Beach Park

LAHAINA PALI

30

12

Olowalu

10

380

Ukumehame Beach Park

30

11 *tunnel*

31

Papawai Pt.   McGregor Pt.

N W E S

VALLEY ISLE

T R A I L H E A D S

H	HIKING
SN	SNORKELING
P	KAYAKING, CANOEING
SF	SURFING, BOOGIE BOARDING, WIND SPORTS

10 - 20

TH = Trailhead
mm = mile marker; corresponds to highway signs
All hiking distances in parentheses are ROUND TRIP.
Elevation gains of 100 feet or more are noted.

10.   LAHAINA PALI EAST   H

Best For: This snaking trail, to an open ridge with panoramas, which was the easiest land route from Wailuku to Lahaina until about 1900.

Parking: Take Hwy. 30, the Hoʻonapiʻilani Hwy., north from its jct. with Hwy. 31, North Kihei Road. After about .25-mi.—just south of the jct. with Hwy. 380—look for trailhead sign on your left, near a huge power pole. Drive through the gate on a dirt road for .25-mi., turn left for another .5-mi. and park at a marked trailhead. *Be Aware:* Traffic is usually heavy at the highway turnoff. Also, if the gate is closed at the highway, walk in and add 1.5 mi. to your round-trip distance. You can make this a car-shuttle hike by leaving a second car at Lahaina Pali West, TH11.

H: Lahaina Pali East (5 mi., 1,500 ft.)

The Lahaina Pali Trail—pali means cliffs—was constructed in 1825 over Kealaloloa Ridge as a way for missionary school children to get from Wailuku to the Mauna Olu Seminary in Lahaina. Think about that when you're slogging up its famed zigzags in the noonday sun. But it wasn't easy for them, either. One of the teachers called it "the crookedist, the rockiest road ever traveled by mortals." Prior to this trail, most people going this direction traveled via canoe. In the early 1900s, a crude road was built nearer the coast, and the trail was abandoned. In 1993, the trail was restored and made part of the state Na Ala Hele hiking system.

For the **Lahaina Pali East** hike, leave the shade of kiawe trees at the trailhead enclosure, following a rock-lined path. The shade will soon be a distant memory as you begin open switchbacks with big views unfolding at your back. The trail levels out after several miles (distances are marked on Na Ala Hele trails) and you'll contour a short distance on the rough road that comes up from McGregor Point. Then follow signs, taking the trail leading from the road to your right to the turnaround and viewpoint at sign number 10. *Be Aware:* Bring plenty of water, sturdy shoes, and a hiking pole. An early morning or late afternoon start is recommended on sunny days. *More Stuff:* The rough road from McGregor continues up Kealaloloa Ridge, for another 2-plus miles, to Pu'u Anu at an elevation of almost 3,000 feet.

11. LAHAINA PALI WEST   H, SN, P

Best For: Get sweaty on one of the west side's best view hikes, and cool off with a snorkel at a colorful cove that is known mostly by tour boats. Then whale watch at sunset from several cliff lookouts.

Parking: Take Hwy. 30, the Honoapi'ilani Hwy., west from Ma'alaea toward Lahaina. Pass through the tunnel after mm10, continue for .5-mi., and look for a signed, dirt turnout on the right at the bottom of the hill, amid trees. *Note:* As the highway rounds the cliffs before the tunnel, you will see several turnouts on your left. Due to traffic conditions, these vantage points are best visited while heading the other way, toward Ma'alaea. See *More Stuff,* below.

H: Lahaina Pali West (5.75 mi., 1,600 ft.)

From the **Lahaina Pali West** trailhead parking lot, you hop up to a portion of the old highway that was constructed by prisoners in the early 1900s. This old highway, in turn, covered up parts of the ancient King's Highway, or alaloa—the long road. The Lahaina Pali Trail leaves the old road, to your left, after about 100 feet, beginning its steady climb up red dirt and boulders to a high point on Kealaloloa Ridge. During the climb you'll cross several gulches, all signed since this is a Na Ala Hele state hiking trail. On the way, keep a watch for pioneer petroglyphs—rock etchings made by missionary school children and paniolos, or cowboys, who trod this path in the 1800s. Most are before and after the number 9 signpost.

You cross the canyonlike Manawainui Gulch almost 2 miles from the trailhead, and then walk an open grassy area. The high point comes near signpost number 10, serving up views toward Haleakala, Molokini, and Kahoolawe. But for a slightly more enticing view, continue just 10 minutes more, as the trail joins the McGregor Point road and contours Malalowaiaole Gulch—at signpost 11 you'll be able to see down toward the Lahaina Pali East trailhead, and also get a look at the ruins of a trailside shelter. *Note:* To make this a car shuttle hike, see TH10. *Be Aware:* Wear hiking shoes and bring water. The trail is well constructed, albeit steep. Shade is scarce on this hike, but its western exposure means full sun doesn't hit until later in the morning.

More Stuff: To access several whale-watching turnouts, and McGregor Point Light, head back toward Ma'alaea on Highway 30 from the trailhead parking. After leaving the tunnel, within the first .5-mile, look for two dirt turnouts that were part of the old highway. Inspiring viewpoints await. Farther along, after mm9, is the well-marked and popular turnout at Papawai Point. Turning lanes, along with the great view, mean you might have to take a number to park at sunset. For more solitude with your view, continue a bit farther—past mm8 and just before mm7—and take a right on the dirt spur road that leads a short distance to the beacon light at McGregor Point. Safe, but steep, fishermen's trails lead down to weirdly shaped formations at water's edge.

SN: **Coral Gardens** is a small cove featuring acres of coral heads and waters that are calm on days when trade winds make other snorkeling spots choppy. To get there from the Lahaina Pali West trailhead, drive back toward the tunnel and park up the grade a short distance, on the shoulder where the guardrail ends. Make your way down the rugged trail to the point, and walk the rocks around to your left. To first take a look at Coral Gardens from above, drive through the tunnel heading toward Ma'alaea and pull off on the paved shoulder. Often, at mid-morning, you'll see the big catamarans anchored below, discharging snorkelers into aquamarine waters. *Be Aware:* Coral Gardens, due to the hike to the entry point, is for intermediate to advanced snorkelers.

For easier access, go to **Papalaua Beach Wayside**, which is across the road from this trailhead; walk down the beach to your left and swim out toward the rocks. Or, if more difficult access is what you seek, advanced snorkelers can try **Manuohule**, or **Wash Rock**, which is below McGregor Point; walk down from the historical maker near the light and curl around to your right on the rocks.

P: To kayak Coral Gardens and the shores of Lahaina Pali, put in at Ukumehame Beach Park, which is near mm12 on Highway 30 headed toward Lahaina. The park's lawn, palms, and sandy beach also provide an attractive lunch stop. Of course, you can also paddle north from here, catching views that demonstrate why this is called the Valley Isle—Ukumehame, Olowalu, and Launiupoko valleys yawn inland.

12. OLOWALU H, SN, P, SF

Best For: All the makings for a dream day: two classic tropical valleys, lots of snorkeling coral, rideable surf, and historical curiosities that span centuries.

Parking: Take Hwy. 30, the Honoapi'ilani Hwy. toward Lahaina. Pass mm13. *Note:* Further directions follow at the start of each activity description below.

H: Olowalu to: Petroglyph hill (1.25 mi., 200ft.), or Olowalu Valley (2.25, mi., 375 ft.); Olowalu Landing (.5-mi.); Launiupoko to: Village site (.25-mi.), or Launiupoko Valley (3.75 mi., 450 ft.)

To **Olowalu Valley** and **Petroglyph hill**—a yellowish mound whose real name is Kilea cinder cone—turn right at the Olowalu Store and Chez Paul, which sit side by side at mm15. Drive around the left side of the store and jog left on a road near a small water tank. Within a few hundred feet, you reach a gate for trailhead parking. *Note:* If you drive past this gate, as many people do, you can drive all the way to the petroglyphs and subtract 1 mile from the round-trip hiking distances. The first .5-mile of the hike leaves the huge monkey pod trees near the store and crosses fallow cane fields; the rock platforms you see stacked in this area, which look like heiaus, are actually piles workers made when clearing the fields.

The road goes to the north side of the hill, where on its vertical face you will see the picture etchings made centuries ago. Look for old pink pipe railings and decrepit steps. The exact origins of the pictures are the subject of Hawaiian legend and anthropological consternation. To the **top Kilea cinder cone**, keep right on the road past the petroglyphs and curl right and up. Global warming tip: Sea shell fossils indicate that during geological yesteryear, when the earth had small polar ice caps, sea level reached within 15 feet of the top of this cone, making it a tiny island.

To **continue to Olowalu Valley**, cross the stream over the bridge that is just left of the petroglyphs, and stay on the road as it heads for a water tank that is about .25-mile distant. This hike is a trailblazer's special: there is no maintained trail in the valley. But if you cross the irrigation ditch at the tank, and go left, you'll see a feeder trail that heads toward the stream bank. Keeping the stream to your right as you head up, you'll see paths of people who have attempted this hike. The forest is dense, but you can find adequate passage. The fascination with this trail is that it was the escape route in 1790 for Chief Kalanikupule when his troops were slaughtered across the island in the Iao Valley by the forces of Kamehameha the Great. *Be Aware:* Although you can find a decent route heading upstream, finding the same route back is difficult. Don't hike alone or wander too far from the stream.

It takes time to fully soak in the beauty from the wharf at **Olowalu Landing**. At mm15, turn left across from the store and restaurant. Go left immediately on a road that then turns right to a parking area about .25-mile from the highway. The grounds here, adorned with coco palms, Norfolk pines, and several large native Hawaiian trees, were in 1864 the site of one of Maui's earliest sugar mills and its most active pier. For the supreme vistas, head out the rock-and-dirt wharf. Sea turtles often pass, as do whales, just off the point. Lanai is the backdrop. Inland is a museum quality view of Olowalu Valley, a jagged "V" above the treetops. This tranquil place was the setting of the Olowalu Massacre, also in 1790, when American merchant Captain Simon Metcalf slaughtered about 100 villagers in a dispute over a stolen boat. Later, one of Metcalf's men, John Young, was kidnapped from another ship and forced to become a military advisor to King Kamehameha I. Years later, Young's granddaughter became beloved Queen Emma, wife of Kamehameha IV.

To **Launiupoko**, the next valley north, take Highway 30 to the beach park of the same name at mm18. Turn right on Kai Hele Ku, toward upscale homes inland. Continue 1.25 miles and turn right on Wailau Place. The sign noting the **Launiupoko Ahupua'a,** or Village, is at the end of the cul-de-sac. An ahupua'a is a wedge of land running from the mountains to the sea and containing a valley and stream. A short trail leads down to the site; much of it is overgrown.

To **Launiupoko Valley**, and the best interior valley view in West Maui, walk up the dirt road to your left as you enter the cul-de-sac. After about .5-mile, on an upward grade that follows an easement for big power poles, you'll come to a lava-rock reservoir. *Note:* You may want to drive to the reservoir, thus subtracting 1.25 miles and significant elevation from the hike. Use caution as road can be rutted after rains.

With the reservoir on your left, go right on a grassy track that follows an irrigation ditch up the valley. The track becomes a trail, and soon you will find yourself walking the tops to lava rocks that form the ditch. You lose the valley view for good when you enter trees, as century plants, guava trees, and wild coffee trees encroach on the path. About a mile from the reservoir, you cross the stream on a short, falling-down bridge supporting a water pipe. You have to enter the ditch in places over the next two hundred yards, until reaching its end, where the stream spews uncontained out of the dark shade of the jungle. Trailblazers can proceed with caution on a pig path that continues up the valley. *Be Aware:* Launiupoko, a defunct cane field, is being developed for resi-

Launiupoko

dences. Future access is uncertain. Use caution on this slippery route, and be aware that landowners are not responsible for persons using trails through private property.

SN: For some of the best and most readily accessible snorkeling on Maui, try **Kaili'ili Beach**, commonly called, **Olowalu Beach**. Use roadside parking on either side of mm14. Coral shelves spread close to shore, as well as several hundred feet offshore, where tour boats anchor. *Be Aware:* Olowalu has a reputation for being a shark hangout; but only three attacks, including one fatality, have been reported over a 12-year period, making the drive here a bigger risk than swimming. **Olowalu Landing** is also a good snorkeling area, far less frequented. Look for the sandy ramp to the left of the long wharf, and in between a smaller boat landing. A coral bench is to your left within the reef, or, on calm days, swim out next to the wharf through a reef opening to explore deeper waters. You may spot a turtle.

Launiupoko Beach Park, at mm18, has a nice keiki pool, formed by a curve of rocks in the center of the park. Low tide can leave this pool high and dry. Offshore the park are good snorkeling reefs, but shallow waters and breaking waves can make this an iffy proposition. Launiupoko is a choice spot for a picnic, among palms and banyan trees. For swimming with a sandy bottom, try **Awalua Beach**, which borders the highway south of the beach park, between mm16 and mm17.

P: Though not many paddlers do so, you can put in at Olowalu Landing. After a short carry, use the sandy ramp to the left of the big wharf. Then paddle out through an opening in the reef that is just to your left, at the end of the wharf. During late winter and spring, whales often come well within a mile of Olowalu Point. Both north and south of the landing are several miles of undeveloped beach. You'll see plenty fishes beneath your hull.

Olowalu Landing

SF: During the summer, either side of **Olowalu Landing** is surfed, but a shallow reef break can be a problem. Just north of the wharf, a left-break surf spot also pops up during the summer. More reliable surfing in this area is to be had at **Launiupoko Beach Park** and **Awalua Beach**, directions to which are in the snorkeling descriptions. In between these two is called **Kulanaokalai Beach**, but it's all the same run of sand. Small offshore reef breaks are reliable in the winter, and high surf will roll in during summer.

13.   LAHAINA   H, SN, P, SF

Best For: Lahaina has always been where the action is—as the beachside en-clave of kings and queens, as the bustling whaling town that was the capital of Hawaii, and, today, as night-life city and the point of departure of vessels of all sizes. Hike the hills, swim the beaches, roam the town.

Parking: Take Hwy. 30, the Honoapiʻilani Hwy. to Lahaina. On the south end of town, turn toward the ocean on Shaw St., and park in the lot at the corner of Shaw and Front streets. *Note:* More lots, plus on-street spots, are avail-able a few blocks farther north on Front St.; parking spots are at a premium from noon onward. The Shaw Street lot has fewer parking restrictions.

H: Lahaina Town stroll (up to 3.25 mi.); Lahaina Seawall (.5-mi.); David Malo's Grave (up to 5 mi., 1,400 ft.)

In 1802, his immense eminence Kamehameha the Great, fresh from battles that made him the first ruler of all the southern islands, kicked back along the Lahaina shores with his entourage of several hundred family members and hangers-on, while his crafts-men fashioned some 1,000 war canoes, the peleleu fleet, in preparation for the inva-sion of Kauai, far to the north. A treaty was signed in lieu of an invasion.

By the early 1820s, Liholiho, or Kamehameha II, was king. Lahaina saw the arrival of both the whaling ships and missionaries—two disparate forces if there ever were. The whalers—by the 1840s, some 400 ships called each year—believed "there is no God beyond Cape Horn." Whoring brought disease, and alcohol fueled violence. Liholiho, along with his mother Queen Kaʻahumanu and Chief Hoapili, embraced the mission-ary influence. They built a stone prison to quell unruly whalers, and set into motion a series of social reforms that abolished the patriarchal system born of the previous de-cades of war. They developed an educational system that was more advanced than all but a few schools in America. After 34 years, in 1854, the kingdom's capital was moved to Honolulu, whaling subsided, and Lahaina became a sleepy cane town. Recent de-cades have seen its resurgence as a tourist destination.

As you begin the **Lahaina Town stroll**, head to the corner of the lot by the ball field. You'll find a plaque commemorating Moku'ula Island, the most sacred spot on Maui, where kings and queens had palaces and were interred. Common folk were prohibited. Plans to restore the site are underway. Then head down Front Street, on the ocean side. The lawn area open to the beach is Hale Piula, and the foundation remnants are those for the never-completed palace of Kamehameha III—the king preferred sleeping in his grass hut nearby. Behind the hale is Lahaina Beach; see snorkeling below. Continuing on Front Street, after Kamehameha III school, you reach Canal Street.

Veer left at Canal Street, diagonally across the Banyan Tree Square. The sprawling tree was planted in 1873 by the sheriff on the town's fiftieth anniversary. Its canopy of limbs is now an aviary of chattering birds and an umbrella for scores of local artisans. Near the shore behind the tree are the old courthouse, now a visitor's center, and the ruins of the first coral-block prison, which housed unruly whalers.

The Lahaina Harbor is in front of the old courthouse. For the **Lahaina Seawall**—the must-do hike for the town—walk over to the prominent Lahaina Lighthouse. The 30-foot high beacon, dating from 1866, was the first in Hawaii, and sits next to the Carthaginian, a sailing freighter that replicates those from the old days; now a museum, the ship was used in the filming of *Hawaii*. Then walk down the paved road along the water, past an array of commercial boats, and take a right onto the seawall. You'll be walking on big flat boulders. The seawall, completed in 1938, is a spot to view surfers, the outer islands, and boating activity. But the real reason for being here is the romantic look you get looking back toward Lahaina: The opening shot for a South Seas adventure flick, with jagged green peaks as a backdrop to the coco palm shore.

To **continue the town stroll**, return to the lighthouse and head over to the grassy area just north to see the remains of Kamehameha the Great's brick house, built in 1800,

Pu'unoa Beach, Hale Pa'ahao "stuck-in-irons house"

Lahaina Lighthouse, Carthaginian

and the Hauola Stone, used by ancient Hawaiians as part of a birthing ceremony to portend healthy futures for their children. The ancient taro patch was also here, where the kingdom's first monarch labored to demonstrate the dignity of work. From here, cut back up to Front Street. There you'll find the Baldwin House Museum, the former home of Dwight D. Baldwin, one of the earliest missionaries, whose progeny became sugar cane producers and owners of vast tracks of land.

Then, continue north on Front Street—and you're on your own. For several blocks, until things settle down again at Papalaua Street, you'll be in the heart of town, libation only steps away, galleries and shops plentiful, with brokers hawking adventure activities and tunes blaring from open windows. For the full effect, jog up Lahainaluna Street, the main drag that comes in from the highway. Follow your nose, but any history buffs will want to stop in at the Wo Hing Museum. Built in 1912 as a gathering place for Maui's society of Chinese workers, the structure was restored as a museum in 1984. Behind the museum is the rustic cookhouse, in which is shown the Thomas Edison black-and-white footage of Hawaii. Shot in 1898 and 1906, these silent flicks impart volumes in a few memorable minutes.

More Stuff in town: Kids—and most everyone else—will want to see the Lahaina Prison, Hale Pa'ahao, or "stuck-in-irons house." From the parking lot, drive down Front Street two blocks and turn right on Prison Street. You'll see the high prison walls, built from the coral stones of the old fort at the banyan tree, on your left at the corner of Waine'e Street. During the 1850s, the prison housed sailors guilty of awa (kava) drinking, furious riding, and violating fishing taboos, along with your more run-of-the-mill adulterous fornication and assault. Making noise of any kind was prohibited.

Turn right on Waine'e Street and walk to the Waiola Church and Waine'e Graveyard. Buried here are Hawaiian royalty, including Queen Keopuolani, Kamehameha the Great's wife, and Governor Hoapili, as well as missionaries from the 1850s, such as William Richards. Commoners, sailors, elders, and children also rest here, persons of many races reflecting the multifaceted times when the world discovered Hawaii.

One last thing: If you're looking for an inexpensive, local-style plate lunch, try the Lahina Cannery Mall, located at the far north end of town. Yes, it is a mall, but locals hang out here and they showcase excellent free hula performances, which have quite a following. Call the mall for current times; see *Calabash*.

For the hike to **David Malo's Grave**, with its commanding vistas, turn toward the mountains on Lahainaluna Street, in the middle of town. (Before you go, look for the big "L" on the hill way up there—this school marker is your eventual destination.) You'll pass through the hulking remains of the Pioneer Sugar Mill, and continue several miles uphill to Lahainaluna High School. The school, begun in 1831, is the oldest west of the Great Divide. The original schoolhouse—veer left at the top of the hill—is a historic landmark, Hale Pai, where Hawaii's first newspaper was printed in the 1830s. The view from campus makes you wonder how the kids get any studying done.

For the hike, veer right at the top of the hill toward the gym, and park at the cane road gate. *Note:* Some people drive up the next .75-mile, eliminating 1.5 miles and nearly 1,000 feet from the round-trip hike; heed signs and use your own judgment. The

Keiki hula at Lahaina Cannery Mall, Jodo Mission

partially paved road tops out after passing two large water tanks. Where the road ends, follow the fence line uphill, with the deep valley to your left. You'll top a first rise, pass through a low lava wall, and come to an opening in a slack barbed-wire fence. The "L" will be up to your right. The gravesite is a short distance above the "L." David Malo, among Lahainaluna's first graduates, went on to be the kingdom's leading educator. But later in life he requested to be buried high on this hill, away from Western influence he felt would destroy the essence of Hawaiian culture. *Be Aware:* More than one trail leads to the top. Be prepared to trailblaze the last portion.

SN: **Lahaina Beach** at the south end of town, is a .75-mile sand strip bordered by shade trees and quiet neighborhood homes. A sheltering reef offshore makes for safe swimming and decent snorkeling. Some locals call this Baby Beach. This was the beach of choice for Kamehameha I, a man who could do whatever he pleased. From the Shaw Street lot, access the beach behind Hale Piula to your right; or better yet, go to the more private end of the beach, by heading south to a Shoreline Access sign near 409 Front Street. You can beach walk from here to town.

Pu'unoa Beach, a local's favorite, is at the north end of town. From the highway, turn toward the ocean on Kenui to Front Street, and then go right. Two access points: For the south end of the .5-mile long beach, turn left on Kai Pali Place, and look for the Shoreline Access sign. This end of the beach features a popular baby, or keiki, beach. For north-end access, and easier parking, continue on Front, turn left on Ala Moana, and park just past the Jodo Mission. A huge bronzed Buddha rests within the manicured mission grounds, a striking sight with the jungle ridge as its background. Before hitting the beach, you may also wish to walk north through the Pu'upiha Cemetery, to Mala Wharf, a monument to folly, since it was condemned just after completion in 1922 because offshore currents rendered it unusable. A reef just offshore Pu'unoa Beach provides a wave-free snorkeling zone, which can be shallow in spots at low tide.

Wahikuli Beach Park, alongside the highway just north of Lahaina, offers good snorkeling and numerous picnic huts set on the grass margin above the coast. The place can be busy on weekends. Use the second parking lot to the north. This spot has rocks at the shoreline, but you can walk both left and right to find sandy entrances to the water.

P: Although kayakers need to keep a watchful eye for boat traffic, paddling inside the reef at Lahaina is a thumbs-up experience. The best put-in is at the north end Pu'unoa Beach on Ala Moana, as per the snorkeling description above. Also try the Shoreline Access for Lahaina Beach, near 409 Front Street, and Puamana Beach Park, which is off Highway 30 at the south end of Lahaina.

SF: **Puamana Beach Park**, at mm19 just south of Lahaina, attracts low-key locals, both winter and summer. So does the **Lahaina Seawall**, both the north tip and off the elbow at its base. Access is via Lahaina Beach, behind Hale Piula, just north of Shaw Street. **Mala Wharf** also offers a long left-break, best during the summer.

14. KA'ANAPALI COAST

Best For: Take your pick between a glitzy resort path and a hike along a pristine beach. All manner of surf-and-sand sports are happening here.

Parking: Take Hwy. 30, the Honoapi'ilani Hwy., north of Lahaina. Turn left before mm24, into Hanako'o Beach Park. Go to the right in the lot and park near the cemetery. *Notes:* An alternate parking spot is mentioned in the beach resorts' hike. Also, further parking directions, beginning from primary parking and heading north, are given in the hiking and snorkeling descriptions.

H: Ka'anapali Beach Resorts (2.25 mi.); Kahekili Beach walk (2 mi.)

Ka'anapali is comprised of two long beaches, which are north and south of Black Rock, or Keka'a Point, which is midway. The path alongside the resorts is to the south of Black Rock. For the **Ka'anapali Beach Resorts** coastal path, cross over the little bridge at the north end of the beach parking lot. You'll join the paved path that begins at the Hyatt Regency. *Note:* To park at the Hyatt, which will begin the hike at the same place, continue north past the beach park and turn left at Ka'anapali Parkway. Then go left on Nohea Kai Drive, past Shoreline Access 209, to parking for Shoreline Access 208. A paved path leads to the beach path.

The gardens and man-made lagoon of the Hyatt will highlight the first section of the walk. Joggers, pool boys, and people wearing name tags may share the flagstone walkway. You then pass the Marriott, followed by the Westin, each with poolside gardens. Then Whaler's Village, an open-air mall, adjoins the path, presenting an opportunity to Hawaiianize your wardrobe and stock up on macadamia nuts. Not far after the mall, about 1.25 miles into the walk, the path ends, and to continue you must drop onto the long, deep run of sand that stretches in front of the Sheraton to Black Rock—visible ahead. The action-oriented surfer crowd dubbed this zone, Dig Me Beach, a name that has become outmoded, yeah baby, along with many '70s fads.

For the wide-open **Kahekili Beach walk**, you must drive around to the north of Black Rock. Take Highway 30 past the Ka'anapali exits, and turn left at a traffic signal on Kai Ala Place. *Note:* To the right at the same traffic signal is Pu'ukoli'i Road, which is the northern terminus to the Sugar Train, an amusement ride. Keep right on Kai Ala and you'll soon come to the big lot for Kahekili Beach Park, with its pavilion, carefree palms, and grassy banks. This is also called Ahumanu Beach, or Old Airport Beach, or, at the south, Ka'anapali Beach. You can walk left on the beach for about .5-mile to Black Rock, with the Royal Lahaina Resort looming on the bluff above. To the right, is open beach for about .75-mile, with ironwoods buffering the sloping sand and Molokai beckoning offshore.

Black Rock

SN: The south end of **Hanako'o Beach Park**, by the lifeguard platform, is a calm area with sandy bottom, suited for novice snorkelers. This park is also called Cemetery Beach. Most snorkelers in the area head for **Black Rock**. The easiest access is to take Ka'anapali Parkway to the Sheraton and use the Shoreline Access parking garage, just south of the hotel. If that lot is full, try the lot just south, for the Whaler's Village. Either way, you hit the sand just south of the point. Swim out along the steep walled Keka'a Point, where spirits of the dead were said to leave the island in ancient times, and where intrepid swan divers launch themselves these days. You can also access Black Rock from the north side, by continuing to the end of Ka'anapali Parkway, walking down from the Royal Lahaina off Keka'a Drive, or taking the beach walk from Kahekili, as described in the hiking section.

P: Hanakoʻo Beach Park is home to three canoe clubs, with a dozen or more different-colored, sleek outriggers lined up on the beach. Local paddlers are generous with information, so ask. Kahekili Beach Park is the put-in for some local outfitters. From either spot, the usual route is to the waters off Kekaʻa Point. But paddling north for a couple miles, you can discover some excellent sandy coves that are hard to reach on foot because of residential gates.

SF: Boogie boarders and surfers like the area just south of **Hanakoʻo Beach Park**, sometimes called **Sand Box**. Winter rides are available, though summer is better, and this is not in the top ten Maui surfing beaches. When the surf is too hairy elsewhere, the right-breaks here are the choice.

15.   KAPALUA BAYS   H, SN, SF

> **Best For:** A series of sandy bays that nature has scooped out of the rocky coast——providing surfers, snorkelers, strollers, wave-watchers, and sun bathers lots of intimate places to hang out amid the condos and resorts.
>
> **Parking:** Go north past Kaʻanapali on Hwy. 30, the Honoapiʻilani Hwy. Near mm29, turn left on Napilihau Rd. Then turn right on Lower Honoapiʻilani Rd. *Note:* Additional directions are provided in the activity descriptions.

H: Napili Beach to Kapalua Beach (1.25 mi.); Kapalua Beach to: Hawea Point Shoreline Conservation Area (1.25 mi.), or Oneloa Bay (2 mi.); D. T. Fleming Beach Park to Dragon's Teeth (.75-mi.)

Once the domain of Chief Piʻilani, who controlled six bays and the three islands— Molokai, Lanai, and Kahoolawe— that are visible from the shores, this 5-mile coastline today might well be called the Condo Coast. Creative site planners have blocked light from squeaking between the buildings in places. Yet Kapalua Beach was named "America's Best Beach" in a nationally researched university study, and many attest that its neighboring beaches are equally charming.

The coast walk from **Napili Beach to Kapalua Beach** is on a highly scenic path hidden in plain sight. The hard part is finding Napili Bay: From the above directions, continue north on Lower Honoapiʻilani and, at about mm29.5, go left on Hui Drive; you should see a Shoreline Access sign, and signs for Hale Napili. The access path is where Hui Drive bends right. Park at will, amid lots of no-parking signs and weekend car jams. From the beach, head to your right around the pretty crescent of sand, and hop up to the railed path with paved stones that goes in the direction of the point. Before the point, the path ends, and you'll need to step down to a route that is plainly visible on a lava shelf. This fisherman's trail hooks around the point, passing tide pools.

Napili Bay

Notice footprints carved into the lava. After rounding the point, you need to step up to a lawn area of a resort, from which your route to Kapalua Beach will be visible. *Be Aware:* Don't try this walk during high surf.

In spite of its scenic charms, the hike from **Kapalua Beach to Hawea Point and Oneloa Bay** is taken by few people. To get to Kapalua Beach, turn left from Lower Honoapi'ilani Road, just north of an uphill S-turn near mm30. A Shoreline Access sign points to a large parking lot. To the beach, walk down the lot through a short tunnel. Walk to your right along the sand, or the grassy fringes of the Kapalua Bay Hotel that sits above it. Stay on the fringes of the coastal bluff—there is no trail—turning slightly uphill to your right along a fence line. Then go left at a Public Shore sign, and make your way out to low-lying Hawea Point Shoreline Conservation Area—the most *au naturel* spot around these parts. Tide pools on its north side make for soaking tubs, when the conditions are right. To continue to Oneloa Bay, double back from the point, and head north on the lawn at the margin of nicely spaced condominiums. You'll see the bay ahead. An easy path drops from the lawns down to the south end of the beach. *Note:* For direct access to Oneloa Bay, also called Ironwoods Beach, see *Surfing* description below.

The **D. T. Fleming Beach Park to Dragon's Teeth** walk is a wave-watcher's special, leading from beach to the buttresses of Makaluapuna Point below the golf course at the Ritz Carlton Hotel. To get there, take Highway 30 past both Napilihau Road and Office Road, which leads to the Ritz and Kapalua. At the bottom of the grade after mm31, turn left at a Shoreline Access sign, onto Lower Honokahua Road. A .25-mile drive takes you to the beach park. *Be Aware:* Shore break along the beach park can present a hazard, even for walkers.

At the park, go left along the sand until it peters out, and then make your way up to the low bank that skirts the golf course, following the out-of-bounds markers beside the trees. This route is easier than the alternate route along the rocky coast. The Honokahua Burial Site, dating from 850 AD, covers some 14 acres to your left. Respect for this site, and years of legal haggling, is what caused the Ritz to be set back so far from the coast. You then cut right through scraggly ironwoods, and pass the Dragon's Teeth, a line of sharpened tufts of whitish trachyte, four- or five-feet high. Beyond the teeth are lava flats and a grassy area where on most days you can watch combers explode. Oneloa Bay is around Makaluapuna Point to your left.

More Stuff: The ancient trail to Pu'u Kukui, at 5,788 feet the highest peak in West Maui, is not open to the public. Permission to enter is required from Maui Land and Pineapple Company, which owns the Kapalua Bay Hotel. Once a year, people pay $1,000 to enter a drawing for the privilege of taking the hike, which is sponsored by the Kapalua Nature Society. See *Resource Links* section.

Driving north from the beginning of Lower Honoapi'ilani Road—which is a left turn off Highway 30 before mm26—you will see a number of Shoreline Access points with fair-to-good recreational values. Going from south to north: The Keka'a Point Open Space Recreation Area is an immediate left on a scruffy dirt road that provides access to the north end of Old Airport Beach, which is described in TH14. Then, if you hang a left on Ka'anapali Shores Place, you'll find a strip of beach at Shoreline Access 214A. Continuing north is the minor gem of Honokowai Beach Park (see *Snorkeling*). After that, as the road gets curvy, past Akahele Street that leads to airport, is Pohaku Park, or S-Turns, a scenic turnout in view of the Kahana Beach Resort. North of mm28 and Hale Makai Place, is beach access to a small cove. The best access, is just north here. Go left on Hui Road E, to the end of the cul-de-sac. A tree-tunnel trail leads out to a small point with tide pools, and you can make your way to a sweet cove to the north, which otherwise is blocked from access by gated homes.

SN: Go to the right at **Kapalua Beach** for easy entry and good snorkeling, as you stroke out toward the point. People also swim and snorkel below the bluffs on your left, as you come out of the pedestrian tunnel. **Napili Beach**, Kapalua's kissing cousin to the south, also has great swimming and decent snorkeling—to the right as you face the water. See hike descriptions for driving directions. *Note:* Though infrequently, Kapalua Beach is also called Fleming Beach, which confuses it with the beach park—where swimming is not safe. *Be Aware:* Although these beaches are generally safe, currents can be a factor offshore, near the tips of land.

Honokowai Beach Park is a bright spot at the south end of the Condo Coast. Go left from Highway 30 after mm25, and continue on Lower Honoapi'ilani Road for .5-mile. The park's protective reef makes for decent snorkeling and forms a very good keiki pool, with sandy entry. Bring the family and a cooler full of hulihuli chicken.

SF: During the winter, surfers ride the tiers rolling into **Oneloa Beach**, a.k.a., **Ironwoods**. This is a big curve of white sand, not known for swimming, but the high-end condos that rim it are set back enough to score high marks among beach strollers. To get there directly, go north on Honoapi'ilani Road, past mm30 and the Kapalua Hotel, and turn left at the low sign for Ironwood Lane. You should see a sign for Shoreline Access 30, a parking lot, and an improved path that leads a short distance to the beach. You can also get here by turning left off Highway 30, towards Kapalua and the Ritz, on Office Road. Go downhill past the rows of ironwood trees, turn left, and then make a right on Ironwood Lane. Bodysurfing is sometimes good at **D.T. Fleming Beach Park**, but the shore break and undertow can be dangerous when surf's up; lifeguards post hazard signs.

16.   HONOLUA MARINE PRESERVE   H, SN, SF

Best For: A snorkeling sanctuary, a dramatic bluff walk, and world-class surfing waves—watch 'em or ride 'em at the beginning of Maui's wild north coast.

Parking: Take Hwy. 30, the Honoapi'ilani Hwy., north of Kapalua. The road narrows. *Mokuleia access:* Just beyond mm 32, look for a Marine Conservation District sign and paved turnout on your left at a chain link fence. *Honolua access:* About .5-mi. past mm32, on a sweeping left bend, park at marginal turnouts; more parking is on the left at a one-lane bridge just before mm33. *Lipoa Point access:* Continue past mm33 and look for a dirt road on your left, just past the guardrail at the top to the hill.

H: Honolua and Mokuleia Marine Conservation District (up to .75-mi.); Lipoa Point (1.75 mi.); Windmill Beach (up to .5-mi.)

Concrete steps with a piped rail aid the short walk down to the small sand beach at **Mokuleia Bay**—which is sometimes spelled, Makuleia, and is known to surfers as Slaughterhouse Beach. To the right is Kalaepiha Point, the protuberance that separates this bay from its twin to the north. A .25-mile trail—within a dense forest that includes banyans and dripping vines—takes you to the boulder shores of **Honolua Bay**. You'll find a concrete boat ramp, small patches of grass and sand, but no beach. In 1976, recreated Polynesian sailing canoes took off from this bay and proved that the trip back to Tahiti would have been possible by the ancient voyagers.

With weird formations, crashing surf, and offshore views, **Lipoa Point** is a place you'll long remember if you sit for a while. From the highway, a rutted but passable dirt road curves down and right to where it's blocked by a gate and berm. If you drive this part, subtract .5-mile from the round-trip walk. Before the berm, as this road bends right, surfer-goat paths lead down to water. One drops down to an overlook—the northernmost point of the marine conservation district—where below surfers rip the big ones.

From the berm and gate, walk down the dirt road, keeping to your left. A pineapple field will be on your right, as you descend gradually. In the 1940s this was a golf course, and this point is sometimes called Golf Links. You'll pass a grove of palms and then one of Norfolk pines, where a lava wall marks the remains of the old golf club-house. Bear left toward the point, through ironwood trees, and drop down through grassy patches and a rock-bordered path to the tip of the point. A smooth shelf is low enough to catch sea spray, but you can scramble up to perches on the craggy wall of trachyte that forms the point to get a point-blank view of Molokai. Little coves are pocked with caves, and you'll also see smooth tide pools that invite soaks.

Windmill Beach, officially called Punalau Beach, is north of Lipoa Point. Look for a gate and road to your left, near mm34.5. A path leads a short distance down an embankment, through a stand of nicely spaced ironwoods, to a long run of sand that is punctuated by sharp lava boulders. Net fishermen like this beach, as do surfers. This is the last sandy beach going north, and its relatively quiet shores are right for a picnic or short stroll. *Be Aware:* Leave your car unlocked and free of valuables.

SN: In spite of having no beach, **Honolua Bay** offers some of the island's best snorkeling. Enter at the boat ramp and swim out channels in the coral both left and right. Snorkeling tour boats often anchor farther out in the bay. Kalaepiha Point, to your left, hosts lots of fish but be mindful of choppy waters on days when surf is breaking. **Mokuleia Bay** is usually only suitable in the summer; flipper out to the point on your right. *Be Aware:* Avoid Honolua after a heavy rain.

The northwest side of **Lipoa Point** has snorkeling pools waiting for trailblazers willing to do the rock hopping it takes to find them. Also, at the outset of the hike as described above, look for a small coco palm beach down a ravine to your left, where snorkeling is good. *Be Aware:* Days when surfers gather indicate large surf that makes snorkeling at Lipoa Point a poor choice.

SF: Surfers like the right-break at **Slaughterhouse Beach**, that is, **Mokuleia**, just off the point on its north side. Bodysurfers also like Mokuleia, but rock hazards are present. The real action at this trailhead is at the north side of **Honolua Bay**—reachable via the Lipoa Point access—where fabulous right-breaks draw intermediate to advanced surfers. The overlook is a magnet for surf photographers. **Windmill Beach** is less crowded. Scope out the offshore rocks before paddling out to these left- and right-breaking tiers.

17.   NAKALELE BLOWHOLE   H

   Best For: A sea geyser that erupts from a multicolored shelf on a rugged coast.

Nakalele gusher, Honolua Marine Preserve entrance

Parking: Take Hwy. 30, the Honoapi'ilani Hwy. north of Kapalua. At mm38, look for a paved turnout on the left with a gate, from which a Coast Guard light is visible. *Be Aware:* Leave your car unlocked and free of valuables.

H: Nakalele Blowhole (1.25 mi.)

The **Nakalele Blowhole** is a 3-foot circular opening in the roof of an underwater cave beneath a lava reef, where wave action compresses air with a hollow whooshing sound, followed by towering blasts of white water, some 50-feet high. From the parking area, head down the red cinder road through the eroded grassy area, bearing to the right of the Coast Guard light; several routes are possible. Then go down the gray-rock gully to the right of the light, to a sandy spot at the bottom. The blowhole is about .25-mile away, to your right, on a trail leading though sea-scoured rocks that may remind you of a Nevada desert—gray, black, and red; pock-marked and smooth; swirled together at their seams, or lying about in cobbles and boulders. You'll cross a large sandy area, make passage through a tuft of these rocks, and come to the blowhole—set to your left, maybe 40 feet from the sea and 15 feet below on a broad, smooth reef.

You can view from above or circle around inland to drop down to the lava shelf for an eye-level perspective. Unless you'd like a shower, which is not a bad idea on hot days, get a fix on the spray's direction and magnitude before circling the hole. *Be Aware:* Stay away from the actual opening. It may lull you for awhile on calm days, but anyone slipping into that foamy maw is not coming out.

More Stuff: On the way to the blowhole, Honokohau Bay is at the big bend north of mm36. An intriguing wide stream flows into a rocky surfer's beach. There's no inland access, but Aloha Fruit Stand is a recommended stop, when it's open. Also, at mm37, look for a gated red-dirt road on the sea side. A .25-mile walk from here gets you to the flowered, grassy view area of Kanounou Point, as far north as you can get on Maui.

18.   EKE CRATER TRAIL   H

Best For: An inland journey from the grassy upsweeps of the north shore to the fringes of the jungle at the wet heart of the island.

Parking: Take Hwy. 30, the Honoapi'ilani Hwy., north of Kapalua and continue as the road narrows along the north shore. After entering Kahakuloa Game Management boundary just before mm40, turn right on dirt Poelua Rd., near speed limit sign—just before mm41. Drive in a short distance and park at the small hunter check station. *Note:* Hunter's gate is open to vehicles on weekends and holidays.

H: Poelua Road to Eke Crater Trail (6 mi., 1,600 ft.)

Eke Crater, also called Mount Eke, is in the center of West Maui, at an elevation of nearly 5,000 feet, with some 30 feet of rainfall each year. You can't walk there—too far and too dangerous, with tangles of greenery, muddy rockslides, and lava tubes ready to slurp up a wayward hiker. But you can hike a few miles in toward the interior, where the jungle laps at your knees, and take a peek.

For **Poelua Road to Eke Crater Trail**, walk up the road to your left. You'll soon cross a metal gate, and curve to the right. Avoid two right-hand options as you arc around a red-cinder amphitheater, and stay on the main road. The route climbs on a switchback amid koa trees, and then ascends straight up a ridgeline, with green Poelua Gulch down to the left. A little over a mile from the trailhead, you'll cross a grassy area—to the left across the field is a game-watering station—and reach a second gate. Then ascend a long straightaway through a tunnel of planted pine trees, after which you'll pop out to a view. Looking up from here, you'll see a knoll at the head of the gulch, where the trail will take you if you're willing.

After the steep walk to the top of the knoll, you'll be greeted by a garden of several kinds of ferns, and a forested bench that affords a view from the high rim. After this point, the plants that have been slapping shin-high start to reach above the knees. Continuing upward, you lose Poelua Gulch on the left, and start picking up views of a deep valley to your right, which contains Honokohau Stream. Through the greenery which chokes the trail, look up to head of the drainage to see a portion of inaccessible Honokohau Falls, which is one of the highest in the nation. Pick your own turnaround point. Foliage presents a defeating obstacle and rain at this point would be downright demoralizing. On the way back you'll enjoy the seaward views as you drop to the airy slopes that lead to the trailhead. *Be Aware:* Prepare for a full-fledged day hike, anticipating sun and rain.

More Stuff: Beyond Poelua Road, the highway sweeps down to Hononana Bay. Near mm41, after a one-lane bridge, a path leads down to the boulder shores of the bay. If you rock-hopped for about .5-mile to your right at the coastline, you may find a seldom-seen blowhole.

19.   WAIKALAI PLATEAU   H

Best For: A getaway hike, from the cliffs of the north shore to the grassy plateau and pine forests high above them, with close-ups of the landmark peaks at Maui's interior.

Parking: Take Hwy. 30 north of Kapalua, as road narrows around the north shore. After mm41, Hwy. 30 becomes Hwy. 340, the Kahekili Hwy., coming around the other way, from Wailuku. Pass mm16—the numbers descend in this direction. At near mm15.5, before the road makes a steep descent, park on right at shoulder next to gate for Waikalai Game Management Road. *Note:* Hunter's gate is open to vehicles on weekends and holidays.

H: **Waikalai Plateau (5.75 mi., 1,400 ft.)**

You'll feel like you've been someplace after this moderately strenuous jaunt, beginning on the green slopes of West Maui Forest Reserve and ending at the lip of the Kahakuloa Natural Area, home to the endemic dwarf greenery that sprawls northward from center of the West Maui Mountains. For the **Waikalai Plateau** hike, start up the road from the gate and pass the hunter check station. After ten minutes you'll hook around to a view of Kahakuloa Head, the shark-fin-shaped landmark that rises above the village. About a mile into the hike, after a switchback up and a straightaway beside koa trees, you'll reach a grassy field. A wildlife watering station provides a viewpoint to the coast, and inland you get a first look at buttelike Mount Eke, which lies far inland at the head of Kahakuloa Stream.

From above the watering station, you'll walk a narrow shoulder inland, and then dip down across a saddle, which is like a land bridge spanning a gorge. Atop the other side is a freshly scented pine forest. A little more than 2 miles in, the road leaves the ridgeline, alongside a cut bank that reaches the stream. You then embark on a serious uphill segment, which leads to a grassy tableland that is planted with pines. From here is a commanding view seaward, but press on as the route snakes gradually up and in. In a few minutes you'll see a plateau, a green hillock that is your destination, rising just above the tablelands.

Take the road to the top—spurs lead elsewhere—and you'll get a view of green, stepped ridge that climbs to flat-topped Mount Eke, a.k.a. Eke Crater. Pu'u Kukui, is also visible, to the right, as are the other topographical features of the interior. Notice that the vegetation changes here, transitioning into the West Maui Natural Area Reserve, which is home to many plant species unique to Hawaii. At this end point, you may feel the hike is just beginning, such is the allure of the view. Go, if you must. *Be Aware:* Prepare for both hypothermia and heat stroke. Bring a hiking pole and plenty of water.

20.   KAHAKULOA VILLIAGE   H

Best For: Although wood-frame homes with electricity belie the image of "my little grass shack," this tiny village, with its dramatic location, is the island's best example of how Hawaiians lived in ancient times.

Parking: Take Hwy. 30 north of Kapalua as road narrows along the north shore. Continue past mm41, when route becomes Hwy. 340—and road *really* narrows. Dip into the valley and park after steel bridge near mm15. *Note:* You can also get here by taking Hwy. 340 north of Wailuku; that option involves more narrow-road driving.

H: Kahakuloa Village (up to 1.5 mi.); Kahakuloa Head (.5-mi.)

After enduring the precipitous road into **Kahakuloa Village**, most drivers are anxious about getting out, so not many take the time to stop and appreciate the place—which is a blessing since there are few parking places. But the village is Maui's best example of how people lived in ancient times in an ahupua'a—a wedge of land that contained a seacoast with agricultural plain, bisected by a stream that originates in the mountainous woodlands. These were the geographic ingredients for generations of survival.

You may wish to start your stroll at Ululani's by the Bay Shave Ice, for refreshment and to talk story with Ululani. Then, from the parking by the bridge, take the dirt road that passes homes, whose stream-irrigated gardens display an array of Polynesian fruits. Ubiquitous wild chickens and poi dogs will sound a greeting. The road follows Kahakuloa Stream through large trees to the rocky beach. Then, backtrack and continue up the main road, past a fruit stand and garden terraces. On your right will be the driveway leading to the Francis Xavier Mission. Sitting on a rise above the village, the tiny church is open to all who want to come in and light a candle. *More Stuff:* From the steel bridge, a trail leads upstream for some two miles. Local residents are generous in granting access to this route; ask permission if you see someone.

Kahakuloa Head is the 600-foot "Tall Lord" that presides in his feather cape over the northern end of the bay. For a close-up of this angular landmark often seen from afar, you need to drive through the village. After surviving the one-lane road along the cliff, the road bends right. You'll see the head on your left. Pull off on a dirt loop by a fence that provides parking for two or three cars. *Note:* If you're approaching the head from the south on Highway 340, look for this turnout on the right near mm14. You'll pass Pu'u Kahulianapa, a twin hillock that sits just inland from the head. The turnout is between the two.

From the pullout, walk through an opening in the fence and across the grassy swale between Kahakuloa Head and Pu'u Kahulianapa, which is to your right. Social trails lead seaward, down through an eroded area with large pocked-lava boulders. If you continue down to the ledges closest to the ocean, and go left, you'll get a look at Moke'ehia Island Seabird Sanctuary. It sits close to shore beneath a high cliff and is visible from few other places. Frigate birds, sherwaters, and tropic birds may grace you with a fly by. You'll also see Haleakala and the east shore. Trade winds are often in your face from this perch, but on quiet days during the whale migrations in the winter, you'll be in a natural echo chamber that amplifies the exhales of the big mammals as they laze by.

Be Aware: Ragged trails lead up Kahakuloa Head, but coming down is more difficult and using these trails contributes to harmful erosion. Birds nest here, and you may disturb them. If you feel like climbing, try a route up less-steep Pu'u Kahulianapa, a volcanic dome.

Ferns, Francis Xavier Mission, highway to Kahakuloa

Windward Coast

Kanaha Beach Park

WINDWARD COAST

The reef-protected beaches and mountain ridges on this working side of Maui are often bypassed by visitors—but not by surfers and windsurfers. Several strolls invite wave-watchers and history buffs, and adventurers will find roads to hidden heiaus, lofty mountain ridges, and sea cliffs where gargantuan waves arrive.

DRIVING TOUR
PICKING THE RIGHT DAY

Select Saturday for this driving tour to see locals at play at the Maui Swap Meet, and avoid the traffic in town during the workaday week. On days when clouds hang in the West Maui Mountains, avoid the high stuff and retreat to the sunnier coast. Featuring some indoor activities, this is a good tour when the weather is not the greatest.

THE ROADS

You'll at least be on regulation sized roadways during this drive, although traffic bogs down mornings and evenings in Kahului, like sand going through this hour glass-shaped island. Traffic also clogs headed into Paia late in the afternoons, as commuters head Upcountry. Also respect Mother Nature, by avoiding Highway 340 north of Waihe'e during or after heavy rains, as flashflooding occurs. For those wishing to circumnavigate West Maui from this directedion, one-lane road segments begin about mm8 and continue for some 9 miles—but the only white-knuckle segment is the short stretch through Kahakuloa.

THE COURSE

Follow along on the Windward Coast map, page 80. Refer to trailhead descriptions beginning on page 81 for more details.

BEGIN EARLY MORNING. MAUI SWAP MEET, KAHULUI. People-watch, souvenir shop, pick up exotic flowers, and expand your art collection at this Saturday morning extravaganza. Good deals abound. Items range from strictly tourist stuff to some guy selling what's left of his apartment before moving back to Des Moines. A good time to arrive is about 7:30 a.m., after the early birds. Think about picking up some homemade bread, organic veggies and fruits for a fresh picnic lunch.

MID-MORNING. TAKE KA'AHUMANU AVENUE, WHICH IS HIGHWAY 32, TO IAO VALLEY STATE PARK. Every day is a weekend at Iao, and you're bound to see a tour bus or two in the parking lot. The Needle is Maui's signature landmark, and it deserves it reputation. Stop at Kepaniwai Heritage Gardens on the rebound. After that, if you feel like getting high on an out-of-the way trail, try Kapilau Ridge.

HEAD UP THE COAST ON HIGHWAY 330, WHICH BECOMES HIGHWAY 340. This route takes you up Market Street in Wailuku, where you can pop out of the car to take some of the old-town stroll. Then continue north on the highway. You can use pullouts or the short trails to check out the coast at Hulu Island Seabird Sanctuary. Hikers can also take side trips for the stream walk at Swinging Bridges, or the uplands of Waiheʻe Ridge. But the best bet for a daylong tour is the short walk to the Kukuipuka Heiau, a big-mana viewpoint for the Kahului coastline, which you'll explore during the rest of the day. It's at the same parking for Waiheʻe Ridge.

NOON. HEAD BACK DOWN HIGHWAY 340. In a few minutes you can take a side-trip in Waiheʻe to see the town's hidden, pleasant beach park. Then roll the wheels south, making sure to keep left on Highway 340, which is Waiehu Beach Road. This will give you a chance to pull in to see the Halekiʻi-Pihana Heiaus State Historical Monument, hiding in plain sight.

HUG THE COAST AS THE ROUTE BECOMES KAHULUI BEACH ROAD, AND KEEP LEFT AT A MERGE WITH HIGHWAY 32. Keep left, turn left on Hobron, and turn right on Amala to get to Kanaha Beach Park. Here you can enjoy your picnic and be entertained by kite-boarders and windsurfers. This place is a never-ending action movie. Across the street is the Kanaha Pond Wildlife Sanctuary.

Iao Valley, Kite-boarding at Kanaha, Kepaniwai Heritage Gardens

AFTERNOON. DOUBLE BACK AND GET ON THE HANA HIGHWAY, HIGHWAY 36. You'll want take to a few minutes to do a drive-by at the locals' beaches mentioned in the Spreckelsville trailhead—and, hey, nobody's going to sue you if you decide to flop back for the rest of the afternoon at one of them. Or, continue driving, through Paia to check out some country scenery, either by taking the fairly long walk to Pauwela Point, or a shorter one to Halehaku Heiau and Kahuna Point. The Halehaku option is a respite among tropical trees, before you backtrack to Paia.

SUNSET. PULL IN AT HOʻOKIPA LOOKOUT. The world has few better places to finish out the day than from this overlook of the surfer and windsurfer scene. You can follow up with a meal and stroll of Paia after dark. Don't worry about a dress code. Or, if you need to get back to another part of the island, cruise down the road to Baldwin Beach Park for sunset. Coco palms fringe a long sand trip, giving way to a view of the Iao Valley and, far to the north, Kahakuloa Head. It's easy to pop a whole roll of film here—big sky, ultra-aquamarine water, perfect light. Island-style rules, as locals gather to savor another day in paradise.

Baldwin Beach entrance, Kanaha Beach Park, Hookipa Beach

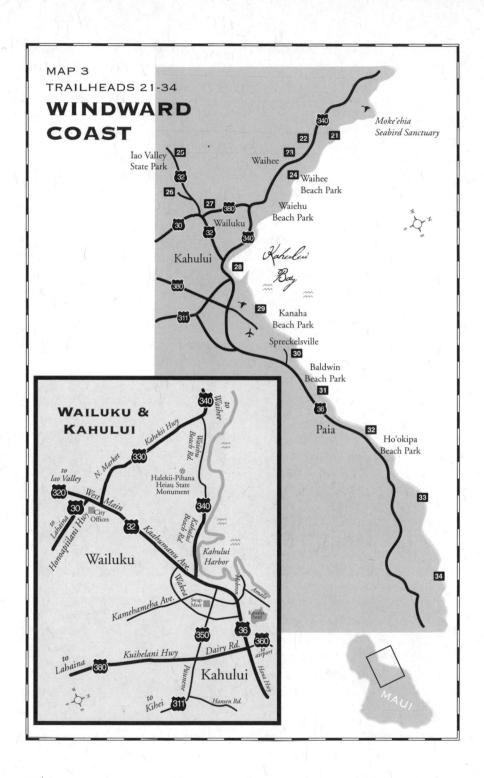

MAP 3
TRAILHEADS 21-34

WINDWARD COAST

Iao Valley
State Park

25

32

26

27 380

30

32 Wailuku

340

Kahului

28

380

311

29

Waihee

22 23

21

24 Waihee
Beach Park

Waiehu
Beach Park

340

*Kahului
Bay*

Kanaha
Beach Park

Spreckelsville

30

Baldwin
Beach Park

31

36

Paia 32

Ho'okipa
Beach Park

33

34

*Moke'ehia
Seabird Sanctuary*

WAILUKU & KAHULUI

340 *to
Waihee*

Kahekii Hwy 330

N. Market

*to
Iao Valley*

320

30 *West Main*

*City
Offices*

32

*to
Lahaina*

Wailuku

Kamehameha Ave.

350 36

*to
Lahaina* 380 *Kuihelani Hwy* *Dairy Rd.* 360 *to
airport*

Kahului

*to
Kihei* 311 *Hansen Rd.*

Waiehu Beach Rd.

Halekii-Pihana
Heiau State
Monument

340

Kahului Beach Rd.

Kaahumanu Ave.

*Kahului
Harbor*

Wakea

Swap
Meet

*Kanaha
Pond*

Halona

Amala

Honoapiilani Hwy

Paihene

Hana Hwy

MAUI

TRAILHEADS

H	HIKING
SN	SNORKELING
P	KAYAKING, CANOEING
SF	SURFING, BOOGIE BOARDING, WIND SPORTS

TH = Trailhead

mm = mile marker; corresponds to highway signs

All hiking distances in parentheses are ROUND TRIP.

Elevation gains of 100 feet or more are noted.

21. SEABIRD BLUFFS   H

Best For: Wandering grassy bluffs above a wild coast and tiny islands that are a sanctuary for seabirds.

Parking: Take Hwy. 340, the Kahekili Hwy., north of Wailuku and Waihe'e. Look for a large turnout on right at mm5.75., at wooden, gatelike opening a fence. *Notes*: You will see other similar openings after mm5, before this one. This trailhead is apparent public access on private property. Use your own judgment. Landowners are not legally responsible for your safety.

H: Seabird Bluffs (up to 2 mi., 200 ft.)

Extending several miles north of Waihe'e is a roadless coast with cliffs and bluffs that embrace the trade wind's waves. The bluffs were the Western world's first glimpse of Maui, by Captain James Cook in 1778. Offshore the southern end of this coast is Hulu Island, a nationally designated bird sanctuary. Its sister sanctuary, Moke'ehia Island, is to the north, just offshore of the 500-foot Hakuhe'e point. Coastal walls are hundreds of feet high. The solid lava on this side of Maui does not so easily erode into the valleys that are typical of the leeward side of West Maui. For the **Seabird Bluffs** hike, hop through the wooden bracing in the fence and take one of the social trails down the grassy hills, among trees braving the windswept creases.

If you veer right—toward the other fence openings you may have seen before the primary parking—you could drop way down to the coast on a dirt road. Horseback tours make the swing through this country. For a better look at the bird islands, you'll

Moke'ehia Island

want to veer north, or left, a few hundred feet. You'll drop down to where Hulu Island is just offshore. Moke'ehia Island is tough to make out without binoculars, since it is so small and partially behind the 500-foot cliffs of Pu'u Makawana, a volcanic dome. You can make your way in that direction, but steep terrain and stream ravines make the going tough. *Be Aware:* Maui is a geologic work in progress. Some bluff edges are precipitous and unstable. Stay back.

22. WAIHE'E RIDGE   H

Best For: Starting high above the coast on a trail that takes you higher, to the gateway of the mountains at the center of the island.

Parking: Take Hwy. 340, the Kahekili Hwy., north of Wailuku and Waihe'e. Turn left at mm6.75, across the highway from Mendez Ranch and call box 4. Drive .75-mi. up a partially paved road to a signed trailhead on the left in a pasture; the road continues to Maluhia Boy Scout Camp.

H: Waihe'e Ridge (4.75 mi., 1,500 ft.); Kukuipuka Heiau (.25-mi.)

From a cow gate, trudge up the steep concrete ramp that begins the **Waihe'e Ridge Trail**. Part of the state's Na Ala Hele trail system, the route is well constructed and marked. At the top of the ramp, go left through a gate and ascend through a tree tunnel that includes Norfolk pine and guava trees. At .5-mile and beyond, you'll come to an overlook of Waiheʻe Valley—the site for the hike in TH23—a worthy end-point for hikers with less time, or on days when the clouds are hanging on the interior ridges.

From this first overlook the trail climbs with the aid of staircase sections, to a knob and spiny ridge that affords both the big look back toward the windward coast and the ridges that rise inland. The trail then veers away from the valley, across a depression of native scrub, before exacting another climb that is made easier by stair sections. Trail's end is an open hillock at 2,500 feet, offering a picnic table from which to enjoy the vista. Inland, about a mile away and not much higher, is Mount Lanilili. Puʻu Kukui, West Maui's highest, is behind that peak, and flat-topped Eke Crater is north and inland. *Be Aware:* Prepare for rain and slippery conditions on this hike. The trail beyond the fencing is hazardous and not maintained. Watch your step.

Kukuipuka Heiau is a place that radiates beauty in all directions. Walk or drive toward the ocean from trailhead parking toward the hill that rises above the meadow. Pass through a gate and up the improved trail. You reach an open promontory, and the heiau, whose low, white-limestone walls—about 75-feet square—invite visitors to stop and enjoy. Native flowers and trees accent sweeping coastal views. The heiau has been restored by Leiʻohu Ryder and other community members; see *Resource Links.*

Kukuipuka Heiau

Second swinging bridge, Waihe'e Ridge Trail

Best For: An exciting hike over plank suspension bridges that lead upriver in a tropical canyon—to where waterfalls drop from thousands of feet.

Parking: Take Hwy. 340, the Kahekili Hwy., north from Wailuku. Pass the school in Waiheʻe and turn left Waiheʻe Valley Rd., before the bridge at mm5. Go .4-mi. and park at grass turnout on the right across from telephone pole #12, before the end of the paved road. *Be Aware:* Leave your car unlocked and free of valuables. Access is via an easement on lands of an irrigation district.

H: **Swinging Bridges (4.25 mi., 250 ft.)**

This popular trail follows the river up Waiheʻe Valley, which is nearly 3,000 feet deep. Waiheʻe means "slippery waters," made so by algae, so be extra careful with your footing. For the **Swinging Bridges** hike, walk up the street and turn right on the dirt road. At a decrepit cable gate, the road starts up through dense subtropical forest, with the river down to your right. You'll gain much of the hike's elevation on this stretch.

About .75-mile in, the road begins a contour alongside an irrigation ditch, which periodically disappears into dripping tunnels. You may see a waterfall or two coming down from the ridge inland to your right. Less than .5-mile later you drop to the first

First swinging bridge

bridge, a plank-and-cable strand some 150 feet long and 10 feet above the water. Just after the first bridge is the second, set in a profusion of jungle greenery. The second span is maybe 50 feet long, with a slightly uphill grade nearly 20 feet above the river.

Okay, you made it. From the second bridge, the trail rises a little, and pierces a thicket of hau trees. Then you drop down and cross the river, and weave up the other bank. Several hundred yards ahead, the official trail ends at an old dam, with pools. Steep terrain and foliage prevent the postcard shot, but you will glimpse the great walled amphitheater carved by the Waiheʻe River, falling thousands of feet from one of the wettest spots in the world. *Be Aware:* Flash floods in this valley present a significant hazard. Stay out during rains, keeping in mind that rains can be falling inland when the coast is sunny. Don't cross the bridges unless the river is low enough to cross through the water in a pinch. If you get stuck on the wrong side of a torrent, wait it out. If the water rises suddenly, immediately head to high ground.

24.   WAIHEʻE BEACHES   H, SN

Best For: This long, scenic beach offering a quiet relief from resort strips; and nearby heiaus are a historical surprise, hidden above the neighborhoods.

Parking: Take Hwy. 340, the Kahekili Hwy. north of Wailuku. In Waiheʻe, just after the ball field and before mm4, turn right on Halewaiu Rd. At the bottom of the hill, veer right toward Shoreline Access sign, and then turn left, before the golf course, into beach park. *Note:* Additional parking is described for heiau hike.

H: Waiheʻe Beach Park (up to 3 mi.); Halekiʻi-Pihana Heiaus (up to .5-mi.)

At Waiheʻe Beach, the 600-foot-high walls of the northeast shores have tapered down to sea level. This long curve of tree-fringed sand and coral reef is seldom visited by tourists. Tall ironwoods surround a spacious lawn, creating a choice beachside picnic spot. From **Waiheʻe Beach Park**, you can walk about .75-mile north, or left, on the sand, but cliffs and rocks make the going tough before reaching Waiheʻe Point. A sand road inland, with questionable public access for trailblazers, leads toward the Kealakaihonua Heiau, located just south of where the Waiheʻe River joins the Pacific.

Going to the right, you can walk about a mile to Waiehu Beach Park, which abuts the other side of the golf course. The sand dwindles along the fairways, and you may have to skirt margins of the golf course or pick your way along driftwood and black boulders for a short stretch. You then hit the sandy, open beach at Waiehu. *More Stuff:* To drive this unimproved park, turn left on Lower Waiehu Beach Road, which is off Highway 340, a.k.a. Waiehu Beach Road, just south of the junction with Highway 330. Follow the lower beach road to the golf course.

The **Haleki'i-Pihana Heiaus** are a State Historical Monument, with some ruins dating from the late 1500s. Take Highway 340, or Waiehu Beach Road, south of its junction with Highway 330; you could also approach from Kahului Harbor on Highway 340. Turn inland on Kuhio Place (across from Ka'ae Place) and then turn left on Hea Place. The monument takes up 10 acres atop the hill, with views of the Iao Valley and Kahului coast. The Pihana Heiau remains are farthest from the parking lot. This site, some of which was partially eroded by floods, is thought to date from the 1500s. The Haleki'i Heiau ruins spread from the lot's interpretive signs and beyond. Kamehameha the Great made human sacrifices here in 1790 to prepare for his conquest of Maui in the Iao Valley. Both these heiaus were partially dismantled when kapus against sacrifice and other decrees were made in the 1800s. Below the vantage point, housing tracts and metal warehouses provide historical juxtaposition.

SN: A coral reef offshore **Waihe'e Beach Park** limits shore break and provides for colorful swimming, when conditions are right. But this is more of a place to take a dip than snorkeling destination; waters may be shallow. The park is an excellent picnic choice. *Be Aware*: Waves breaking on the reef mean rip currents may exists. Watch the bottom when you get in and observe whether current is carrying you someplace.

25.   IAO VALLEY   H

Best For: Maui's signature tropical ridges, cascades, gardens, and ocean panoramas woo hikers and strollers alike. Take your pick.

Parking: *For all hikes,* take Hwy. 320, or Iao Valley Rd., from Wailuku. Iao Valley Rd. is where Hwy. 32 meets Hwy. 30, near city hall. *For Kepaniwai Heritage Gardens,* look for county park near mm1. *For Iao Valley State Park hikes,* continue 2 miles to the end of road at a large paved lot.

H: Kepaniwai Heritage Gardens (.25-mi.); Iao Valley State Park to: Botanical Gardens and Iao Needle Overlook (.75-mi), or Iao Tablelands vista (1.5 mi., 250 ft.), or Iao Stream (1.25 mi.)

The **Kepaniwai Heritage Gardens** are at the gateway to Iao Valley, where steep green ridges narrow, alongside rushing Iao Stream. The park features banyans, coco palms, taro, and a variety of Polynesian flora, growing amidst a stone-foundation grass hut and other exhibits that recreate village life on Maui. A Japanese garden and Chinese pagoda also grace the park, along with the architectural styles of Portugal, the Philippines, and New England—all meant to pay tribute to the many people who have called Hawaii home. On a less harmonious note, Kepaniwai means "damming of the waters," in reference to the mounds of fallen warriors who virtually stopped the flow of Iao Stream during the great battle of 1790. If you're headed to the state park, these gardens are the best spot to stop for a picnic on the way back.

Most tourists, some in buses, visit **Iao Valley State Park** to pay homage to the Iao Needle, the poster-boy for Maui travel photos. Nonetheless, you'll find plenty of room to roam. For the hike to **Botanical Gardens and Iao Needle**, take the paved path past the rest rooms, and go left down the stairs before the bridge. You can wander around among the signed plants, both indigenous and Polynesian-introduced, and ponds. At the far end of the gardens, face upstream to observe the confluence. Kinihapai Stream, which flows under the bridge from the Needle, joins Iao Stream, which comes from the valley to the left. Then retrace your steps out of the garden, cross the footbridge— a Kodak moment—and take the paved path to the right. After hopping up a few dozen stairs, you will come to the small covered viewing area for the Iao Needle. The boundary for the 6-acre state park is the railing at the Needle Overlook.

To continue to the **Iao Tablelands vista**—the choice hike for the valley and one of the best on Maui—you need step over the railing at the overlook and continue up the well-used trail. *Note:* This trail has been walked continuously from ancient times to most recent. Signs note that you are leaving the state park and trespassing. Property owners are not liable for injury to persons using their lands for recreational purposes. Use your own judgment.

The Iao Tablelands is the area between and above the two streams, which join below at the botanical garden. The trail at first is cut into the side of a narrow ridge, with an embankment rising to your left and a steep valley on the right. As you climb, during the first .25-mile, you'll rise above the Needle and be able to observe that the backside of the spire is anchored up high to a ridge, eliminating the needle effect. After less than .5-mile, you'll see the first of several spur trails on your left—steep climbs up about 15 feet—that take you to the top of the a small ridge. Take one of these, or continue until the trail climbs so that there is no rise to your left. Then double-back a few hundred feet down the trail that runs along the ridge, parallel and slightly above the main trail.

Either way, near the top of this little ridge are astounding views: You'll see inland up the Iao Valley and seaward to the Kahului Coast. Both streams are visible. On the north is the Wall of Tears, a 3,000-foot fissured cliff that at times will have a half-dozen silvery falls. And then turn around. The craggy green topography of the Kapilau Ridge is equally captivating. *Be Aware:* Prepare for a slippery surface and stay back from trail edges, where drop-offs are very dangerous.

More Stuff: From the vista point, the trail continues into the tablelands for more than a mile, and gradually up. Although flora encroaches the trail at times—ferns, koa, ti, bananas, guava—the route is easy to walk. You won't achieve a view comparable to the vista point, and forget about taking the ancient route to the Olowalu Valley: It's overgrown and washed out. *Be Aware:* The trails are easy to walk, but make sure to memorize your trail junctions, as coming back can be confusing.

Iao Tablelands shrine, Kepaniwai Heritage Gardens, Kapilau Ridge

For the **Iao Stream** walk, cross the bridge at the stream on the improved path. At the stairs leading to the Needle, go to your left on a path and stairs down to the forested banks of Iao Stream. A social trail leads upstream, the first part of which is easy to follow. If you wish, take that and then backtrack. The improved trail makes a loop downstream, passing near the confluence across from the botanical garden. *Note:* The Iao Valley has become known for the gruesome battle. But for centuries is was also the place on Maui where the Makahiki was celebrated in the fall—when the god Lono returned to bring peace and renewal, and to bless of the land's bounty.

26. KAPILAU RIDGE   H

Best For: A little used trail that takes you way up to a sweeping view of the isthmus' two coasts and a goat's-eye look at Iao Valley.

Parking: Take Hwy. 320, or Iao Valley Rd., from Wailuku. After about .5-mi., veer left toward Wailuku Heights on W. Alu Rd. Continue about .5-mi., to where guardrail ends and the road makes a big left. On the right is telephone pole #5, with a smaller #7 beneath it. Reverse course and park at a shoulder on the right.

H: **Kapilau Ridge to: Wailuku Cross (1.5 mi., 850 ft.), or Pu'u Lio (4.5 mi., 2,100 ft.)**

Almost 50 years ago, parochial school students from Wailuku erected a large cross on the Kapilau Ridge, which is the one to the left as you look toward the Iao Valley. Repairs and improvements have been made on yearly pilgrimages. You can see the white cross from Highway 30 south of Wailuku, and from Highway 340 going north. Pu'u Lio is several pitches up the ridge from the cross, the pointed knob just below the top.

For **both Kapilau Ridge hikes**, step up the embankment at telephone pole #5 and begin the steep climb through trees made less dense by a recent fire. Roots help with footing. The trail flattens before you reach the wooden **Wailuku Cross**, contouring along through koa, ironwoods, and even paperbark trees. You can see the Needle up the valley, but flora prevents the big view in any direction.

For the aerial views from **Pu'u Lio**, continue past the cross. The trail makes several steep rises, followed by flatter segments on knolls. Not far above the cross, century plants may block the trail in one spot, but good passage follows for the rest of the hike. The first big pitch from the cross reaches a clump of ironwoods. From there you'll ascend two eroded, red-dirt ramps. The more forested Pu'u Lio is above these; a small grassy area, which is often at cloud level, lets you look through leaves and century plants, down at the Iao Needle, and the Kinihapai Stream side of the valley. Helicopters, if present, will be several hundred feet below. Unfortunately, the ridge you are climbing occludes a view of the Iao Stream side of the valley.

Since the Puʻu Lio is often in clouds, you may prefer the open, red-dirt knoll that lies below it as an end point to this hike. Coming down, of course, you'll have vistas of both coasts of the isthmus, and Haleakala. *Be Aware:* Although drop-offs are not much of a hazard on this hike, a slip-and-fall is likely. Use a hiking pole if you have one.

More Stuff: Waikapu Valley is west of Iao Valley, to the left as you face West Maui. Trailblazers can explore there by taking W. Waiko Road off Highway 30, south of Wailuku. Pass Kilohi Street and look for telephone pole #17 about midway in a pineapple field on your left. Roads through the field lead to the stream, and upstream. The going is off-trail, advised for experienced hikers only. *Be Aware:* Access is via private lands. Use your own judgment.

27.   WAILUKU TOWN   H

Best For: Doing some quirky souvenir shopping while you get a sense of small-town Maui, circa 1950.

Parking: Go north toward Wailuku on Hwy. 30, which becomes S. High St. At a traffic signal, S. High St. meets Hwy. 32, which is also Main St. Two parking spots: *For the Historical Buildings:* Park at public lot across the street from the library, just before reaching Main. *For the Old Town Stroll:* Turn right on Main St. and then turn left on N. Market St. Park on-street, or in a public lot that is on the left before reaching Vineyard St.

H: **Historical Buildings Tour (.25-mi.); Old Town Stroll (.25-mi.)**

At the opening to the Iao Valley, Wailuku's site was the chosen spot for the kings, or aliʻi, of ancient times. This is also where Kamehameha I's forces won the final battle that united all the islands as a kingdom, where the missionary movement and educational reforms were centered, and, finally, the capital for sugar industry's growth during the late 1800s and well into the 1900s. All of these historical threads are braided together within a few blocks on the **Historical Buildings Tour**, featuring some 10 buildings listed on the National Register of Historic Places.

The Old County Building, under the huge monkeypod trees at the parking lot, dates from 1925. Next door, the Circuit Courthouse, was built 18 years earlier. Both are National Historic Places. So are the Wailuku Public Library across High Street, and the Territorial Building, which sits with a lawn buffer just above it. Next to these sites, toward Main Street, are the Kaʻahumanu Church, built in 1876 to honor Hawaii's favorite queen, and a small cemetery—easy to miss—where Hawaiian aliʻi and missionary families lay side by side.

Walking to your left, toward Iao Valley, on Main Street, you'll see the Alexander House, built in 1836. And just up the street is the Bailey House Museum. Built on lands donated to the missionaries by Hawaiian royalty, the plantation-style structure was home to the Wailuku Female Seminary from 1832 to 1932. Today, you'll find native Hawaiian artifacts, paintings, and furnishings, set among informative displays that tell the story of Maui's golden era, when educational and cultural reforms took place in the 1800s. Outside amid an exotic garden is a canoe, hand-hewn from a koa log, and a long board used by the daddy of wave riders, Duke Kahanamoku.

Although the county seat since 1905, the high tide of commerce has been receding from Wailuku since the 1960s, as evidenced in the charming, art deco-meets-Old West buildings along the **Old Town Stroll**. Antique stores, bona fide junk stores, Hawaiian crafts, used records, galleries, second-hand clothes, old books, and espresso cafes, are strung along one block, all set around the crown jewel of funk deco, the Iao Theater. Old Wailuku is not trying to be cool, although some brochure writers have dubbed Market Street, "Antiques Row." It is what it is. *Note:* Plan this walk for Monday, Tuesday, or Thursday to pick up some island fruits and veggies at a farmer's market at the corner of Market and Vineyard.

You can also turn left on Vineyard and meander up toward Church Street, which is a one-way in the opposite direction of Market. On side streets, are neighborhoods with sugar shacks covered with sprays of flowers and tropical greenery. Way at the end of Vineyard, at the corner of Ilina Street—you'll probably want to drive—is another cemetery. The headstones are a history of Maui, and the view of the Iao Valley from here is one to make most of us take time to reflect. Alright, back to the beach.

28. KAHULUI HARBOR   H, P, SF

Best For: Catching the gargantuan open market and swap meet on Saturdays. Then see if there's a canoe race or big surf at the harbor.

Parking: Take Hwy. 311, the Mokulele Hwy., to Kahului. Mokulele becomes Hwy. 350 and Pu'uhene Ave. Follow several blocks to Kamehameha Ave. *Alternate route:* Take Hwy. 30 to Wailuku and turn right on Hwy. 32, which is W. Main St. Follow as Main St. becomes Ka'ahumanu Ave., and turn right on Hwy. 350, Pu'uhene Ave. *Note:* Additional directions follow in activity descriptions.

H: **Maui Swap Meet (about .5-mi.); Kahului Breakwater and Keopualani Park (up to 1.5 mi.)**

Locals gather before 7 a.m. on Saturday for the **Maui Swap Meet**, in search of good deals on fresh flowers, sunglasses, T-shirts, books, jewelry, ethnic snacks, native crafts, castaway junk, baked goods, trinkets, and a mind-boggling assortment of locally grown

Maui Swap Meet, Kahului Bay

fruits, herbs, and vegetables. You may arrive just to roam the several-acre scene, but few will depart empty handed. The event winds down around noon.

From the swap meet, drive to the **Kahului Breakwater** and **Keopualani Park**. Head up Pu'uhene Avenue to Ka'ahumanu Avenue, or Highway 32. Turn left, and then veer right on Highway 340, which is Kahului Beach Road. At the far end of the harbor, turn right on an unpaved road that goes out onto the wide breakwater that forms the west side of the harbor. This is Kahului Harbor Park, an undeveloped place. Park near the end and walk about to view the big ships, incoming surf, fishermen and surfers—and an inland look at the Iao Valley. Keopualani Park, home to the Maui Art Center, spacious play areas, and Maui Nui Botanical Garden, is across the main road. A jogging path leads through the park to the gardens, which are growing into one of the better exhibits of Polynesian and native plants. To drive directly to the botanical gardens, turn right after leaving the breakwater and make your first left on Kanaloa Avenue.

P: The Hawaiian Canoe Club puts in at the grassy shores of Hoaloha Park for paddles out Kahului Harbor. At the harbor entrance, you can head right toward Spreckelsville, or stroke north toward the bird islands on the northeast coast. A long reef offshore moderates the swell. Hoaloha Park is at the east end of the harbor. Continue on Pu'uhene Avenue, crossing Highway 32 toward Shoreline Access. If you're driving east on Highway 32, Ka'ahumanu Avenue, turn left past Lono Avenue on Pu'uhene. The small park offers a big view of Pier 2, where the big container vessels dock. *Be Aware*: This is a summer adventure, as high surf usually creates unsafe conditions during the winter. You need to be aware of ship traffic at all times.

SF: The breakwater at **Kahului Harbor Park** presents a choice for surfers: a left-break inside the harbor, or a larger, right-break outside on the ocean side. The outside break is often better reached from the **Paukukalo** neighborhood. In addition to the breakwater spot, locals like the winter surf just up the coast at **Nehe Point**, a left-break that can reach 12 feet or more. Take Highway 340 north as Kahului Beach Road veers right as it becomes Waiehu Beach Road. Several Shoreline Access points are to the right on dead-end roads: Kainalu, Linekona, Kaiko'o, and Kailana. The Paukukalo neighborhood gives you an unvarnished look at Maui's more modest homes.

29.   KANAHA BEACH PARK   H, SN, SF

Best For: A historic wildlife sanctuary and pond sit across the street from a coral reef beach that beckons windsurfers and kite-boarders from all over the globe.

Kanaha Beach

Parking: *For Kanaha Beach:* Go east on Hwy. 32, Ka'ahumanu Ave., and continue straight at the jct. with Hwy. 36, the Hana Hwy. Turn left on Hobron Ave., and then turn right on Amala Pl. Continue for 1.75 mi., as Amala becomes Alahao St., and turn left into the second paved entry to the beach park on your left. *Alternate route:* Go to the airport, loop all the way around the terminal, and turn right toward the rental car returns on Ka'a St. Ka'a joins Alahao St.; turn right for beach park.

For Kanaha Pond: From its jct. with Hwy. 32, take Hwy. 36 and then veer left toward the airport on Hwy. 36A. The viewing kiosk parking will be on your left. For the pond paths, veer left off 36A toward the airport on Keolani Pl., and make the first left, on Palapala Dr.

H: **Kanaha Beach stroll (up to 2.25 mi.); Kanaha Pond Wildlife Sanctuary to: viewing kiosk (.25-mi), or pond paths (up to 1.75 mi.)**

Head to **Kanaha Beach Park** in the afternoon, when the kite-boarders are going airborne and the breaking waves are accented with dozens of colorful windsurfer sails. Many visitors overlook this scenic park because it is off main roads and near the airport. About .5-mile after making the right on Amala, you'll see the wildlife sanctuary on your right, although there's no entry on this boundary. Then, on the left is the unimproved beach area that is the kite-boarders' hangout. These guys, and gals, stand on a short board with toe clips and hold onto a kite—that has just enough lift to swing them into the air in a pendulum motion, but not enough to yank them into the wild blue yonder.

From the farthest lot at Kanaha Beach Park, the take-off spot for the windsurfers, stroll down the beach to your left and continue past the rounded point to the kite-board

Kanaha Beach

beach. You can also weave through the expansive picnic area, shaded by ironwoods and tall broadleaf trees. The county camping area is at the end of the park on its Kahului side. Along the coast, you may notice just offshore a few concrete boxes. These are WWII-vintage pillboxes that were just onshore in the 1940s—that much erosion has taken place since then. *Note:* The east end of Kanaha is sometimes called Airport Beach. *More Stuff:* Continue past the beach park to where Alahao Street ends, and you'll find a bike path that skirts the airport fields and takes you to Spreckelsville, TH28.

The **Kanaha Pond Wildlife Sanctuary viewing kiosk** is a short walk over the water on a man-made peninsula, from a very busy street. The pond was built to raise fish and waterfowl, more than 200 years ago by King Kapiʻiohoʻokalani. Today this National Natural Landmark provides habitat for native Hawaiian species, such as the coot, stilt, and duck—all endangered. Migrating waterfowl and shorebirds also touch down here in the winter, along with the tourists, from Asia and the mainland.

At the east end of the fenced, 150-acre sanctuary are **pond paths**, four of them running parallel, creating a walking track with options. Wandering these tree-shaded land patches between still waters will be a memorable experience for bird watchers. *Note:* You'll need a permit—available from September through March, when birds are not nesting—from the Division of Forestry and Wildlife; see *Resource Links*. The free permits only take a few minutes to process on the day of your request.

SN: The long Spartan Reef offshore **Kanaha Beach Park** provides for a wave-free and colorful snorkeling area, but windsurf action makes swimming chancy. A roped-off pool near the lifeguard stations is a safe place to take a dip; or, show up before 11 a.m., the prescribed start time for the wind worshipers. Summer is best here, when surf usually subsides. Hawaiian spear fishermen like this beach, some of them venturing out at night.

SF: **Kanaha Beach Park** is a windsurfing and kite-boarding Mecca, both for those who take part and those who want to kick back and watch the spectacle.

30. SPRECKELSVILLE

H, SN, SF

Best For: Three beaches to get away from it all, without having to go far to do it.

Parking: *For all beaches:* Take Hwy. 36, the Hana Hwy. past its jct. with Hwy. 37 and mm3. *For Spreckelsville Beach:* As Hwy. 36 bends to the right, turn left on unsigned Spreckelsville Beach Rd., a.k.a., Stable Rd. *For Sugar Cove, Baby Baldwin:* Continue as Hwy. 36 bends right, pass the senior center, and turn left on Nonohe Pl. Further directions in hiking descriptions.

H: Sprecksville Beach (up to 2.5 mi.); Sugar Cove (up to 1.25 mi.); Baby Baldwin Beach (1.25 mi.)

Claus Spreckels came to Maui already a millionaire in 1877. He left 20 years later a multi-millionaire known as the "Sugar King" of Hawaii, after he bought up thousands of acres and built mega-irrigation ditches that captured stream flows on the north slope of Haleakala. Known also by some as a robber baron, Spreckels' former compound, Spreckelsville, was where the Maui Country Club is today.

You'll see several potholed spur roads to **Spreckelsville Beach** after you pass coco palms. Dunes and beach succulents appear on your right. The access roads are from .5-mile to 1 mile from the highway turnoff, before reaching homes at road's end. Park off the pavement at the farthest, and walk through the pinkish sand dunes to the beach. To your left, less than .5-mile away is Kanaha Beach Park, TH29. To your right you can walk about 1.25 miles, passing rounded Papaula Point, to Sugar Cove. Small black-rock points intrude into the sand along the way. *Be Aware:* Jet traffic from the airport goes overhead. But this is Maui, with infrequent takeoffs, and this beach is devoid of car traffic. *More Stuff:* To your left, across from the beach access roads, is the bike path that goes to Kanaha Beach Park.

To **Sugar Cove**, drive to the bottom of Nonohe Place and turn left on Pa'ani Place, which may be unsigned. Park at road's end, near a sign for Shoreline Access 302. A short sand trail leads along a lava seawall to a .25-mile cove set below unobtrusive, high-end condos. You can walk left to Spreckelsville Beach—the reverse of the hike described above—but this beach is more a place to catch a few winks or count grains of sand. To **Baby Baldwin Beach**, go right on Nonohe at the bottom, and then turn left toward Shoreline Access, on Kealakai Place—instead of going to the golf course. The unimproved parking is at Wawau Point, where a mosaic of red banks, black rocks, and white sand make for an interesting stroll. The beach hike seamlessly connects with Baldwin Beach Park, TH31.

SN: A finger from Wawau Point's reef curls just offshore for several hundred feet at **Baby Baldwin Beach**, making a sandy-bottomed oval that can accommodate large numbers of swimmers. The beach is a well-known dipping pool for families, safe even during trade winds—although be mindful of the current flowing to your right as water returns out the open end of nature's pool. Soft sand buffets the shore. Not many fish in the pool, but this is a five-star swimming spot.

SF: Windsurfers catch the breeze off **Wawau Point**, near Baby Baldwin, but offshore rocks make this less popular than other spots not far away, both up and down the coast.

31. BALDWIN BEACH PARK H, SN, SF

Best For: One of Maui's sweet spots, where coco palms fringe golden sand and turquoise waters, the perfect place to enjoy life on a waning afternoon.

Parking: Take Hwy. 36, the Hana Hwy., past the Maui Country Club to mm6. Turn left into signed beach park lot.

H: Baldwin Beach to: Baby Baldwin (.75-mi.), or Paia (1.5 mi.)

The beach park is the former home for families who worked the sugar cane for Harry A. Baldwin—whose grandfather Dwight Baldwin was one of Maui's original missionaries in Lahaina in the early 1800s. Harry furthered the efforts of his father, Henry P., and the family by the 1930s was one of the Big Five, who controlled more than 90 percent of the state's sugar production—and virtually ran Hawaii's government. Local mills have shut down, but you'll still be able to talk story with some of the workers and their descendents who hang around the park. If you're lucky, you'll arrive on a day when blade-wielding Tongans are climbing the park's willowy coco palms to trim.

Late afternoons are a good time for **Baldwin Beach**, as locals gather to frolic in the surf and unwind. **Baby Baldwin Beach** is a sand-and-surf walk. In the background is the jade tunnel of the Iao Valley, and to the right in the distance you'll see the shark fin of Kahakuloa Head. See TH30 for direct access to Baby Baldwin. Going to your right from the pavilion, toward **Paia**, you'll round a sandy point, with a Zen center just inland. Riprap protects the shore in places, but you can use a dirt path—a joggers'

Baby Baldwin Beach

Sugar Cove Beach, Baldwin Beach Park

favorite—that parallels the beach and takes you to the beach park at the youth center in Paia. Ironwoods, palms, and kiawe trees shade the way.

SN: **Baldwin Beach** is not known as a snorkeling beach, but you will find spots to take a dip. The best swimming is during the summer, as trade swells usually foam over the barrier reef and make unsafe conditions during winter months. Ask the lifeguard, on duty until late afternoon.

SF: The shore break to the left of **Baldwin Beach** parking draws bodysurfers and boogie boarders in the winter. But be careful, as head plants can be scary at times. The lifeguards normally post signs when the hazard is greatest, but you shouldn't rely on them. Board surfers head for the reef break, to the right of the pavilion in the direction of Paia.

Best For: Shopping for surf shoes, espresso, or island art in this quirky beach town, and then head down the road to watch the show at the world capital of windsurfing.

Parking: *For both hikes,* take Hwy. 36, the Hana Hwy., past mm6. *For the Paia stroll:* As you approach the first buildings, at the first crosswalk and reduced speed sign, look for public parking sign on your right. *For Ho'okipa Beach walk:* Drive beyond Paia. At about mm8.5, pass the first entrances to the beach park and turn left past a sign for Ho'okipa Lookout. Park at the upper lot. *Note:* Additional directions given below in activity descriptions.

H: **Paia stroll (.75-mi.); Ho'okipa Beach walk (1 mi.)**

For the **Paia stroll**, wander up the Hana Highway to its T-intersection with Baldwin Avenue. All the action is a block or two on either side. If you need a beach break, begin your stroll by doubling back a short distance to the Lower Paia Beach Park, at the youth center, where you can take a look at Paia Bay.

Paia reinvented itself in the 1980s, when the studly new sport of windsurfing married the fetching waves of nearby Ho'okipa Beach. The fading Old West wood-frames, plantation cottages, and sugar shacks got new coats of pastel paints, as the sandy-footed set created a demand for a host of low-key tourist shops—boutiques, hemp-reggae wear, surfer Joe outfitters, espresso internet cafés, seafood grills, and some of Maui's best art galleries. Missing your pooch? In Paia you can rent a dog for a day, at the Maui Grown Market. Although traffic clogs the center of things, you can still stroll and people watch, read the plastered community bulletin boards, and veer into quiet sugar-shack neighborhoods. Don't bother to shave or blow dry beforehand, since this is a dress-down place, even for island-style.

Surfers catch the point break below the **Ho'okipa Beach** lookout, riding in toward the shore as spectators view from a pipe railing. At the far end of the railing, you can take a social trail down a grass embankment to the smooth lava shelf to get a board's eye view on the action, looking down the waves instead of at them. You'll also find tide pools and a small natural arch on this formation. A side trip to your right leads toward sloping pastures. Then, for a closer look at the beach scene, double back to the lookout and take the road down to the pavilion—or you can contour around to the beach below the lookout. Late in the day, the long parking lot along the beach is filled with surfers of every stripe, enjoying their day at Hookah, er, Ho'okipa. The lower part of the beach extends for about .25-mile, with a reef close in on the east end below the lookout. Windsurfers often gather where a point extends on the west end of the beach.

Ho'okipa Beach, Paia

SN: Paia and Ho'okipa, with reefs close in and wave action, aren't good for swimming, particularly in the winter. To take the plunge, try **Mama's Cove**. Driving toward Ho'okipa from Paia, turn left at Shoreline Access sign at mm7.75, on Kaimao Place; this is about .25-mile before the venerable Mama's Fish House. With no help from signs after making the turn, drive until you have to turn right on Aleiki Place and then go all the way, as if you're entering someone's driveway at a block wall near 133 Aleiki. You'll then see another sign. Park at a grass strip, and walk down a path between two homes. At last you'll pop out to this sandy cove, just down the beach from Mama's. The cove has a reef close to shore that creates a keiki pond, normally safe for swimming.

SF: Bodysurfers and boogie boarders ride the tiers at **Lower Paia Beach Park**, which is on the left as you come into Paia. **Ho'okipa** has been home to the world championships of windsurfing; they normally gather at the west end of the beach, where the Spartan Reef begins offshore and runs all the way across Kahului Harbor. Bodysurfing is sometimes good at the other end, below the pavilion, close to shore. Some of Maui's best board surfing waves are off the lookout, several tiers of wedges that break to the right.

In the little settlement of Kuau, about .5-mile from Paia, are two Shoreline Access spots that host a lower-key surf scene. The best is near mm7 at **Kuau Beach Place**. A dimple of a cove creates wave action. Ask locals, since shallow reefs create hazards.

33. PAUWELA POINT   H, P

Best For: Behemoth waves that meet the land at this grassy bluff high above an otherwise inaccessible coastline.

Parking: Take Hwy. 36, the Hana Hwy., past mm11 and the turnoff to Haiku. After another .5-mi., park on right near the Haiku Community Center, which is between Pauwela Rd. and Pili Aloha. *Note:* On dry days, you may be able to drive the first part of the hike, eliminating some 2 mi. from the hiking distance.

H: Pauwela Point (up to 3 mi.)

Across the highway from Pili Aloha, an unpaved and unsigned Lighthouse Road skirts the east end of the broad wedge of pineapple fields that slope downward toward **Pauwela Point**. People drive down about a mile, but mud and ruts can make this a foolish gambit for rental cars. As you walk down, the fields will be on your left, while on your right, bananas and tropical trees will give way to a steep gully that eventually falls to tiny Kuiaha Bay. Keep heading for the white light beacon, which is on the point.

Acres of grassy bluffs surround the light beacon. You can loop to your left along the edge for a view toward Paia and West Maui, and then peel off right, following concrete stanchions along a path with the view toward the Hana Coast. The path eventually comes around to the road you walked in on, making a semi-loop of the hike. A goat trail, perfect for surfers, drops steeply through dense foliage to Kuiaha Bay. To the east of Pauwela Point about 1.5 miles, winter surf can bring waves 50- to 60-feet high, attracting psycho surfers from all over the world. Jet skis from Maliko Bay—see *Paddle* below—tow these guys out to ride the big ones in the Jaws surf competition.

More Stuff: Traffic jams will let you know when the Jaws competition is underway. At that time small buses shuttle people out to a viewing area, which unfortunately is far from the surf. To explore the Jaws coast, go left on Lower Ulumalu Road, just past mm14. And just past that road, at telephone pole #44, is a trailblazer's road that goes toward Uaoa Bay. New, gated homes have blocked access to much of this coast.

P: Maliko Bay, which is off the highway before Pauwela, has a sheltered boat ramp at a county park that is an ideal place to put in. Continue on the Hana Highway past Hoʻokipa. On an inside bend at mm10, turn right and wind around under the old bridge that takes you along a stream out to the rocky bay and boat ramp. Paddling south from here, begins a run of sea cliffs with few beaches and little public access. Kayaking is a good way to see this coast. *Be Aware:* Avoid this spot in the winter and during storms.

34.   HALEHAKU HEIAU   H

Best For: Contemplating the sea overlooking this secluded bay, or taking a short walk that leads centuries into the past, to the ruins of a village.

Parking: Take Hwy. 36, the Hana Hwy., past the Haiku turnoff. Just after mm16, turn left on Haumana Rd. Continue .4-mi., veer right on Kulike Rd., and follow 1 mi. to its end, which becomes gravel but is still okay. Park near guardrail.

H: Kahuna Point (.25-mi.); Halehaku Heiau (1 mi.; 200 ft.)

Halehaku Heiau is a place you may not think much of as you go on your merry Maui way, and then two weeks later you won't be able to get it out of your mind. Voices of the past and a quiet beauty resonate. For the short walk to **Kahuna Point**, take the trail that leads from the left of the guardrail, and walk straight out the visible perch that sits about 200 feet above the west side of Halehaku Bay—which is also called Pilale Bay. The spot affords both details and a panorama of the wild bay and the steep, lush walls that frame its opening to the sea. You're bound to see whales offshore in the winter, and down below don't be surprised if sea turtles swim by. The cliffs only get higher over the next 15 miles down the coast.

To get to the heiau, double back from Kahuna Point and take the trail that traverses inland. You'll switchback down through koa and hau trees, which provide hand supports when this hippie trail then drops straight down. Cross the stream at the bottom, and make your way across the grassy bench that sits just above a boulder beach. After a few hundred feet, hook right and walk in to see the big heiau remains, built into the hillside under a canopy of trees. In 1790, King Kamehameha, having ventured from Hana during his invasion of Maui, won a decisive battle near here, bolstering his flagging confidence on his way to the final victory at Iao Valley. Trees grow through places in this landmark, but its terraces and platforms are fundamentally intact. Built of beach rock, its duel platforms each measure roughly 125-feet square. Some remains in this area date from the 1500s. *Be Aware:* As with all such sites, be careful not to disturb anything. Many ruins on Maui, including this one, have not been studied completely.

Hana Highway

North from Keanae Peninsula

HANA HIGHWAY

More than 50 one-lane bridges allow passage on a squiggly blacktop that hugs the cliffs and valleys of a rain forest—and in typical Hawaiian fashion, each has a name, such as, "open laughter," "heavenly mist," "land of deep love," and "lightning flash." Waterfalls are strung like confetti. The coast is wild with waves doing battle with sculpted lava. Then you reach Hana and its hidden beaches, pastoral slopes, historical strolls, and freshwater pools. After Hana, the twisting highway takes a curtain call, offering more waterfalls and forest, as the journey continues to the Pools of Oheo.

DRIVING TOUR
PICKING THE RIGHT DAY

Every day is a weekend on the Hana Highway, although you'll see less local traffic on the real weekend. The main concern is to avoid this tour during and right after tropical storms, when mudslides and flash floods present a hazard. Of course, a safe time after storms is when the road's greenery sparkles and waterfalls are most plentiful. Overcast weather will not spoil a day here, since this is not a fun-in-the-sun adventure, and the rain-forest greens deepen under cloud cover.

The wisest advice is to depart early, if you would like a more private experience. Rental cars seem to form a train beginning from about 8 a.m. to 10 a.m. If you are taking the half-trip—see below—you could also opt to depart after the rush.

THE ROAD

Provided the weather is fair, the Hana Highway is not in the running for Maui's most dangerous drive. Cars tend to plug along in a mellow samba line. The one-lane bridges have clearly marked yield lines. Although some publications say that cars headed toward Kahului yield to cars headed toward Hana, this etiquette is rarely practiced. The car that gets to the bridge, or one-lane road segment, first goes through, along with the cars in the same posse. If you arrive behind that stream, pull over and yield to the oncoming traffic from the other side of the bridge.

Exceptions to the yield rule are surfers hell-bent on catching the next wave down the road, and pick-ups and other commuters who drive the highway with a certain reckless abandon. If cars are on your tail, pull over. Everyone will be happier. Also remember to fill up on gas before leaving Paia. You also want to cart any garbage you produce back with you, since the Hana landfill is nearly full.

THE COURSE

Follow along on the Hana Highway map, page 12. Refer to trailhead descriptions beginning on page 113 for more details.

Note: Visitors who have an extra day on Maui can consider breaking this tour into two trips: The first would end at Nahiku, where the highway leaves the rain forest, and the second would begin there, and continue around to the pasturelands of Hana and the Pools of Oheo. If you want to do two trips, then take advantage of the side trips and hikes. Otherwise, take the side trips sparingly. The times outlined in the course below are for the longer tour.

BEGIN EARLY MORNING. TAKE HIGHWAY 36 PAST MM16 TO WHERE IT BECOMES HIGHWAY 360. Consider grabbing a steaming caffeinated beverage and baked goods to-go in Paia, just before sunrise. Just before the road narrows, you'll pass Twin Falls, which is one of the best and longest inland hikes on the coast. After that, the road starts living up to its reputation.

Over the next 10 or more miles, you weave in and out, on the fringe of the Ko'olau Forest Reserve, where the Waikomo Ridge Nature Trail and Garden of Eden, as well as several state hunter's roads, lead into a rain forest that gets denser the farther you go. Waterfalls appear at inside bends, beginning around mm6, highlighted by the short walk to Puohokamoa Falls near mm11.

St. Augustine Shrine, Wailua

Wailuaiki cascade, Keanae Arboretum

MID-MORNING. After mm12 you come to the Kaumahina State Wayside, an excellent rest stop, with a short path leading to a view that previews the Keanae Peninsula that lies just down the road. Beyond the wayside, down in the next valley, is rugged Honomanu Bay, the only place the highway reaches the water until you get to Hana. After climbing out of this valley, you reach the Keanae Arboretum. If you were to take just one short walk along this stretch of the highway, this is it. Just after the arboretum are the side trips to Keanae and Wailea, both of which impart a sense of Old Hawaii.

NOON. After Keanae, the Hana Highway really does the hokey-pokey, offering cascades and steep hillsides dripping with flora in a constant turn of the wheel. Inland is the Hanawi Natural Area Reserve, one of the wettest places on earth. A side trip to mysterious Nahiku awaits at mm25. After rounding the bend in Nahiku, fruit stands

Hana Highway, Hana Wharf and shore

and occasional homesteads appear, as the highway changes character. The overhanging jungle lifts, giving way to bucolic slopes, pocketed by tropical woodlands.

Just before Hana, at mm31, is one side-trip that is tough to pass, to Kahanu National Tropical Botanical Gardens and Pi'ilanihale Heiau—where you can appreciate the Hawaiian culture at its zenith. And just down the road from these attractions is the Blue Pool, unsurpassed in scenic beauty by any of the island's other pools. Beyond the turnoff to the gardens is the road to Waianapanapa State Park. You could easily spend the day here, and the park's picnic grounds are the best around. If you're looking for a long coast walk next to exploding waves, this is the place.

AFTERNOON. If you're on a day trip, and plan on doing some walking around at the Pools of Oheo, you might have to give Hana short shrift. But make time for the Hana Cultural Center and a stroll out the wharf—and for that matter, the .25-mile hike to Kauiki Head and the Queen Ka'ahumanu Birthplace is a bell ringer. For an overview of Hana, hump up to Fagan's Cross on Pu'u o Kahaula. Come to think of it, Red Sand Beach isn't that far, and it is a sight you'll never forget; although the trail can be hazardous, this beach is unique.

As you head out of Hana—and Highway 360 becomes Highway 31—you'll have time to hook seaward and see Koki Beach Park and Hamoa Beach. Haneoʻo Road loops back out to the highway. Unless you bypassed all the stuff early in the day, you may have to skip Venus Pool. About five miles later—passing waterfalls through deep forest on some fairly hairy one-lane segments—you reach Kipahulu Visitors Center at the lower part of Haleakala National Park.

Papaʻaea Road, Hamoa Beach, Keanae pasture

At Kipahulu are the Pools of Oheo Gulch, formerly known as the Seven Sacred Pools, scooped out by Pipiwai Stream before it enters the ocean. Fantastic as they are, the pools are not the epitome of the Hana Highway tour. In fact, they may play second fiddle in this neighborhood to the trail that leads inland to the Falls at Makahiku and Waimoku Falls—up a jungle crevice and bamboo forest, over a hard-rock stream on bridges. If pressed for time, do the falls walk to the bridges—for a big scenic payoff. Darn it, we wish we were there now instead of writing this book.

SUNSET. Unless you left yesterday, your waning hours will be spent behind the wheel going home. But that's good news, no matter which route you select. One choice is to continue around on Highway 31, past Kaupo. The road is actually an easier drive than the Hana Highway—with the notable exception of a mile-long segment about three

Hana Wharf, Hana Cultural Center, Ko'olau Forest Reserve

Koki Beach, Wishard Grove at Kahanu Garden, Wailua taro field

miles from Kipahulu, near mm39 at Lelekoa Bay. If you go back this direction, you can dip in to see Charles Lindbergh's grave, before that difficult stretch. Look at the Haleakala driving tour for more on this route. You'll see sunset on the backside of the big volcano, as well as have a sunset ocean view.

An equally good choice is to retrace your route on the Hana Highway. You may need to do this just to believe all the sights you beheld earlier in the day. Certainly, you can drive the Hana Highway a dozen times and see fresh sights. The place is overflowing with them.

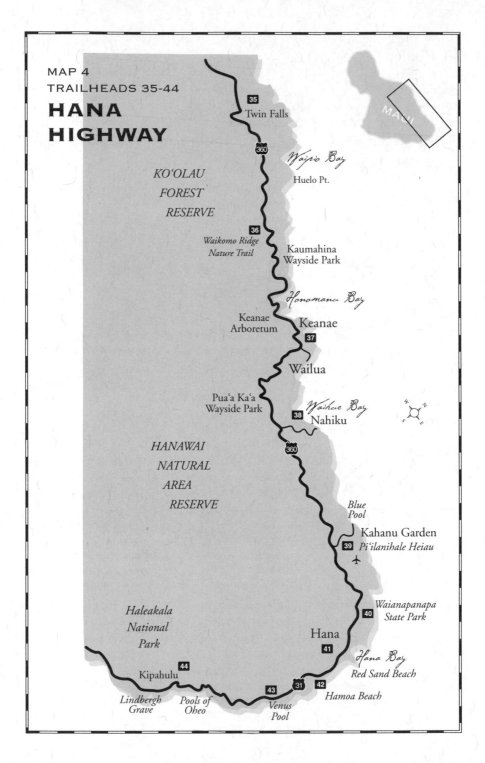

MAP 4
TRAILHEADS 35-44

HANA HIGHWAY

MAUI

35 Twin Falls

360

Waipio Bay

Huelo Pt.

KOʻOLAU FOREST RESERVE

36
Waikomo Ridge Nature Trail

Kaumahina Wayside Park

Honomanu Bay

Keanae Arboretum

Keanae

37

Wailua

Puaʻa Kaʻa Wayside Park

38 *Waihue Bay* Nahiku

360

HANAWAI NATURAL AREA RESERVE

Blue Pool

Kahanu Garden

39 Piʻilanihale Heiau

Waianapanapa State Park

40

Haleakala National Park

Hana

41

Hana Bay

Red Sand Beach

Kipahulu

44

43 **31** **42**

Hamoa Beach

Lindbergh Grave

Pools of Oheo

Venus Pool

T R A I L H E A D S

H	HIKING
SN	SNORKELING
P	KAYAKING, CANOEING
SF	SURFING, BOOGIE BOARDING, WIND SPORTS

TH = Trailhead
mm = mile marker; corresponds to highway signs
All hiking distances in parentheses are ROUND TRIP.
Elevation gains of 100 feet or more are noted.

35. TWIN FALLS   H

Best For: Cascades falling through multitudinous tropical flora that preview the Hana Highway to come.

Parking: Take Hwy. 36, the Hana Hwy., beyond mm16, where route becomes Hwy. 360 and mile markers restart at mm1. *For Twin Falls:* At mm2, pull out to the right on the shoulder of a wide, curving bridge. *For Lower Falls:* Backtrack on Hwy. 360 about .1-mi. and turn right on Ulalena Loop. Continue .4-mi. to an old concrete bridge at the stream, and park. *For Kaulanapueo Church,* continue past mm3 as road narrows. After about .5-mi., turn left at a bus stop at a turnout with a public phone and mailboxes. After .25-mi., toward Huelo, turn left on a short, rough uphill driveway to the church.

H: Twin Falls and Upper Falls (1.75 mi.); Lower Falls (.25-mi.); Kaulanapueo Church (.25-mi.)

Twin Falls is where two streams with very long names join together, fall some 20 feet over a lava ledge, and depart as one: Ho'olawa Stream, which then descends over another few miles to reach the ocean at Ho'olawa Bay. Hop through the gate at the organic produce stand, and within a few minutes on the unpaved road you'll see access trails to the stream on the left . You'll hear the falls before you see them, less than .25-mile from the trailhead, set below the road among banyans and other large trees. Access trails put you both below and above the cataract. After school lets out, you may catch some zany local boys who climb the cliffs and jump into the frothing waters.

To the **Upper Falls**, continue up the road, which is an easement through private homes.

Exotic gardens of the homes—papayas, hibiscus, ti, guava, bananas—rival the falls as this hike's main attraction. A bamboo forest blankets the ridge in the background. About .5-mile from the trailhead, the stream crosses the road on a spillway, and then, just ahead, go left on a path where you may see a hand-painted rock. Then go right— don't take the path that dips down to an irrigation ditch. On the right-bearing option, you climb slightly, past paperbark trees, and come to a plank that bridges a flowing ditch. Cross and go left along the wall of the ditch, then across roots and rocks, and you'll reach the Upper Falls—cascading 25-feet from a curved cliff into a pool, all of it under a leafy ceiling.

The **Lower Falls** parking was the main access from the old highway. Head upstream in deep shade, with the water on your left. A cliff encroaches after a few hundred feet, and you have to get wet feet to proceed the last short distance to the 15-foot cascade. The sky opens enough at the falls pool to make this one of the better swimming spots on Ho'owala Stream. Relatively few people visit the lower falls. *More Stuff:* Continue on the road toward the ocean to see the tropical gardens that produce the goodies sold at the Twin Falls Fruit Stand. Park and walk down the stream valley toward the bay.

Built in 1853, on a grass clearing in a jungle setting, **Kaulanapueo Church** is poetically situated. The church's thick walls are plaster-covered basaltic boulders that rise to a majestic steeple. Palms and Norfolk pines accent several acres of lawn, and a garden frames French windows. Sitting next to the building is a small cemetery whose tombstones link history to the 1990s. There are no hiking paths. This is more a place to wander around and appreciate.

Lower Twin Falls

Waikomo Nature Trail, Garden of Eden, Twin Falls Fruit Stand

36.   WAIKOMO RIDGE NATURE TRAIL   H

Best For: Turn your adventure into a thrill by choosing from among these walks to the rain forests and waterfalls just off the Hana Highway.

Parking: Take Hwy. 36 toward Hana past mm16; route becomes Hwy. 360 and mile markers start at zero. See hike descriptions for further directions.

H: Waikomo Ridge Nature Trail (1.25 mi., 200 ft.); Garden of Eden (up to .75-mi.); Puohokamoa Falls (.25-mi.)

The Koʻolau Forest Reserve runs for about 10 miles along the road to Hana, extending inland to an elevation of about 4,000 feet. Interior roads connect an elaborate system of tunnels and irrigation ditches, many dating from the late 1800s, a remarkable engineering feat led by Henry P. Baldwin. Son of missionary Dwight Baldwin, Henry gained fame in 1876—one month after losing his arm in a sugar mill accident—when he belayed 120 feet down a jungle gorge after his work crews balked at the precipice. The massive water conveyance project was completed in the nick of time to prevent a takeover by the rivals of Baldwin, and his partner and boyhood friend, Samuel T. Alexander.

Featured in many brochures and clearly marked at mm9.5, the **Waikomo Ridge Nature Trail** attracts a fair number of visitors stopping midmornings on the way to Hana. The hike climbs through native and planted trees, many identified, with view benches along the way, and picnic areas at the trailhead and at the top. To start, go to the left as you face inland, and keep left to the first lookout—an inside trail at the bottom joins this outer loop at the first lookout. From there the trail makes a long switchback among pandanus at eye level, with a canopy of other limbs high overhead. Then comes a second lookout, above the dense flora of a bend in the highway.

From the second overlook the trail levels, as you walk through a lovely paperbark and bamboo tree tunnel, at the end of which is a picnic hut in a clearing. To your right as you enter the clearing is the Kolea Road, a hunter's route that descends through bamboo to trailhead parking. Take that way back to make this a loop hike; or backtrack to the first lookout, where you can take the inside trail back, making this a semi-loop.

Look for the entrance to the **Garden of Eden** on your right near mm10.5. The 26-acre garden and arboretum has family walking trails, one of which features a look at Keopuka Rock, which appeared in the opening sequence of the movie *Jurassic Park*. At several picnic tables you can commune with coco palms, mangoes, ti, bananas, and a host of flowering plants. On the way out, visit the small flock of exotic birds who are willing to pose for snapshots. *Note:* A small admission is charged.

For the short walk to **Puohokamoa Falls**, pass the Garden of Eden and park at a small inside turnout near mm11. A picnic shelter at trail's end provides a vantage point, looking across a large pool beneath the 30-foot cascade. In drier conditions, trailblazers can cross the stream and take a trail that leads to a bigger, upper falls. A third waterfall lies below the highway, but this one is even harder to access; use caution.

More Stuff: Several roads lead into the Koʻolau Forest Reserve rain forest lands leased by East Maui Irrigation Company. To enter lawfully, you need permission from the irrigation company, or a hunting permit from the State Division of Forestry and Wildlife. You will see the brown-and-yellow signs marking the gated roads. After passing a bamboo forest on a long uphill S-turn—at mm6.75—a gate is on your right marking Papaʻaea Road, which passes a large reservoir at the outset and leads over several streams to an immense hillside of ferns. Next to the Garden of Eden at mm10.5 is Wahinepeʻe Road, leading to what some call Little Jurassic Park. Old-growth native forests drip with flora too profuse to perceive unless you stop for awhile.

37. KEANAE   H, SN, P, SF

Best For: Wild seascapes, village taro fields, historic churches, pools, falls and a tropical arboretum: Old Hawaii lives on.

Parking: Activities take place over a 6-mile section of Hwy. 360, the Hana Hwy., beginning before and ending just after the Keanae Peninsula—from near mm12 to mm18. See each hike below for specifics.

H: Kaumahina Wayside Nature Trail (.25-mi); Honomanu Bay (up to .5-mi.); Keanae Arboretum (1.25 mi.); Keanae village and pools (up to 2 mi.); Wailua churches, beach, taro fields (up to .5-mi.); Wailua Wayside Overlook (less than .25-mi.)

After mm12, pull off at an outside bend into the **Kaumahina State Wayside**. Follow the pipe railing uphill on the park's nature trail. From a stand of hala trees is a look straight down to the bay and toward the low lava peninsula that is Keanae. Wild **Honomanu Bay**—the only place the highway reaches the sea level between Paia and Hana—features a large jungly stream, trees dripping with vines, and a smooth-rock

Hana Coast

beach, all enclosed by high cliffs drilled with sea caves at water level. You can drive there on two spur roads, each leading about .25-mile in from the highway.

The first access is easier to drive but puts you on the opposite stream bank from the beach; turn left on an unpaved road near mm13.5 as you descend into the valley. The second access is after the bridges at the bottom. At mm14, veer left and drive down to a flat area just above the water. At the boulder beach, walk right to the sea caves beneath the cliff. *More Stuff:* Trailblazers can explore dank Honomanu Forest Reserve by taking a signed trail at the bridge in the bottom of the valley. Foliage engulfs a seldom-used streamside path.

The **Keanae Arboretum** is the best family leg-stretcher on the coast, featuring a wide path alongside Pi'ina'au Stream, in the shade of huge trees brought here from both sides of the equator. Look for the signed turnout on your right near mm16.5—and heads-up because the mm16 sign may still be missing. A paved trail slopes to a grove of tropical trees from around the world, extremely large considering the arboretum dates only from 1971. A giant bamboo is awe inspiring. Roam among other species with their interpretive signs. The paved path becomes dirt as you continue upstream and enter the native Hawaiian and Polynesian-introduced species, including taro, papaya, and ti. From here the path becomes a trail that crosses a tributary stream, then deteriorates into a trailblazer's special that heads into the rain forest along a second tributary. Pick your own turnaround.

The Keanae Peninsula came into being after one of Haleakala's more recent eruptions, when lava flowed out the Ko'olau Gap (see TH46), filled a gorge that had eroded for eons, and fanned out into the Pacific. For the **Keanae village and pools** hikes, turn left just down the hill from the arboretum, before reaching mm17. Continue on the sleepy road for almost .75-mile, and park at the big turnout on the left across from the church and ball field. Start out by walking to the point toward lava stacks, nature's statuary that fight a losing battle against oncoming waves. Down the coast to your right, is Pauwalu Point. A seabird sanctuary, Moku Mana, is a tiny island just offshore.

Village life centers around a little church with a big name—ihi'ihio lehowa ona Kaua—sitting dreamily below green ramparts and on the edge of taro fields. The edifice dates from 1860, as its garden tombstones will testify, but it was substantially rebuilt in the 1900s. From the church you can curl over to the cottages you passed on the way in—stopping to munch a petite loaf of the righteous banana bread at the Keanae Landing Fruit Stand. Then walk the road or meander through the salt spray, saying hello to the occasional grazing horse, back to the parking. Don't forget to look inland down the coast where, after rains, you'll see a half-dozen waterfalls.

The **pool** is large lagoon formed where Keanae Stream, hemmed in by the cliff above the peninsula, meets a gravel bar at the beach. From the parking area, walk with the

ihiʻihio lehowa ona Kaua Church, Keanae Arboretum, Poi Dog, Keanae Peninsula

ocean on your left, and keep left as the road passes by several farmhouses. Signs not-withstanding, it's okay to walk here, but do so lightly. The road becomes grassy. Veer left from the road, before reaching the ironwoods and palms, and descend several feet to lagoon level, where swimmers will find easy entry. Under most conditions, you'll be able cross the stream or just walk onto the gravel bar that separates the lagoon from the ocean. At the far end of the long pool, is a cascade of Keanae Stream.

More Stuff: Higher upstream are several popular swimming pools, locally known as Sapphire Pools. Trailblazer access is from the highway. Turn toward Hana and park after the second bridge. You need to walk down from the bridge. If stream flows are low, you'll find clean, pure tubs. *Be Aware:* Flash floods make this a bad choice during or after rains. Also, for the supreme view of Keanae, look for a turnout near mm17, headed toward Hana—at a guardrail, where a tidal wave siren hangs above telephone pole #41. This vista may inspire you to paint.

To visit the **Wailua churches, taro fields, and beach**—which get far fewer visitors than Keanae—veer left from the Hana Highway near mm18.25, on Wailua Road. Just down the blacktop on your left are St. Gabriel's Church and, in the gardens behind it, St. Augustine Shrine. The taro field is down a red-dirt road, a right turn just past the churches. Park a respectful distance from the few homesites (this is a non-tourist attraction), and ask permission if you happen to see anyone. The rich valley is like the floor of a vast, green coliseum, with the walls rising a thousand feet in an curve. Continuing down the road, look inland to see Waikani Falls, which you'll later see from the highway above after mm19. At the road's end, a short dirt road leads to rocky beach at Wailua Bay, where two streams join the ocean.

Leaving Wailua, look for the **Wailua Valley Overlook** on the right as you come up the grade, before mm19—it's before the turnout on the left where most people stop. The parking is through a cut bank. The overlook is up a mere 40 steps to railed area that offers an on-high view of Wailua. *More Stuff:* A road leads from the overlook parking into the Keanae Valley. Trees occlude an inland view initially, but after a short downhill grade, the road swerves right into an open area, rich bottomlands frequented by numerous birds. Permission to enter may be required.

SN: No snorkeling here, but you can get a swim in at the **Keanae Pool**, and take a dip at the **Sapphire Pools**, which lie above it. Watch your step.

P: Kayakers put in on the west side on Keanae Peninsula; look to the left as the road gets to sea level as you drop down from the highway. Paddling scenery both ways on this coast is superlative, but some weather and wave conditions are not for amateurs. Going west are the steep cliffs that descend into Honomanu Bay. Paddling the other way, you'll get close-ups of the peninsula's sea stacks, and, as you round the point, a look at Moku Manu sanctuary and Waiokilo Falls.

SF: Surfers who want to get away from it all ride the tiers of offshore wedges at **Honomanu Bay**. Winter swells of 4- to 8-feet break within the mouth of the bay.

38.   NAHIKU   H

Best For: Discovering what grows where subtropical sunbeams strike rich soils moistened by 300-plus inches of rain per year. To find out, follow some of the water down to the coast at remote Nahiku.

Parking: Take Hwy. 360, the Hana Hwy., past Keanae. Hikes for this trailhead take place over a 4-mile section from near mm21 to mm25. Further directions are given below in *More Stuff.*

H: Nahiku (up to .75-mi.)

The Hana Highway climbs inland from Keanae and zigzags to a crescendo over a 4-mile run that crosses some 10 streams. Steep valleys are inscrutably tangled by forests that shed the rains from one of the wettest spots on earth. To explore **Nahiku**, veer left from the highway after the bridge at mm25. Getting there is half the fun, as the narrow, but well-paved road descends 1,000 feet over 2.5 miles before coming to an end at ocean-scoured Opuhanu Point. The descent reflects the transition that takes place along the Hana Highway, as the stream gorges and cliffs give way to the more gradual and open slopes that sweep around to Hana.

Botanists counting species will hit triple figures in no time. Prominent among them are huge banyans and rubber trees. Some 25,000 rubber trees were planted near the coast, launching the Nahiku Rubber Company in 1905, which failed in spite of fabulous production due to geographic isolation. In more recent times, the Nahiku environ gained famed as a retreat for former Beatle, the late George Harrison.

The road snakes deeper and deeper through overgrown forests. About a mile from the top is a cavelike lava tube, which is near Big Spring, the largest on Maui. As the road level, .25-mile from the ocean, you'll see an old road to the right that invites further exploration, among tin-roofed sugar shacks and the occasional honor-system fruit stand. The Catholic church near the school dates from the early 1800s, a time when Catholics were persecuted on the island. You'll cross a stream and bridge, snap a picture, and come to road's end. Big-boulder Honolulunui Bay does not invite walkers, but you can walk the point's lava tongues that extend seaward. *Be Aware:* Keep an eye peeled for monster waves in the winter.

More Stuff: Pua'aka'a State Wayside is a 5-acre developed park at mm22.5. It can be dreary in rains, or idyllic when sun shines on the lush greenery, waterfall, and pool. A number of roads lead into the Ko'olau Forest Reserve; to enter you need permission from the East Maui Irrigation Company, or a hunting permit from the State Department of Fish and Wildlife. Look for Wailuaiki Road near mm21.25, just after an uphill grade and sharp right turn; the gate and sign sit above the road making it difficult to spot. A waterfall and deep gorge lie less than .5-mile in on Wailuaiki Road. Just past the wayside, at mm23.5, is hunter's access to Kapa'ula Gulch. And just before the bridge and turnoff to Nahiku at mm25 is Makapipi Road. It leads toward the Hanawi Natural Area Reserve, nature's storehouse of endangered plants. Finally, not far from the turnoff to Nahiku, look for a gated road to Kuhiwa Valley. *Be Aware:* Take care not to disturb plants or wildlife.

39. PIʻILANIHALE HEIAU   H, SN

Best For: A huge temple dating from the 1500s sitting within a National Tropical Botanical Garden, and a nearby blue pool resting beneath a waterfall next to crashing surf: the makings for a fantasy island.

Parking: Take Hwy. 360, the Hana Hwy., almost to Hana. At mm31, turn left on Ulaino Rd. *For Kahanu Gardens and Piʻilanihale:* Continue 1.5 mi. on the partially paved road to the entrance on the right just after a stream crossing. *For Blue Pool-Ulaino Village ruins:* In dry conditions, you will be able to drive 1.5 mi. to road's end near the beach. You can also opt to walk the road from the garden entrance; if you drive, subtract 3 miles from the round-trip hike.

H: Piʻilanihale Heiau-Kahanu Garden loop (1.25 mi.); Blue Pool (up to 3.25 mi.)

Kahanu Gardens is a 123-acre living exhibit of Hawaiian culture, and also one of only five National Tropical Botanical Gardens set up by an act of Congress to preserve and study endangered plants. From the entrance station you drive almost .5-mile across a sprawling lawn, through a grove of 200 breadfruit trees, as well as other species. On your left is one of Hawaii's last pandanus forest ecosystems. You can backtrack to roam this grove later on.

From the parking area, cross through the gate and go left. Immediately on your left are kamani trees and a "canoe" garden, so named because it replicates the planting cycles for some 27 plants the voyaging Polynesians brought with them across uncharted seas nearly 2,000 years ago. But you may not notice this garden at first because, across the grass field, **Piʻilanihale Heiau** looms out of the jungle foliage. This House of Piʻilani is named for a beloved king of the 1500s, a time that in many ways was the zenith of Hawaiian life. The platform stone structure—roughly 300 feet by 300 feet, with walls terraced about 50 feet high—will remind some of the ancient civilizations in the Americas. The path continues toward the heiau, dipping in and out, and then up a short distance to an interpretive hut. *Be Aware:* Visitors are not allowed to climb up or use trails that circle around behind the structure.

From the interpretive hut, the path loops away from the heiau, along low lava cliffs at the ocean's edge, before reaching a cabin, Hale Hoʻokipa. The cabin was part of the area's former life as Kaeleku Plantation in the 1800s. Old Hawaiian and homesteader gravesites are nearby. Several families, and the Hana Ranch, donated property to form the gardens in the 1970s. Complete your loop by circling right to the lava ledges behind the hale, and continuing through the Wishard Coconut Grove, back to the parking area.

Pi'ilanihale Heiau, Heleleikeoha Stream

To see the **Blue Pool**, drive or walk from outside the garden entrance on the undulating main road for 1.5 miles. This perfumed and shaded journey ends about 100 yards in from the surf at a green lagoon of Heleleikeoha Stream. This lagoon, with rock terraces, pandanus and large kukui trees, is also a good swimming hole. But to get to the fabled pool, follow the steam to the boulder beach, and go left for less than .25-mile. You'll see a whitewater sheeting down about 100 feet of ferny cliff—known as Blue Angel Falls—and, walking up a few boulders, you'll come to the Blue Pool. From the lip of the 30-foot oval, the ocean's waves are a short throw away.

More Stuff: To explore Ulaino Village ruins, walk downstream from the parking area, but hook right and inland. The village was one of the larger in the region, though its walls are now overgrown. It spreads along the coast, toward Pi'ilanihale, extending inland at streams.

SN: Flippers are not necessary in the **Blue Pool**, but swimming will be very tempting on hot days. *Be Aware:* People skinny-dip here, but nudity is not allowed at Hawaiian beaches.

Blue Angel Falls and Blue Pool

40. WAIANAPANAPA STATE PARK H, SN

Best For: The ancient King's Trail along a sea-sculpted lava shelf, which features fountains of whitewater and historical sites. Or enjoy the tropical flora, caves, and Black Sand Beach on the park grounds.

Parking: Take Hwy. 360 nearly to Hana. At mm32, turn left at sign to Waianapanapa and follow the road .4-mi. to the state park. Go left and park at the picnic area.

H: Waianapanapa Caves (less than. 25-mi.); North coast-Kapukaulua Burial Site (1.25 mi.); South coast to: Ohala Heiau (1.5 mi.), or Hana Bay (5 mi.)

Coco palms, pandanus, hala, and a wealth of other flora soften the flows of sharp lava that fan to meet the coast at the 122-acre Waianapanapa State Park. The picnic grounds are picturesque, and the park's 12 coastal cabins offer the best rustic lodging on Maui.

The **Waianapanapa Caves** trail dips down from the parking area into the lush pockets of a streambed, where caves are carved at the base of mossy rock knobs. Legend proclaims these dripping caverns were the tryst for a Princess Popoalaea and her lover, until her husband found out and killed her here. In the spring, the waters turn red with the memory of her blood—or from tiny shrimp hatching, take your pick.

For the **North coast** walk toward the **Kapukaulua Burial Site**, take the trail from the railing at the picnic area, which drops to the Black Sand Beach, a.k.a., Pailoa Bay. Trod the sand-slash-pebbles and climb up to the low point at the far end of the beach. Part of the King's Trail, circa 1550, the rocky path weaves through the pointed-leaf pandanus, and passes two small, black-boulder coves—Pokohulu and Keawaiki. Then watch your footing as the path heads across the sharp lava to the north side of Pukaulua Point, where the burial mounds and heiau remains are located. *Note:* The trail continues to the Hana Airport.

For the **south coast walks**, curl right along the railing at the picnic area, at a signed trailhead. You'll pass the park's buildings as the trail hugs a frothing coast and passes a natural arch. Within .25-mile you'll pass the cabins, set back from the trail; a road to the right just after them leads back to the park, making for a .75-mile loop option. As waves battle the shore, you cross a lava bridge and, a distance farther, reach the walls of the **Ohala Heiau**. Stay the course, hugging the ragged coast over lava, to continue to **Hana**. You'll pass a fishermen's shrine. Some 2 miles from the trailhead is the boulder beach at Kainalimu Bay. To get to Hana Bay, you need to cross over intervening Nanualele Point. From there, an unpaved road curves right, and meets the road coming into Hana. *Note:* The south coast hike works better as a car shuttle; drop off at the park, and pick up in Hana.

Wainapanapa State Park

SN: **Black Sand Beach** is the best snorkeling spot along a coast with few choices. If surf is small, under 2 feet, you can swim out to the right toward the natural arch, and also to the left toward Pokohulu Cove. *Be Aware:* Rip currents may exist in the bay. Watch for posted signs and ask park personnel about swimming safety.

41. HANA   H, SN, P, SF

Best For: After the precipitous curves through the rain forest to get here, Hana's sloping pasturelands and open bay will come as a surprise and a relief. Pick from several short walks—a cultural stroll, powerful seascapes, or a panorama.

Parking: Follow Hwy. 360, the Hana Hwy., past mm33. *To Fagan's Cross-Pu'u o Kahaula:* Keep right on Hwy. 360, pass Keawa Pl., and park in a lot across from Hotel Hana Maui. *For all other hikes and activities:* Veer left on Uakea Rd., continue 1.5 mi., and park at Hana Cultural Center, which is just past Keanini Dr. *Note:* Directions from this point continue in the hike descriptions below.

H: Fagan's Cross-Pu'u o Kahaula (1.75 mi., 500 ft.); Hana Bay stroll (.75-mi.);
Kauiki Head-Queen Ka'ahumanu Birthplace (.25-mi.); Kaihalulu (Red
Sand) Beach (1 mi., 200 ft.)

Don't come looking for action in Hana. Low-key aloha rules here, with quiet cottages
set above the harbor, and a few Hawaiiana shops and cultural sites spread about. **Fagan's
Cross** is atop **Pu'u o Kahaula**, which is in view from the thatched gazebo at the
parking lot. Follow the paved path as it takes a gentle rise through the pastures of Hana
Ranch. As you near the base of the pu'u—also known as Lyon's Hill—the trail curves
around to the right and does its serious climbing. The cross on top is a memorial to
Paul Fagan, who introduced cattle in the 1940s to found the ranch, and later started
the Hotel Hana Maui. The view from the top is a geography primer for Hana and its
coastline, but don't forget to look inland toward the array of old volcanic pu'us and the
far ridgeline that climbs toward Haleakala. *More Stuff:* In the pasture not far from the
trailhead, the Hana Maui Trail takes off to the left. Joggers and exercise walkers will
like this 4-mile, round-trip jaunt through the ranch and across two streams. It comes
out near the highway before Haneo'o Road; see TH42.

The **Hana Bay stroll** begins at the Hana Cultural Center and Museum. The interior
of the small center is an educational work of love, with artifacts, crafts, quilts, photographs, and exhibits that reflect both ancient times and contemporary. Outside is a recreation of a village, including a Hawaiian Ethno-Botanical Garden that grows all the
essential plants from ancient times and changes seasonally. Also on the grounds is the
Old Historic Courthouse and Jail, dating from 1871.

Hana Bay is just down Uakea Road from the center, a left turn on Keawa Place; you
can walk or move the vehicle. Hana Beach Park rims the bay, where visitors are released
from shuttle buses to sit under coco palms and ironwoods and enjoy the cuisine of
Tutu's Snack Shop, or perhaps Bill's Lunch Wagon. At the far end of the bay is Hana

Fagan's Cross trailhead, roadside falls

Wharf, a T-shaped intrusion several hundred feet onto the water that provides the best picnic spot in town, as well as postcard shots inland and out to sea.

More Stuff: To see some of the dozen churches and other sites in town, stop by the Hasegawa General Store, which is on your left at the edge of town as you continue south. A free Hana Visitors Guide with map is available. The venerable general store is also one of Hana's main attractions, run by the same family since 1910, as well as being the best place to buy snacks, trinkets, and supplies.

Kauiki Head is the furry 400-foot rise that frames the south end of Hana Bay. The **Queen Ka'ahumanu Birthplace** is at a sheltered rock near its tip. To begin, park at the wharf and take a red-cinder trail that skirts the shoreline among ironwoods. Stay near the shore. At the beginning, one eroded spot requires handholds and will dissuade some hikers, but it's easy walking afterwards.

In the 1700s, the Kauiki Head was a stronghold for warriors during the ongoing battles between Maui and the Big Island—typically these Hana slopes were controlled by the Big Island's forces, since open sea was easier to cross than the terrain of East Maui. Near the end is a plaque commemorating Queen Ka'ahumanu, who was born in 1768 and went on to become Kamehameha the Great's favorite wife, as well as a beloved and enlightened ruler. A tiny island with a light beacon, Pu'uki'i Island, lies a long jump from the tip—too long when the big seas are galloping in. This ten-minute hike gets you a million miles away.

Kaihalulu, also known as **Red Sand Beach,** is on the other side of the head from the bay. To get to the trailhead, continue a few blocks on Uakea Road, past Hauoli Street, and park on-street near the Hana Community Center. The striking cove is scooped out of a towering red cinder cliff, protected by the jagged teeth of a black-rock reef that is just offshore. The trail will be off-putting to acrophobics and hazardous to the careless. Traverse the lawn just beyond the cultural center, and drop down through ironwoods—a cemetery will be on your left, and the sea cottages of the Hotel Hana Maui on the right. You climb a little on the cinder path on a ledge above the water and reach a point. Around this corner is the eye-popping view of the beach. The trail is cut into the cliff as you descend to the red sand. *Be Aware:* Watch where you're going and avoid this trail during heavy weather. Also, in spite of the bare bottoms you may see here, some of which you may wish you hadn't, nudity is not permitted on Hawaiian beaches.

More Stuff: To rocky Waikoloa Beach and Kainalimu Cove, veer left on Waikoloa Road and you come down Uakea Road on the way to the Hana Bay. The rocky beach, which is the north side of Hana Bay, will be on your right. The cove is beyond a spillway and Nanualele Point; you need to veer right off the unpaved road before it curves inland. These places are the terminus of the trail from Waianapanapa State Park; see TH40.

Red Sand Beach

SN: The best snorkeling at **Hana Bay** is between the base of the wharf and the light beacon on Puʻukiʻi Island. Currents sweep out the bay during higher surf, so stay close to shore and avoid swimming when the surf's up. Due to natural silt, the bay is not known for clear waters. Your best chance is during the winter. **Red Sand Beach** is a spectacular swimming hole, inside the black-rock breakwater. Lots of fish reside. You can normally get in here all year round, but a shore break indicates rip currents may be present. Under ideal conditions you'll loll about in an aquamarine bathtub.

P: Hana Wharf has a boat ramp at its base that will suit kayakers wishing to explore the coast. Outfitters are usually set up at the beach park, offering tours, rentals, and advice. Seek the latter at a minimum, as the confused waters here are not to be trifled with.

SF: Mostly during the summer, you'll find the wave riders offshore at the **Hana Wharf**. The bay has a nice deep-water break. This is also a good place to be a spectator.

42.   HAMOA BEACHES   H, SN, SF

Best For: A short side trip from the Hana Highway passes two beaches, including the south shore's sandiest swath and an offshore bird sanctuary.

Parking: Take Hwy. 360 through Hana. After mm33, the road becomes Hwy. 31 coming from the other direction. You begin here at mm51, with numbers *descending* as you travel away from Hana. Turn left on Haneo'o Road, less than .5-mi. past mm51.

H: Koki Beach Park (.5-mi.); Hamoa Beach (.25-mi.)

Koki Beach Park, a tranquil place with an exciting view, will be on your left, .4-mile from the highway at call box 18. From the shoulder parking, an ample strand of sand leads left toward a red cinder cliff. Look for a natural arch near the point. To the right, you can cross a small stream and walk a grassy area shaded by palms, ironwoods, and an occasional Norfolk pine. Offshore the tip of land is small Alau Island Seabird Sanctuary, with a few coco palms pointing askew from its crest like wayward hairs.

Hamoa Beach is around the point on Haneo'o Road, a little more than a mile from the highway. Look for a bus stop and low lava wall on the left. Concrete steps and ramp lead down to a good-sized white sand crescent—the beach used by guests of the Hotel Hana Maui. A lawn and garden, part the hotel's beach facilities, border the sand. From the shore is a spot-on look at the Big Island, rising from the far horizon. From Hamoa Beach, Haneo'o Road travels .5-mile through the quiet homes of Hamoa and loops back to Highway 31.

Hamoa Beach

More Stuff: Near mm33, a dirt road on the ocean side leads to Lehoula Beach; no public access. Also, the Hana Maui Trail, which originates at the Fagan's Cross trailhead in TH41, can be accessed at a gate on your right after mm51, just before Haneoʻo Road. It travels about 2 miles through Hana Ranch.

SN: Enter **Hamoa Beach** to the left as you face the water, and swim out the lava tongues and submerged rocks. Shore break and rip currents may present hazards. Ask the guys working the beach facility, if in doubt.

SF: You wouldn't make the drive just to bodysurf and boogie board at **Hamoa Beach**, but the conditions are often good for both. The same is true for Lehoula Beach, mentioned above in *More Stuff*, although there's no approved public access.

43.   VENUS POOL   H, SN

Best For: Nature has scooped freshwater baths at the ocean's edge, a short walk in from the highway.

Parking: Take Hwy. 360 through Hana. After mm33, the road becomes Hwy. 31 coming from the other direction. You begin here at mm51, with numbers *descending* as you travel away from Hana. Cross a bridge at mm48, and park on the shoulder to the right at telephone pole #88.

H: Venus Pool (.5-mi.)

To reach the **Venus Pool**, walk back across the bridge and hop through a gatelike opening in the fence. A path leads down the sloping pasture, with Waiohonu Stream on your right. A few minutes into the walk you'll come upon a dome-shaped rock kiln, where the path curves right toward the stream. Fringed with greenery, the pool reveals itself only when you come upon it from about 15-feet above.

The waves from a rocky nook in the coast mingle with the leading edge of Venus Pool, while upstream of the 75-foot oval, freshwater enters from bedrock ledges that are carved out in places, forming smaller pools. Pool conditions will vary depending on both the surf and runoff. The pastures above the pool extend seaward toward the black-rock point, providing room to roam with a Big Island view.

More Stuff: Trailblazers may find pictographs in the lower Waiohonu Valley, across the highway but on the same side of the stream as the path. Pictographs are painted onto rocks, whereas the more common petroglyphs are etched into them.

SN: On sunny days, **Venus Pool** is ideal for swimming around.

POOLS OF OHEO

Best For: The Hana pilgrimage, ending at a series of terraced pools that a stream has scoured from bedrock. Inland, the stream tumbles from two of Maui's highest waterfalls, alongside a trail that penetrates a bamboo jungle.

Parking: Take Hwy. 360 through Hana. After mm33, the road becomes Hwy. 31 at mm51—with numbers *descending*. After mm43 you'll pass Haleakala National Park boundary, and then a bridge over Oheo Gulch. Just after mm42, turn left into the parking for the Kipahulu Visitors Center. *Note:* Additional directions are given for Lindbergh hike, and in *More Stuff.*

H: **Pools of Oheo loop (.75-mi, 150 ft.); Pipiwai Trail to: Falls at Makahiku (1.25-mi., 300 ft.), or Waimoku Falls (4.25 mi., 850 ft.); Kipahulu Point Park-Charles Lindbergh Grave (.25-mi.)**

Upper Venus Pool, Pipiwai Trail

Just when you thought it was safe to get back in the car … the pasturelands of Hana give way to a rolling rural area, lush with gardens, which in turn transition to a narrow, twisting road that is punched through steep rain forest and across eight streams over the last five miles—before breaking out to an open bench where the park headquarters is located. As the interpretive exhibits in the visitors center artfully demonstrate, this park is located on the ahupua'a of Kipahulu, a village of antiquity that was one of the largest on Maui. The pools here were dubbed Seven Sacred Pools in the hippie days, although there are considerably more than seven.

For the **Pools of Oheo loop**, walk to the visitors center, and take the signed Kuloa Point Trail. You'll meander in the shade of a huge banyan before reaching the stream and its pools. You can extend this walk by going right to the point, where the lowest pool nears the surf. Interpretive signs explain the ruins. The path then swerves upstream to the highway bridge before looping back to the visitors center. *More Stuff:* A half-dozen or more pools await trailblazers willing to head up Oheo Stream from the bridge. *Be Aware:* All the pools present a danger due to flash floods. Watch your footing.

The **Pipiwai Trail** is the most classic subtropical jungle trek available on Maui. Begin by taking the trail to the left of the visitors center, or backtrack on the highway toward the bridge, to where the trail crosses. On the leg to the **Falls at Makahiku** you cross a pastureland and then climb the forests above the stream, lying steeply below to your right—a free-fall intruded upon by hundreds of branches along the way. You'll come to a falls overlook sign, where the 200-foot watery ribbon is visible. Fine, but be sure to take the spur to the right just afterwards that leads to the top of the falls and a view down the gulch. When water is low, you can proceed, off-trail, up the miniature canyon just upstream from the falls. Stay back during runoff and rains.

Pools of Oheo, Pool at Hotel Hana Maui

To continue to 400-foot **Waimoku Falls**, ascend the trail past a gate and under the boughs of a huge banyan. The trail levels as you get a first glimpse of the higher falls from a stand of guavas. Stream overlooks will be to your right. About a mile from the trailhead, the stream narrows as it crashes through a rocky gorge, falling in cataracts and pools that are spanned by two steel footbridges—for many this will be the hike's highlight. You still have climbing to do, aided by boardwalks through muddy sections of sprawling bamboo forest straight out of Borneo. The trail ends at the forest-shrouded pool beneath the skyscraper amphitheater that has been carved by Waimoku Falls.

More Stuff: For an easy stroll away from the crowds at the pools, go right as you face the visitors center, toward the signed campground. At the shoreline, you pass tiny Kau Bay, and loop inland around small Kukui Bay. At the far side of Kukui Bay is Puhilele Point and the ruins of Kanekauila Heiau. This walk is about a mile, round trip.

Kipahulu Point Park and **Charles Lindbergh Grave** are a mile or two beyond the visitors center. You'll pass St. Paul's Catholic Church and mm41. Then turn left on a narrow lane lined with century plants, and then left again to Palapala Hoʻomanu Church, which sits beside a large banyan. The church is also called Kipahulu Church, and dates from around 1860. The small cemetery is next to the church, and the unassuming gravesite of the most famous American of his time lies farthest from the church. Lindbergh, more concerned with a monumentally beautiful view, was laid to rest here in 1974. Down the lawn from the church is the small county park with shaded tables and a big view back toward Oheo Gulch and across the wide channel to the Big Island. When you leave this area, turning right on Highway 31, look on the left for the big smoke stack and other ruins of Kipahulu Sugar Mill, which shut down in 1922.

More Stuff: Going back toward Hana from the Pools of Oheo—between mm44 and mm45—are the double bridges of Wailua Falls. The turnout at the first bridge is normally frequented by crafts vendors. A short trail leads from the Hana side of the bridge to the pool beneath the thundering falls. Additionally, on the uphill grade after the first bridge is the marker for the so-called trail to Helio's Grave. The route, for trailblazers only, is a dangerous butt-slide 300 feet down an overgrown embankment to Wailua Cove and stream. A 20-foot cross memorializing Helio is down there on high ground, along with the ruins of the village at Wailua. Helio and his brother, Peterto—inspired by legends of shipwrecked Spaniards that predated the English—led a Roman Catholic movement on Maui in the 1840s.

SN: You'd look silly with a mask and fins in the **Pools of Oheo** but not swimming around. The deepest are about 40 feet, and there's enough space to have relative privacy in this popular area, since few visitors actually take a dip. *Be Aware:* Flash flood hazard exists here, so dip only when skies are blue. Some days these pools are brown, even when it's not raining. Experienced scuba divers enter at tiny **Kau Bay** but sea conditions are normally unsafe and snorkeling is generally not recommended.

Kipahulu Sugar Mill, Wananalua Congregational Church, Lindbergh Grave, Falls at Makahiku

Haleakala

Haleakala Ridge Trail

HALEAKALA

You don't need to leave Maui to cure tropical malaise, just drive up 5,000 feet to the rolling hills and pine forests of Kula. Or, put on the outerwear and head up 10,000 feet to leave the planet altogether on a journey into the Haleakala crater. As a third choice, go to the unexplored Kaupo coast for a trip to Arizona with an ocean.

DRIVING TOUR
PICKING THE RIGHT DAYS

Seeing sunrise from the summit of Haleakala is a quest for many Maui visitors, and if you're one of them, bring every stitch of warm clothing you have, plus the beach towels. Perhaps this quest has derived from the myth surrounding the volcano's name "House of the Sun." In ancient times, the demigod Maui snared the sun with his fishhook, thereby insuring a longer planting season and well-being for the people. The sunrise expedition, aside from being cold, also must begin in darkness, meaning you can't reliably check out visibility on the summit from down below, and it's too early to call the rangers for a forecast. When clear, the Haleakala summit is an eye-popper. Consider leaving just after sunrise, which will put you ahead of the tour buses and allows you to enjoy the scenery on the way up in daylight.

Regardless of what your watch says, when the weather appears clear at the top is the time to head for Haleakala. Bear in mind that Kula clouds often hang at about 5,000 feet, making the peak appear socked in when it's not—you wind up with an airplane's view of these clouds. And, aside from full-on storm conditions, clouds get tossed around up there, so be patient. Cloudy days have clear moments.

Kula is a scenic drive any day, but it doubles as a fallback alternative when weather forces a retreat from the summit. The Kaupo coast is Maui's least visited region, and therefore is a good choice if seeking quietude on a busy weekend. In the shadow of Haleakala, it's also the most arid, and the most likely place to find sun, even when rains are lashing West Maui and the Hana coast. During droughts, and mostly in the summer, the Kaupo coast will be dry grasses, save the coastal Kiawe trees and the upper reaches of the Kahikinui Forest Reserve. But during normal winters and springs, a green carpet of low-lying vegetation fills in around the lava formations.

THE ROADS

The Haleakala Highway has the most elevation gain per horizontal mile covered of any paved road on earth. But it's built on the mountain's relatively gentle north slopes, and using long switchbacks without vertigo-inducing hairpins. Provided your brakes hold out on the way down, and you avoid the stream of downhill bicyclists as you go up, the road is a snap. Kula is made for convertibles. Along several miles well below the summit, the Kula and Haleakala highways run on parallel contours—with old Lower Kula Road between them—providing loop options for touring the Upcountry.

The southern Kaupo coast—where Highway 37 circles around to become Highway 31—is also an easy one to navigate. New steel and concrete bridges appear to have been built in advance of commute traffic, and the county crews are extending the pavement toward Kaupo. But currently, the smooth pavement ends before the road reaches sea level at Nu'u Bay, and becomes pothole-patched and dirt-graded after that. Lack of shoulders present hazards in some areas. Just follow the yellow-paint line. Traffic is wonderfully sparse, increasing only in late afternoons when the Hana commute comes through on the clockwise circumnavigation. The only dicey section is past Kaupo, near mm39 when the road narrows to one lane at Lelekoa Bay on its 8-mile finale to Kipahulu. Even with this challenge, you might consider visiting the Pools of Oheo from this direction, rather than coming around from Hana. Go in the morning, and double back to visit the Kaupo coast in the afternoon.

The Course

Follow along on the Haleakala map, page 146. Refer to trailhead descriptions that follow on pages 147 for more details.

Note: Three tours for this trailhead section: Haleakala, Kaupo coast, and Kula. The Kula tour can be combined with either of the others, or done independently, but to do all three would be more like work than a vacation.

Haleakala Highway

Kula

HALEAKALA TOUR. BEGIN EARLY MORNING. THE HALEAKALA HIGHWAY STARTS AS NUMBER 37, CHANGES TO 377, AND FINALLY BECOMES 378 AS IT MAKES ITS SWITCHBACKING ASCENT INTO THE HALEAKALA NATIONAL PARK. The highway segment, after Pukalani, is through rolling horse country, sensuous hills dotted with eucalyptus as well as native Hawaiian trees. The tight turns of Highway 378 at first cut through the flower farms and gardens, and then the road tops out on the broad shoulders above the tree line. Keep your eyes peeled, because you pass through different biological zones in minutes.

You enter Haleakala National Park at mm10, where an entrance fee is charged. Consider saving Hosmer Grove—to the left after the park entrance—for the return leg of the tour, but a visit to Park Headquarters is a recommended stop for an introduction to the visit. Then, push the wheels toward the top. The Kalahaku Lookout, after mm18, can only be accessed on the downward trip.

Must stops are the Red Hill observation area at the summit, and the White Hill walk at the Haleakala Visitors Center, just before the road's end. At the summit, observe the sinking phenomena described by author Jack London when he rode a horse up here: Since you see more of the horizon as you climb, the summit of Haleakala can be perceived as a downward journey. After taking in the summit, energetic travelers will want to immerse themselves in the red cinder of the crater, by taking the Sliding Sands Trail.

Haleakala Visitors Center

On the way down, check out at the Leleiwi and Kalahaku overlooks. Highly recommended is Halemau'u Trail to the Ko'olau Gap overlook—a place that exceeds imagination. You'll be able see most everything on this tour, since Haleakala is the right size for a full-day visit. And you'll feel like you've been gone for a week after descending to the sandy beaches and coco palms.

KAUPO COAST TOUR, BEGIN EARLY MORNING. TAKE HIGHWAY 37 PAST KULA AND CONTINUE AS IT BECOMES HIGHWAY 31. Traditionally, people see this area on the last leg of a long day, coming around from Hana. Consequently, it's passed over as an "eerie moonscape" you pass by on the way back to the resort for the evening's Mai Tai. For many visitors, however, the Kaupo coast will be Maui's most pleasant surprise—gulches becoming canyons along a rugged wilderness coast rich with archeological sites, and all of it under the towering relief of Haleakala.

After rounding the bend at Kula, you may wish to take a first rest stop at Sun Yat Sen Park at mm18. But save a refreshing wine-tasting and historical tour at Tedeschi Winery, just down the highway, for the homeward leg. *Note:* You can just as easily visit the Pools of Oheo, by going this way rather than taking the Hana Highway, though neither is a short trip. If you choose this option, read the above notes in *The Road*, and proceed directly to Oheo, and make your Kaupo stops on the return. The drive from Kaupo to the pools at Kipahulu is wildly scenic.

A couple miles past Tedeschi, which is on the grounds of Ulupalakua Ranch, the road narrows, and you start to pick up views down to the lava flow on the Kinau Peninsula at La Perouse Bay. Cinder cones rise from the desert flora of the slopes. The road

Tedeschi Winery

begins a long descent, passing the Lualailua Hills and reaching near sea level at Manawainui Gulch. From the turnout at Manawainui, you can walk a short distance to see the natural arch and fishing shrine ruins on a remote portion of the King's Trail.

The highway stays near sea level for the next several miles. Stop at will. Along this coast, you truly can explore. You will mostly likely want to see the petroglyphs at Nuʻu Bay, as well as the view of Haleakala you get from the boulder beach there. After Nuʻu, the highway climbs to Puʻu Maneoneo, where you can hop out of the car for a perspective on where you've just been.

Huialoha Church

For the next several miles, the partially paved road winds through ranchlands, passing St. Joseph's Church, and reaching the sanctum sanctorum of this coast, the Kaupo Store. That this country-funk place is the center of commerce for the entire coast speaks wonderful volumes. From here, adventurers wanting the area's best hike can try the Kaupo Trail, that scales Haleakala and reaches the park through the Kaupo Gap. As mentioned above, the remaining 8-mile trip to the Pools of Oheo is one of Maui's most scenic. But even if you don't go that far, be sure to check out Huialoha Church, which is about a mile from the Kaupo Store.

KULA TOUR. ADD ON TO THE HALEAKALA OR KAUPO TOURS, OR DO SEPARATELY. The Kula, or Upcountry, portion of Maui runs along a contour at several thousand feet in elevation on the west slope of Haleakala. Cool temperatures, moderate rainfall, and trade-wind clouds prevail here, an ideal environ for gardens, forests, and arboretums. Put Bruddah Iz Kamakawiwoʻole's version of John Denver's *Country Road* on the CD player and roll.

TAKE HIGHWAY 37 TO HIGHWAY 377. A horse's life may seem appealing as you see them grazing up here on the rounded hillsides, with enough shade and windbreak offered by eucalyptus and native tree groves. Near mm5 is Kula Lodge, a venerable eatery with an art gallery downstairs. Next door is Upcountry Harvest, where souvenir shoppers will be interested in local crafts and Maui Protea bouquets. You'll see protea

Haleakala from Puʻu Maneoneo

Kaupo Trailhead, Hosmer Grove, Sliding Sands Trail

flower farms farther down the road, on either side of the junction with Highway 378, and then pass Kula Gardens, which is a short drive up the hill to a 23-acre site that is one of the island's oldest private reserves.

If you're doing a full day in the Upcountry, you'll want to take a spin up Waipoli Road to the Kula Forest Reserve; the road will be on your left before Highway 377 joins Highway 37. Waipoli Road wiggles upward to about 6,000 feet, over hillsides favored by model airplane buffs, before becoming unpaved and entering the sublime trails of the Polipoli Springs State Park. It's the relatively secret side of Haleakala.

JUNCTION OF HIGHWAYS 377 AND 37. Take Highway 37 around the mountain for some 7 miles to Tedeschi Winery that is within Ulupalakua Ranch. On the way you'll pass through the historic Chinese settlement of Keokea, just past which you can veer left up the hill to see the movie-like setting of the Kula Sanatorium. Also on the way, near mm18 is Sun Yat Sen Park, where views of Makena open up. And down the road from the park is Uluapalakua Ranch and the Tedeschi Winery—offering tasting and a history tour of its arboretum.

BACKTRACK TO JUNCTION OF HIGHWAYS 377 AND 37. JUST PAST THIS JUNCTION, TURN RIGHT ON LOWER KULA ROAD. You don't want to miss this slice of old Maui, left intact since bypassed by the newer highways. At the turn is Rice Park, with rolling lawn and a commanding overlook toward West Maui. Down the road is Calasa Service, built in 1932, where gassing the car will be an experience, without having to pay higher prices. Down the street from the service station are the Morihara Store and Café 808, which may not have an identifying sign—both are places for local-style libation. Farther along from these establishments is the centerpiece of Kula, the Church of the Holy Ghost, an octagonal edifice built in 1894.

Note: Beyond the church, Lower Kula Road pops back out to the highway. You can take another section of the road—a right turn shortly after coming out to the highway—to see the Mormon Pulehu Church, built in 1851. This segment of Lower Kula becomes unpaved and joins Highway 37 again.

Olinda Road, Calasa Service, Upcountry bicyclists, Church of the Holy Ghost

Kula wall, Ulupalakua, Waipoli slopes

CONTINUE ON HIGHWAY 37, TURN RIGHT ON HIGHWAY 377, AND TURN LEFT ON KEALALOA HANAMU ROAD. This maneuver takes you through dairylands—also the descent route for Haleakala bicycle tours—and joins up with Olinda Road. *Note:* You could also continue on Highway 37 to Highway 365 and reach Olinda Road a little farther down the mountain in Makawao. Either way, you can turn right on Olinda for a spin to the upper Upcountry, ending at the Waihou Springs Forest Reserve. On the way up you pass flower and succulent farms, near mm11, and the Maui Bird Conservation Center, which is a couple turns higher.

On the way down Olinda are big views toward the Kahului coast. Makawao, the Upcountry's cowboy town is worth a walk through; turn left at the stop sign on Highway 365—across from which Olinda Road becomes Baldwin Avenue. You can then return to the lowlands via the Haleakala Highway, or double back and take Baldwin, which is Highway 390, down to Paia. Just to complicate things, you can also take a longer version down, Highway 398, which is Kokomo Road. The best plan from Makawao may be to plan on getting lost. Just keep heading downhill, exploring country lanes, and you'll hit the Hana Highway someplace.

MAP 5
TRAILHEADS 45-52
HALEAKALA

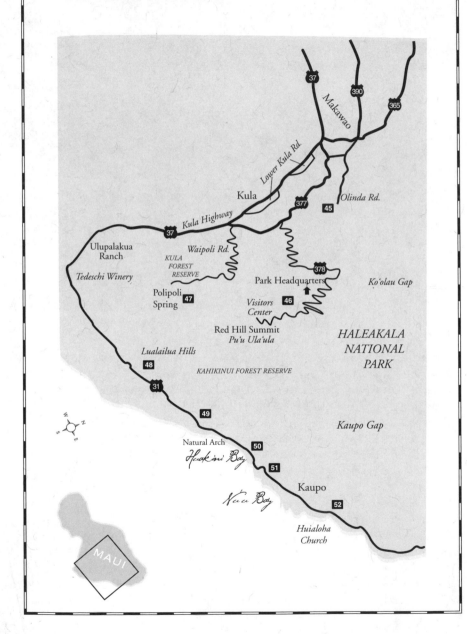

37

390

365

Makawao

Lower Kula Rd.

Kula

377   45   Olinda Rd.

Kula Highway

37

Ulupalakua
Ranch

Waipoli Rd.

KULA
FOREST
RESERVE

Tedeschi Winery

378

Polipoli
Spring   47

Park Headquarters

Ko'olau Gap

Visitors
Center   46

Red Hill Summit
Pu'u Ula'ula

HALEAKALA
NATIONAL
PARK

Lualailua Hills

48

KAHIKINUI FOREST RESERVE

31

W   N
S   E

49

Kaupo Gap

Natural Arch

Hāna Bay

50

51

Nu'u Bay

Kaupo

52

Huialoha
Church

MAUI

T R A I L H E A D S

H	HIKING	45-52
SN	SNORKELING	
P	KAYAKING, CANOEING	
SF	SURFING, BOOGIE BOARDING, WIND SPORTS	

TH = Trailhead

mm = mile marker; corresponds to highway signs

All hiking distances in parentheses are ROUND TRIP.

Elevation gains of 100 feet or more are noted.

45. OLINDA UPCOUNTRY   H

Best For: Take a drive through rural cowboy country, and keep going—to a trail deep into pine forest and a spring at 3,500 feet.

Parking: *For both hikes:* Take Hwy. 36 to Paia and turn right on Hwy. 390, Baldwin Ave. Follow about 5 mi. to Makawao. *For Olinda Rd.-Waihou Springs:* Continue straight at jct. with Makawao Ave., as Hwy. 390 becomes Olinda Rd. Pass mm11 and the Hawaii Tree Growth Research Area. Park on the right at signed trailhead, before mm12. *For Camp Maui-Kauhikoa Hill:* Turn left in Makawao on Makawao Ave., which is Hwy. 365, and then left again on Kokomo Rd., Hwy. 398. After mm4, turn right into signed park on Newman Ln. *Note:* If descending Olinda, turn right on Makawao Ave.

H: **Waihou Springs Forest Reserve to: Springs (1.75 mi., 350 ft.), or Forest loop (1 mi., 150 ft.) Note: The springs trail is a spur off the loop trail; to do both together, the hike is 2.25 mi., 450 ft. Camp Maui-Kauhikoa Hill (up to .5-mi.).**

Getting there is fifty-one percent of the fun on this hike. On the way, you might choose to dawdle in the shops at Makawao or stop at a roadside garden as Olinda Road winds skyward. Waihou Springs is part of the state Na Ala Hele hiking trails system, over lands test-planted with pines and other species in the 1920s. **For both Waihou hikes**, head down the needle-cushioned road through the orderly pine grove. After about .25-mile, turn right toward the overlook, and then, **to reach the springs**, go right again, amid spindly ash trees. You reach an overlook with a bench among sugi pine, where the springs trail drops steeply on switchbacks among koa trees. The springs seep from a 200-foot mossy wall that is bored with cavelike irrigation tunnels—a mysterious Hobbit-land. In summer, and drought conditions, it may be dry. *Be Aware:* Stay away from embankments as even large boulders are unstable.

For the **forest loop**, continue past the second right-leading spur that goes to the springs. The trail continues on an undulating circle, through a variety of trees that include cypress and koa, as well as some good-sized pines. Then you reconnect with the main path back to trailhead parking.

More Stuff: Olinda Road ends just past mm12. From just above the road's gate is the lower part of Waikomo Ridge Trail, which descends from Hosmer Grove. Permission to hike here is required from The Nature Conservancy. Also, if you'd like an alternate route down, take Pi'iholo Road, a left turn just before the end of Olinda. After about 5 miles on Pi'iholo, you come to Makawao Avenue, Highway 365, near the town. About .5-mile *before* that junction, look for an unpaved road on your right near a water tank. The road leads across a stream to Pi'iholo Hill, about 2 miles away. Permission to access this hike may be required. You can also access this road by backtracking down Olinda to Makawao, turning right, and then making your first right on Pi'iholo Road.

Only WWII buffs would make a special trip to **Camp Maui** and **Kauhikoa Hill**, but everyone else will enjoy this airy park as a stop on an alternate route back down from Olinda Road. From 1943 to 1946 a small city of 16,000 Marines lived here, training to fight Pacific battles that included Iwo Jima. More than three-quarters of the men

Waihou Springs forest, Polipoli sign

were killed or wounded. The beloved soldiers were made to feel at home on Maui, and the park is dedicated to their memory. Kauhikoa Hill rises above the park's sprawling lawns. Trailblazers can wander up through eucalyptus for views of the Kahului coast.

More Stuff: Kokomo Road descends to become Haiku Road, Hwy. 366, which joins the Hana Highway east of Paia. Browsers can check out the old pineapple cannery in Haiku. Trailblazers might be interested in Pu'u Umi, a lofty perch named for a Maui king of antiquity. Turn left on Umi Place, after Paia. This area is now being developed with large homes, and the summit has no signed access.

46.   HALEAKALA NATIONAL PARK   H

> **Best For:** A journey to a volcanic planet, two-miles in the sky in the middle of the Pacific. Choose from hikes that will suit every energy level: forests, craters, lava caves—not to mention overlooks with aerial views of Maui and beyond.
>
> **Parking:** Go inland on Hwy. 37, the Haleakala Hwy. After Pukalani-Makawao jcts., turn left on Hwy. 377. Follow for 6 mi. and turn left on Hwy. 378, and enter the national park boundary near mm10. *Notes:* Additional directions for each hike given below, beginning at the boundary and working toward the summit. An admission is charged to enter the park. Bring warm clothes.

H: Hosmer Grove Nature Trail (.5-mi.); Halemau'u Trail to: Ko'olau Gap-crater overlook (2.25 mi., 250 ft.), or Holua Cabin-lava caves (8.25 mi., 1,200 ft.); Leleiwi Overlook (less than .25-mi.); White Hill (.5-mi, 150 ft.); Sliding Sands Trail to: cinder cones overlook (2 mi., 400 ft.), or Ka Lu'u o ka O'o (5.25 mi., 1,400 ft.), or Kapalaoa Cabin (11.5 mi., 2,500 ft.), or Bottomless Pit (11.25 mi., 2,600 ft.); Red Hill Summit (less than .25-mi.)

Climbing to 10,000 feet over a few horizontal miles, the Haleakala Highway is the steepest roadway in the world. Yet its sweeping curves provide for a mellow drive, by Maui standards, unless your brakes fail on the way down. The crater at the top—19 square miles and 3,000-feet deep—is not technically a crater. It's actually a valley created by erosion, whose moonscape is dotted with about a dozen red cinder cones, mini-craters that are called pu'us, each one a vent from a separate eruption. Having had an eruption within the last few hundred years, Haleakala is considered an active volcano. Clouds can bring wintry conditions to the summit, and weather changes rapidly. Frequently a band of clouds hangs near Kula, near 4,000 feet, making the top appear socked in from below when it's actually rising into the sun—Haleakala, "House of the Sun."

The **Hosmer Grove Nature Loop** through native shrubs will be of most interest to botanists and ornithologists. The trailhead is from the campground, a .5-mile drive on a left turn just after entering the park. The first part of the loop goes through cedar, spruce, and other conifers planted in the early 1900s by forester Ralph Hosmer. The second part is through native shrubs, where our feathered friends live.

More Stuff: The more exciting hike from this area is the Waikomo Ridge Trail; the trailhead is near a rest room a few hundred feet from the end of the road into the campground. Permission is required from The Nature Conservancy to enter this area. For this and other hiking information, stop at the Park Headquarters, just up the road near mm11.25. You'll also find an extensive bookstore, as well as brochures and expertise on all aspects of the big volcano.

The **Halemau'u Trail** parking lot is on your left, just after mm14. The hike to the **Ko'olau Gap** and **crater overlook** reaps a big return for the investment of energy. After descending through low shrubs you reach a precipice. On your right is the west side of the Haleakala Crater, a jumble of black lava here, speckled with greenery. You walk the spine of the precipice toward the gap, where a relatively recent lava fall created the Keanae Peninsula off the Hana Highway, which is to your left. Across the gap is the steep relief of Kalapawili Ridge.

To reach the **Holua Cabin** and nearby **lava caves**, the trail takes a herky-jerky descent of nearly 1,000 feet down a weirdly formed escarpment. On the bottom, your feet briefly are comforted by a grass patch, before the trail again ascends up a lava bench. Atop the bench, on a small lawn below the towering Leleiwi Pali, is the cabin. Often waddling around this rustic oasis are the endangered nene, or Hawaiian goose, the state bird. (Please don't feed them.) A trail leads south from the cabin, eventually connecting with trails coming down from the top of the crater. On the left, off the trail leading away from Holua, is the first cave. Its entrance is more of a hole in the ground that requires hands to access. The major cave is reachable by an unmarked trail that leads up to the right near the first cave. *Be Aware:* Lava tubes can be dangerous. Venturing in alone or with only one flashlight is unadvisable. Also, prepare for both cold and

Holua lava cave, Cinder cones overlook

Holua Cabin, Nene, Silversword, Haleakala Crater

hot weather if descending to Holua. A spigot at the cabin provides non-potable water; bring a pump or purification tablets.

The kiosk **Leleiwi Overlook** offers a view from the high cliffs above Holua Cabin, as well as the entire crater. Look for a signed turnoff after mm17. Late in the day at the overlook is a good time to observe the surreal Hoʻokuaka effect, or what the Germans call "Bröckenspector": With clouds in the crater and the sun at your back, your shadow sometimes will appear in the mist, illuminated by a halo of color. The Haleakala Visitors Center, perched on the edge of the crater is almost to the top, at mm20. A trail from outside its door winds to the top of **White Hill**, a.k.a. Pa Kaʻoao. The exquisite view area on top is the prime destination for short-walk specialists.

The **Sliding Sands Trail** departs from the right as you enter the visitors center parking lot. Descending with long traverses over red sand, this trail has a way of drawing hikers deeper than they intended, so begin the trail prepared for a long hike. The **cinder cones overlook** will come up on your left, an unmarked spur. The **Ka Luʻu o ka Oʻo** crater will be directly below. To get there, continue down and make a left at the first junction—at a confusing outcropping and among some silverswords, the darling of the Haleakala plant world. When you reach the crater, be sure to take the thrilling trail around its rim.

To the **Bottomless Pit**, a.k.a. Kawilinau, continue on the Sliding Sands for nearly 2 miles past the above junction. The last part will be a steep descent. Then take a left at a trail junction, beginning a moderate fall over about 1.5 miles, keeping two cinder cones to your right. The pit—with a bottom clearly visible—is on the north side of the cinder cones. To reach the **Kapalaoa Cabin**, keep on trekking past the Bottomless Pit-Halemauʻu Trail junction, for 2 more miles. The cabin lies near the edge of the Kaupo Gap, and the 7,000-foot escarpments that fall to the south coast.

More Stuff: Trailblazers will enjoy a car-shuttle hike from Sliding Sands, past Holua Cabin, to the Halemauʻu trailhead. The hike is 11.5 miles with 2,800 feet of elevation gain, give or take. Hikers without a second car to shuttle commonly hitchhike back to the top.

To **Red Hill Summit**, drive to road's end, which is at mm21. A covered hut with Plexiglas windows provides shelter, informative displays, as well as staggering views, particularly of the Big Island. Red Hill's real name is Puʻuʻulaula—try it, it's easy. To get a view of West Maui, walk across the parking lot and up the low lip of the rim. The summit road continues to the fanciful domes of Science City, a defense department and University of Hawaii research and telecommunications center. God knows what goes on there.

47. KULA FOREST RESERVE

Best For: Ascending to green side of Haleakala, where some trails achieve lofty heights with views way down to breaking surf, while other paths wander misty forests, including a large grove of redwoods. Afterwards, tour a historic winery.

Parking: Take Hwy. 37, the Haleakala Hwy., up the mountain and keep right as Hwy. 37 becomes the Kula Hwy. *For all Kula Forest hikes:* After mm13, turn left on Hwy. 377. Then, after .25-mi., turn right on Waipoli Rd. Follow up and up 5 mi. to the end of the paved road—which is about 1 mi. past the hunter's check station. See hike descriptions for further directions. *For Sun Yat Sen Park, Tedeschi Winery:* Continue on Hwy. 37. See hike paragraphs for directions.

H: Waipoli Road to: Boundary Trial loop (6.5 mi., 900 ft.), or Haleakala Ridge view (7 mi., 150 ft.); Skyline Trail to: Mamane Trail loop (5.75 mi., 950 ft.), or Haleakala Park summit (up to 13 mi., 3,200 ft.); Polipoli Springs-Redwood Trail loop (3.75 mi., 900 ft.,); Sun Yat Sen Park (.25-mi.); Ulupalakua Ranch-Tedeschi Winery (up to .5-mi.)

Note: The Waipoli Road hikes are for those who decide not to drive farther than the end of the pavement. The worst part of road normally is at the very beginning of the unpaved section. After that, the road enters the forest on a contour, and should be negotiable in good weather by careful 2WD vehicle drivers. Clearance is the main hazard in spots. Regardless, the road is a wide path that provides a pleasant forest stroll through the 12,000 acre Polipoli Springs State Park, which is part of the Kula Forest Reserve. *Be Aware:* It's nippy up here, from 6,000 feet on up. Bring warm clothing.

For both **Waipoli Road hikes**, begin walking from the parking pavement's end. After .5-mi., you'll round a bend and enter the forest and pass the junction with the Boundary Trail. The road undulates, but basically maintains a contour. For the **Boundary Trail loop**, go right, after about 2 miles from the parking area, at the right-hand junction with the Waiohuli Trail. You will drop 900 feet and join the Boundary Trail. Turn right and enjoy views toward the Kihei coast as you return on a more gradual climb. For the **Haleakala Ridge view**, just stay on the road. In less than 3 miles from the parking area, you pass the junction with the spur road that drops to Polipoli Springs. From that junction it's another .75-mile up to a big open turnout, where you can look up the Haleakala Ridge and down to the vast sheets of lava that meet the sea on the southern coast. The Skyline Trail begins its ascent to the summit here, and hardy hikers can continue.

For the **Skyline Trail-Mamane Trail loop**, drive in about 2 miles from the end of the pavement, and park at signed junction for the Waiohuli Trail, which crosses the road. This trail gives you a taste of the forest, a cave adventure, as well as big panoramas. You

Polipoli Trail Cave, Red Hill Summit

begin with a steep climb over the first .75-mile, to the junction with the Mamane Trail. There you go right. Near this junction you'll find a small volcanic cone used by the ancients as a cave shelter. Over the next two miles you traverse native shrub, noting the mamane tree, because it's the only one growing. You then meet the Skyline Trail, above its first set of switchbacks on the ascent up the ridge to Red Hill. To return, go right, down to rejoin Waipoli Road and the return leg to the car. The last part of the hike is level, through the forest. *Note:* Since this is a loop, you could begin this hike from the Skyline Trail, the parking described in the hike below, and descend the Mamane Trail.

The **Skyline Trail** takes you higher and higher, to the **Haleakala summit** at Science City. Unless some kind of military alert has been declared, you could walk through to Red Hill at the top. Begin by driving almost 4 miles in on Waipoli Road, past the turnoff to Polipoli. You'll round an open bend and come to a forested saddle—where the road becomes red-dirt switchbacks that thwart passenger vehicles. Park here. Views open dramatically when you reach the top of the switchbacks. Continue climbing to your left—a right hand junction takes you into a scrub-filled ancient crater on Kahua Road, an interesting jaunt for those not wishing to go higher. After about .75-mile, Red Hill will be visible up and to your left. Although you occasionally lose sight of the summit, the trail continues straight up the ridge in that direction for the remaining miles. Much of the hike rises above vegetation, as the road becomes cinders. This is the highest, open-view hike you can achieve on Maui, since the Haleakala hikes within the park descend into the crater.

For the **Polipoli Springs-Redwood Trail loop**, veer right from Waipoli Road about 3 miles after the end of pavement, and drive down about .5-mile to the picnic area at Polipoli Springs. This hike takes you through deep forests of redwoods, cypress, plum, and ash trees, and loops back past a mossy cave and a view area toward the lava coast. From the parking area—a glade surrounded by towering trees—double back 100 feet on the road and go left down a short path that leads to the Polipoli Cabin. Hang a right at a signed trail when you reach the cabin. The soft-earth trail swerves down, at first through cypress and a few sugi pine, and then among redwoods, some with diameters approaching 3 feet. After a little less than a mile, at a shelter, go left on the Tie Trail. You'll drop 500 feet farther through redwoods and then ash trees. If you're quiet you might surprise a wild pig or two. After .5-mile the Tie Trail joins the Haleakala Ridge Trail, where you go left.

Big ferns join ash and redwoods over the next mile, at an altitude where sunlight often mixes with waning fog to produce glowing beams. This zone is above legendary Kahikinui on the south coast; see TH48. You'll get ocean peeks at Kahoolawe, as the trail climbs during the next mile. At a junction above a big climb, go left on Polipoli Trail—where the Haleakala Ridge Trail continues right to join the road and Skyline Trail. The **shelter cave** is about .5-mile farther up the Polipoli Trail, just off the trail at a signed junction. The wide-mouthed cave, in bedrock, is in a depression in the forest. A trail to the right of the cave leads to a big view. The Polipoli Trail contours through eucalyptus and pine before reaching the picnic area parking.

Haleakala Ridge Trail

After coming down the mountain from the Kula Forest Reserve, you may want to finish the day with a quick stop at **Sun Yat Sen Park**, followed by a wine tasting at **Tedeschi Winery** and stroll among the paniolos of **Ulupalakua Ranch**. To do either, continue on Highway 37 to mm18. The park is set on a bucolic vista, on hills that roll down a few thousand feet to the Makena coast. Kula was a prominent Chinese settlement, particularly in the 1900s, when favorite son Sun Yet Sen, who had been educated in Hawaii, returned to Hong Kong where he became the Republic of China's first leader after the revolution of 1912. Statuary and a commemorative plaque accent the park's strolling path.

The Tedeschi Winery is a few miles farther through the countryside on Highway 37. The road turns to Highway 31 near mm20, and a mile after that is the winery, which sits amid Ulupalakua Ranch. Tedeschi Vineyards, featuring sparkling wines made from pineapple, has been around since 1974, taking over the historic buildings of the James Makee estate. The Hawaiian royal family and famous writers, such as Robert Louis Stevenson, frequented the grand estate. Makee planted numerous varieties of trees, now giants, and flowers in abundance. Tedeschi's tasting room staff provide a historical tour, along with the vineyard's libation. Ruins of Makee's sugar mill are across the highway. The Ulupalakua Ranch is still a working operation, and you're likely to see some of the paniolos down the street at the local store. In the old days, they'd run the cattle down the mountain to Makena, and swim the beasts out to awaiting ships.

48.   GREAT TAHITI   H

> **Best For:** Ruins along the hills that tell the story of migrations from Tahiti about 1,000 years ago—to hikers willing to endure the sticker brush, beating sun, and high winds on an unmarked trail to find them.

> **Parking:**   Take Hwy. 37, the Haleakala Hwy., up the mountain and keep right as route becomes the Kula Hwy. After mm20, route changes again, to Hwy. 31. Continue past mm21 and two homesteads on either side of the road. At mm22.5, park on left at a shoulder; another homestead will be on the right and the trailhead gate will be to the left, up and off the road. *Note:* Around mm18, as you come down the squiggly highway, note the two Lualailua Hills, lying ahead to the left, above the highway. At the saddle between the hills, observe a contour line of a road that leads to the left, toward the upper part of the hill that is most inland. This is the route to the ruins.

H: **Kahikinui ruins-Menehune footprints (3.5 mi., 300 ft.)**

Kahikinui—or Great Tahiti—was one of Hawaii's earliest settlements, with a population nearing 2,000 scattered about these arid upslopes. Although fishing was primary for sustenance in the village, freshwater was brackish at the coast and many structures were located near 1,500 feet to trap ephemeral spring water with small dams. In Hawaiian, Kahiki also means "horizon," and the village was set in a location to observe the cinder cone which they named Hokukano, after the star, Hokupukano, which guided the ancient mariners on their 2,500-mile voyage to the Tahitian homelands. The cone is on the ocean side of the highway at mm17.5.

The Menehune footprints are the Holy Grail for archeological enthusiasts. A mystery even to the earliest Polynesians, the footprints, are etched into a smooth lava shelf about 35 feet in diameter—some 30 prints measuring from 4- to 10-inches in length, mostly children's size. They are thought to be a type of petroglyph left by the legendary Menehune, the diminutive precursors to the later Tahitian migrations, who probably came from the Marquesas. The prints are difficult to find, and hard to make out even if you do find them—good luck. *Be Aware:* Prepare for wind and sun on this off-trail excursion. It's possible to avoid thorny underbrush, but wear long pants if you have them. Footing is difficult, due to lava and brush. Also, respect the boundaries of the homesteads in the area.

For the **Kahikinui ruins-Menehune footprints** hike, head up from the roadway and through the gate that seems to be an entrance to nowhere. But you'll be able to follow a rocky path upward, and, after about 10 minutes, turn a right-angle left on an old road. The road levels and leads through the saddle between the Lualailua Hills, which means "dual tranquility." Benign grasses and weeds will slap your shins as you make your way across the saddle to the point that you observed driving in. From the saddle head up to your right, picking your way under some trees just large enough to throw shade. Contour around, ascending a little to stay above the top of a gulch.

From the other side of the gulch—a homestead will be down to the left—you should pick up the trail which contours around the uppermost hill. The trail meets a road,

Statue at Tedeschi Winery, Lualailua Hills

which leads through a rickety, wire gate in an equally rickety fence. Although ruins dot this area, you will find a major site to your left. Walk the smooth lava a few hundred feet and go left out to a promontory marked by a kiawe tree. Here lies the sprawling remains of a Kahikinui village site, that was once covered with a wooden superstructure and thatched roofing. Note the views toward the channel and cones below, the route to the far horizon charted by the kahunas. Inland, Haleakala rises thousands of feet. *Be Aware:* Use caution to leave the site undisturbed.

The footprints lie some 500 yards up the slope from this site, and about 300 yards from the base of the hill. Listen for the hushed voices on the wind from the villagers of the past; perhaps they will guide you to just the right spot. Keep an eye out, too, for lava tubes.

49. MANAWAINUI GULCH   H

Best For: Exploring the fishing shrines on the lost portion of the King's Trail, or taking a short but gnarly hike down to heiaus set at a cove in a canyon.

Parking: Take Hwy. 37, the Haleakala Hwy., up the mountain and keep right as route becomes the Kula Hwy. After mm20, route changes again, to Hwy. 31. Continue past gulches and one-lane bridges near mm25. At the bottom of the long descent, at mm27.5, pull off at a large turnout on the right.

H: Manawainui Gulch heiaus (.75-mi, 300 ft.); King's Trail (1.5 mi. or more, 200 ft.)

From the turnout, walk to the edge and take a gander down the black canyon that is **Manawainui Gulch**, where confused seas meet storm-washed boulders, the alluvium of Haleakala. To reach sea level, walk down the highway to where the guardrail joins the modern concrete bridge. You could also park down here, but there's not much room and the cliffs seem ready to drop a rock on a rental car. Step over the guardrail— there is no trail—and traverse down toward the bridge. At the bottom, cross the drainage and cut back toward the ocean on the brush-and-grass covered bench. Going can be slow. Near the bottom, veer right off the bench, across the boulders to the rough shoreline. There you will find a medium-sized burial platform, built of black rock, and, just behind it, a smaller one built of coral stones.

To explore the **King's Trail**, walk down from the overlook and veer right and down. You won't see a trail or markers on this end of the ancient trail that begins some 6 miles away in La Perouse Bay. Over the next mile or so, walking along the coast, a number of four-wheel tracks come down from the highway, which you may have noticed over the last couple miles on the descent to the Manawainui Gulch turnout. You'll see the first fishing shrine about .25-mile from the parking area, beyond the first shallow gully. Along the lava coast, you are likely to see modern fishermen, who drive down, somehow, and use ladders to get out to their favorite casting spots on sharp reefs that stick out into the waves. Prepared trailblazers can continue, making a true adventure of this little used route. More ruins, a blowhole, and tide pools are in the offing.

50.   HUAKINI BAY   H

Best For: A natural sea arch and a red-rock canyon, which impart a sense of Haleakala's geologic transformation happening in real time.

Parking: Take Hwy. 37, the Haleakala-Kula Hwy. After mm20, the route changes to Hwy. 31. Continue to Manawainui Gulch, near mm27.5. *Note:* Further directions from this point are given in hiking descriptions below.

H: **Natural Arch (up to .5-mi); Pahihi Gulch (2.75 mi., 200 ft.)**

Along several miles of the highway, some half-dozen gulches are gouged into the 9,000-foot high wall that is the southern face of Haleakala. The great shield volcano was once about 5,000 feet higher, as over the eons much of its mass has eroded down gulches and either washed away into the ocean or fanned out to form this rugged coastline.

To see the **Natural Arch** before walking toward it, walk toward the ocean at the Manawainui turnout, as per TH48, and look down the coast, across the gulch. The

Pahihi Gulch, Natural Arch

King's Trail ruins

sloping arch is plainly visible. Then jump back in the wheels and drive to the modern Po'o Po'o Bridge, at mm28.5. (The child in all of us will have fun with that one.) From here you can walk down the top side of the arch, though you'd never know it was below this sloping shoulder. To approach the arch from the coast, get in the car again and proceed to the bottom of the next gulch at Waiopai Bridge, another modern feat. From the black-rock beach, go to your right along the rocky coast to get sort of near the arch. Battered by the sea, it forms an opening some 150 feet in length and about 50 feet high. Up the gorge from the beach is a spur road, leading a short distance into a bedrock gorge. Only good sense and the likelihood of a flash flood or falling rock will prevent trailblazers from venturing farther.

Pahihi Gulch is accessible from Huakini Bay, where the highway crosses a wide wash at sea level, after mm29. The shallow bay is a massive boulder field, easily walked by careful hikers. This gulch is a canyon in the making, as it will continue to deepen over the millennia to become similar to Kauai's Waimea. Park at a shoulder on the left, just as you reach the bay. A hunter's trail leads through the greenery on the left side of the gulch's wide mouth—above the gravel bed that is the low point of wash, but not next to the cliff either. Stay left on this path, headed toward a slide of yellowish rock. When you reach the slide, keep left of a large stand of kiawe trees. Another gulch, Pukai, joins this one from the right. About .75-mile into the hike, you'll lose sight of the highway, as the gulch narrows and you pass to the left of a stand-alone hillock that sits in the middle of the gulch. At this point, look left up the bench, and you'll see a cave below the cliff; hikers with partners and flashlights may want to explore with caution.

Almost a mile into the hike, you'll pass behind the stand-alone hillock, and will be surrounded on four sides by steep, unstable cliffs. Hunters use this area on weekends, and you're likely to find snares made of wire and hear falling rock caused by the movements of the pigs and goats up high. Birdsong practically echoes in this natural atrium. From here the gulch narrows and curves, and you'll have to pick your way across its rocky bottom, deep-grass, and treed banks. Eventually, it becomes too steep and crumbly to safely walk. *Be Aware:* This is not a hike to take alone. Do not attempt during rains, and avoid falling rock by staying away from cliffs.

51. NU'U BAY   H, SN

Best For: Petroglyphs, a birder's marsh, ruins, Haleakala views, and an old landing—put this little bay high on the list if you're looking for the secret side of Maui.

Parking: Take Hwy. 37, the Haleakala-Kula Hwy. After mm20, the route changes to Hwy. 31. Continue to where the road reaches sea level and pass mm30. *Note:* Further directions follow in hike descriptions.

H: Nu'u Bay to: Petroglyphs (.25-mi.), and Nu'u Landing-Kaupo Ranch Wildlife Marsh loop (1.75 mi.); Pu'u Maneoneo (.25-mi.)

At mm30 the highway dips into an oasis of kiawe trees at **Nu'u Bay**, site of an ancient fishing village where you can find ruins by just wandering around. A first road leads in to the right very near mm30, and a second just afterward, where the road dips across a spillway. For the **petroglyphs** and the **loop hike**, look for a gate at mm30.75. After very short distance down the road, curve to your right along a cliff, which is less than 20 feet high. Petroglyphs will be plainly visible in places, etched into the rocks. Closer inspections will reveal reddish pictographs, drawings on the surface. Anthropologists speculate as to the origins of these recordings. Follow the cliff as it loops out to the boulder beach, where you'll find a heiau sitting on a low bluff. *Be Aware:* Take care not to disturb this site.

Nu'u Landing is the low lava point you will see at the far east end of the beach. From the shore is one of the most scenic vistas on Maui: Look inland as the fissured walls of Haleakala and the Kaupo Gap rise some 8,000 feet over the kiawe grove. To reach the landing, it's easier to cut inland and take a sandy road along the edge of the trees. At its end, you have to climb up 15 feet. Fishermen's campsites lie on a grassy bench at the base of the point, and an old concrete ramp leads into the water; this was the point of departure for the cattle raised nearby in the old days. Take the trail past the landing. You'll come to a right-forking trail that lead down to rugged Nonou Bay. You can also stay left on a trail that leads over sharp lava to Apole Point, and to tiny Waiu Bay, which is on the opposite side of the point from Nu'u. *More Stuff:* On the highway, past mm31, is a .5-mile long road that leads down to Waiu Bay. Access is through private property.

Nonou Bay, Nu'u petroglyph, Koa Heiau ruins, St. Joseph Church, Nu'u highway, Haleki'i Bay fisherman

Once you've explored the point, backtrack and take a road that leads from the base of the landing out to the highway. The remains of Koa Heiau, a sprawling site, will be on your right, and an ancient salt pond will be on the left. Also on your left, just before the highway, is the small **Kaupo Ranch Wildlife Marsh**, a pond fringed by grasses which you can see through the trees. Once you reach the highway, near mm31, walk to the left down the road. After about .1-mile, look closely on your left for a chain-link gate in the fence that leads directly to the pond. If you're quiet, you are likely to see water-fowl and shorebirds taking a break at this tiny wetland on a rocky coast.

For the vistas from **Pu'u Maneoneo**, get back in the car and load the camera. After mm31 the road rises inland to a grassy bluff, as the terrain transitions from the arid "dismal coast" to the ranchlands of Kaupo. To the right as the road tops out are a few turnouts and short paths that lead to vantage points. The towering heights of Haleakala will be a crowd pleaser, but don't forget to take a gander up and down the coast. Put a gold star on the map marking this place.

SN: Experienced snorkelers can find relatively safe waters at **Nu'u Landing**, at times during the winter. Use the gate near mm31, which you may be able to drive through. Entry is near the landing, or, better yet, at small **Nonou Bay** which is to the right and down, not far beyond the grass patch at the landing. The walk down to the water is a hands-on affair, but the bay is more protected. This is a deep-water snorkel-ing area not for beginners. *Be Aware:* Don't attempt if the swell is high and test the water for currents. Stay close to shore.

52.   KAUPO   H, SN

Best For: Hike high or savor the coast, but don't just drive by beautiful Kaupo.

Parking: Take Hwy. 37, the Haleakala-Kula Hwy. After mm20, the route changes to Hwy. 31. Continue as Hwy. 31 drops to coast and climbs again, reaching Kaupo Store before mm35. *Note:* Further directions follow in the hike descriptions.

H: Kaupo Trail to: Haleakala National Park Boundary (6 mi., 2,700 ft.), or Kaupo Gap rim (13.75 mi., 5,500 ft.); Huialoha Church-coast (up to 1 mi.)

The front porch at funky Kaupo Store may well be the center of the universe. You'll have to rest a spell with a beverage, watch the world go by, and draw your own conclu-sion. It is open 24 hours a day, except when it's not, a tradition that dates from 1925. To hike the **Kaupo Trail**, get back in the car and make the left turn past the store—before the sign noting that the national park is 8 miles ahead, and before the road drops down to a one-lane bridge. Drive in 1.5 miles on this one-lane, cinder road, which turns ninety-degrees left about halfway. The signed trailhead is off a road that goes left in an open area, where the road forks right up to ranch houses and water tanks.

Note: For both the **Haleakala Park Boundary** and **Kaupo Gap** rim hikes, the hiker's trailhead is marked on the right, as you walk down the road that continues to the left. Tall grass, however, can make the first part of the trail difficult for anyone under 12-feet tall. If the trail is overgrown to the point where getting lost is a likely hazard, walk up the road toward the houses, and go through the gate to the left of the houses along a fence line. This road stays out of the bushes and the trail comes up the grassy gully to join it, after about .75-mile. Whether by trail or road, the first part of the hike is access through private property; heed signs and stay away from buildings and waterworks.

This trail is all about up. Views are with you from the get go, and they only become better. But many people like this trail for its native koa and ahi forests, which attract flocks of woodland birds. Ascending on long switchbacks, you reach the park boundary at an elevation of nearly 4,000 feet, with the steep and jungly Manawainui Valley down to the right. The frozen wave of ancient lava that poured over the Kaupo Gap is to your left. At nearly 7,000 feet, the Kaupo Trail joins the Sliding Sands Trail that comes from the top of Haleakala. From here you are .25-mile from Paliku Cabin, to the right, and about 9 miles from the visitors center, to the left. For trekkers who can't get enough, the Kaupo Trail is Maui's best wilderness experience.

The **Huialoha Church** is a crown jewel, where nature has conspired to craft perfection. To get there, proceed past Kaupo Store and the one-lane bridge. After about .4-mile, turn right on a dirt road that drops down for .25-mile. The church, built in 1859, is set on acres of open grass, accented by coco palms and next to small Haleki'i Bay. Tour the grounds and the bay. You can also walk to the right as you face the water, on a boulder beach path that actually extends for miles to Waiuha Bay.

More Stuff: Three great heiaus in this region date from Chief Kekaulike's rule in 1730. The Loaloa Heiau is upstream to your left just before crossing the bridge after Kaupo Store; the Haleo Kane Heiau is to the right off the road to the Kaupo trailhead, where the road makes its right-angle to the left; and the Popoiwi Heiau is high on a hill off-road to the left, after crossing a second stream past Kaupo Store. A place of worship of more recent lineage—St. Joseph Church, built in 1862—is right on the bumpy road before getting to the Kaupo Store; open grounds and a view of Kaupo Gap combine for a pleasant rest stop.

SN: **Haleki'i Bay**, at Huialoha Church, is the best snorkeling spot along this coast from Kipahulu to La Perouse, which isn't saying too much since most of the coast is totally unsafe. In the winter months, the seas can be flat and the entry okay. You enter deep water, with lots of rocks poking up just offshore, big enough to be called the Mokulau Islands. They provide partial protection from incoming swells. The beach here is also referred to as Mokulau. Net fishermen like this bay, as do scuba divers. *Be*

Aware: If you see a big, fat, hairy guy sleeping on one of the few patches of sand, keep away: It's probably a Hawaiian monk seal, an endangered species for which discretion and the law prescribe a 100-foot buffer zone. But the seal's presence is another indicator that this is the place to snorkel on this coast—as long as the surf is low. In any case, stay close to shore and be mindful of currents.

Kaupo, Huialoha Church and Haleki'i Bay

Outer Islands

Molokai from Maui, leaving Lanai

Father Damien statue, St. Joseph's Church, Molokai

Molokini snorkeler, Hulopoe Beach Park on Lanai, Royal Grove on Molokai

*Take a vacation within a vacation with a day trip to the
three islands that beckon from Maui's western shores.
Molokini is a half-day snorkeling experience. Although you
could spend an entire vacation, or lifetime for that matter,
on Lanai or Molokai, a day on either will seem like a week's
worth of experience.*

53. MOLOKINI   SN

Best For: A marine sanctuary awaiting only a few miles off the coast, with waters so clear you'll think you're flying instead of swimming.

Transportation: A number of vessels make the short trip to Molokini. Some of the best are those of the Maui Dive Shop, which has some half-dozen stores. They offer smaller boats that seat a dozen or fewer passengers, two trained divers who give hands-on help to beginners, and departures from the Kihei Boat Ramp—much closer than some other outfitters, which leave from Lahaina and Ma'alaea. When making a booking, ask your outfitter about these factors, since some of the boats are cattle cars. Also get a reading on the weather, since Molokini's crescent shape opens toward the trade winds, which bring big swells during the winter months. Inquire about cancellation policies. See *Resource Links* for telephone numbers.

Molokini Island came to be in dramatic fashion, when newly formed Haleakala needed to let off steam. Molten lava pushed up from below, super-heating porous rock of the earth's crust until the steam trapped within the rock burst in a gigantic, circular explosion. When the dust and ash settled— viola!—it hardened and eroded from a circle to form a crescent. The fish have come, and Molokini is now one of the world's best spots to snorkel. The island is called a tuft cone, the only one formed in this manner on Maui. Aside from being a Marine Life Conservation District, Molokini is also a seabird sanctuary, but only our feathered friends are allowed to alight on its 70-foot high ridge.

During the winter, waters usually are calmest inside the crescent during morning hours, and the early birds make the 20-minute trip from Kihei starting at 7 a.m. To enjoy warmer sun, take a later departure. Snorkeling boats have their mooring spots inside the crescent, in waters about 30-feet deep near the shore—with better visibility than the air in some cities. On peak days, hundreds of fish lovers will be flopping about, prompting stories about oil slicks caused by sun block and lotions. Regardless, there's plenty of room inside the bowl (the outer edge of Molokini's bowl is submerged). On the convex side of the crescent is a world-famous scuba dive, a wall of several hundred feet. Specialized outfitters take tank divers to this side of the sanctuary.

Molokini

Onboard showers, anchored catamaran, Maui Dive Shop's Captain Rae and Michelle, Kihei Boat Ramp

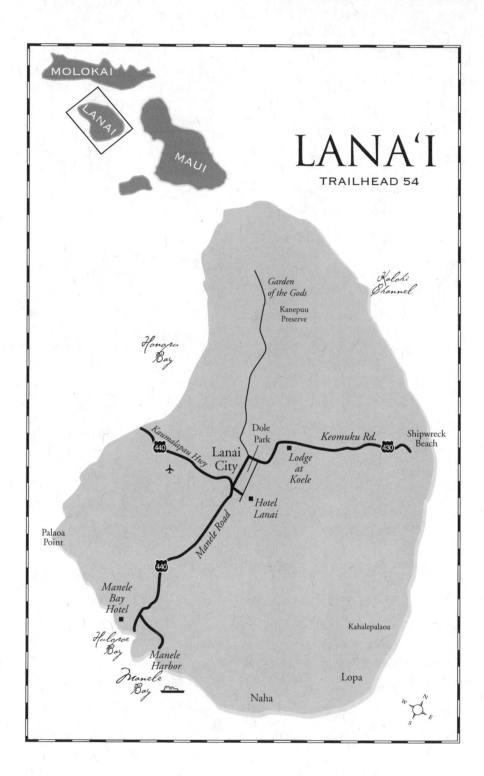

MOLOKAI

LANAI

MAUI

LANA'I

TRAILHEAD 54

Kalohi Channel

Garden of the Gods

Kanepuu Preserve

Honopu Bay

Dole Park

Lanai City

Kaumalapau Hwy

440

Keomuku Rd.

430

Shipwreck Beach

Lodge at Koele

Hotel Lanai

Palaoa Point

Manele Road

440

Manele Bay Hotel

Hulopoe Bay

Manele Harbor

Manele Bay

Kahalepalaoa

Lopa

Naha

N W E S

Best For: Snorking with spinner dolphin and walking the exquisite coastal tide pools. Visit two world-class resorts, one on the beach and another high in the pines with its own sprawling arboretum. Then take a stroll around a sleepy former pineapple town that is nothing but Old Hawaii. A trip to privately owned Lanai is a trip back to 19th century-style vacation resorts.

Transportation: Lanai Expeditions has ferries departing throughout the day from Lahaina Harbor. They are Coast Guard certified. Other vessels take the excursion to Lanai, but Expeditions is the locals' choice, as well as the one used by most tourists. See *Resource Links* for ferry information and overnight accommodations. Advance booking is required. *Note:* Expeditions also offers Jeep rentals and guided tours. The day trip described below is for visitors on foot who utilize the hotels' shuttle buses. You'll want to take a knapsack with lunch and water, and anything else you can think of since finding an open store is not guaranteed. If you plan to snorkel, bring your gear.

Parking at Lahaina: On the south end of town, turn toward the ocean off Hwy. 30, on Shaw St., and park at the lot at the corner of Shaw and Front streets. You'll have to walk a few blocks, but this free lot has no time restrictions.

SCHEDULE FOR A DAY TRIP TO LANAI

BOARD LANAI EXPEDITION FERRY AT 6:30 A.M., LAHAINA HARBOR, PUBLIC PIER. The ride takes about 45 minutes. During winter and spring, the ride doubles as a whale-watching adventure, as the big mammals frolic in Auau Channel on the way over. You board the ferry at predawn and catch sunrise during the trip. *Note:* Check for current ferry schedule.

DEPART FERRY AT MANELE BAY, LANAI, 7:30 A.M. As you look at Lanai from Maui, the Manele Bay harbor is to the left, just out of sight. The ferry rounds the cliff and pulls into a small marina with a dock just big enough to make the landing and a dirt parking lot. The undeveloped coastline you see on the approach previews what's in store.

WALK TO HULOPOE BAY BEACH PARK, TIDAL POOLS, SHARK COVE, 7:45 A.M. TO 9:15 A.M. The park is about .25-mile away. Go up the paved road and take your first left. A drive encircles the park's lawn and pond, and a number of tables are interspersed among ironwoods and palm trees. Hulopoe Beach Park offers great beach camping—call the Manele Bay Hotel or Maui County Parks for details.

To walk to the tide pools, go left at the beach and pick up a trail. After a few minutes, you'll see stairs leading down to a long shelf of pools that extend seaward to the point. These aquariums of nature, at low tide, will let you look in on marine life. Shark Cove is beyond the stairs and to the left, a sandy nook rimmed by 12-foot high, red cliffs. You need to use hands to climb down. The cliffs slope up as you encircle Shark Cove, rising to the 200-foot high head that separates Manele and Hulopoe bays. From the top you're above Pu'upehe Cove and Sweetheart Rock, a.k.a. Pu'upehe, the lava stack that is just offshore. Legend tells of poor Pehe, who drowned while hiding in a cave below, and was taken to the top and laid to rest by her distraught lover, Makakehau. This tale dates from around 900 AD, when the region was a Hawaiian village.

More Stuff: An old Hawaiian trail goes from below the hotel to around Kaluakoi Point, which is the western-most point of the 309-acre Manele-Hulopoe Marine Conservation District. This may be a choice for visitors who want to stay at the beach for most of the day rather than venture inland. Bring sun protection and water on this hike.

Lanai Ferry, Sweetheart Rock, Manele Bay Harbor on Lanai

SNORKEL HULOPOE BAY, 9:15 A.M. TO 10:30 A.M. The spinner dolphin often congregate a few hundred feet offshore at the end of the beach that is closest to the hotel. A stream also enters the bay here, so waters can get murky after heavy rains. The hotel has a snorkel shack at the beach. Gear is only available to hotel guests, but the attendants can give you a dolphin report. Be sure to view the dolphins passively, letting them come to you, rather than pursuing. At the other end of the beach, snorkeling is also good offshore from the tide pools, perhaps better, although the dolphins aren't as frequent. Since 1976, when the marine conservation district was established, it's been against the rules to feed the fish when snorkeling. *Note:* You may want to head up to the front of the hotel to check on the schedule for the shuttle bus before snorkeling; you can also snorkel later in the day.

VISIT MANELE BAY HOTEL. CATCH SHUTTLE BUS TO LANAI CITY, MIDMORNING. The Manele Bay Hotel, whose tiled roofs are slung low over Hulopoe Bay, manages to be grand without being ostentatious. It consistently ranks at the top of tropical travelers' best-places lists among all the world's destinations—six-foot vases, hardwood finish work, floral upholstery, museum quality painting, and chandeliers the size of playsets hanging in front of towering windows that frame the bay. If you're on the cheap, you can snag a room for less than $500 a night.

Make sure you get on the right bus; others go to the golf course and airport. The 8-mile ride to Lanai City takes about 15 minutes, climbing 1,700 feet from the bay—

Shark Cove

Hulopoe Beach Park, Manele Bay Hotel

halfway to Lanai's highest elevation—and crossing arid grasslands that evoke Nebraska. *Note*: The shuttle buses are not public transportation, although the hotels do not seem to prohibit non-guests from hitching a ride. Best not to ask. The buses leave from the front of the hotel, where valets can fill you in on the schedule. You can improve your status by patronizing the hotel's gift store, and make sure to tip the driver a few dollars when you get off in Lanai City. As an alternative, hitchhiking here is acceptable, except for the fact that traffic is virtually nonexistent.

STROLL LANAI CITY AND HOTEL LANAI AND HAVE LUNCH, NOON TO EARLY AFTERNOON. The Hotel Lanai, built during the pineapple heyday of 1923, has a mountain cabin feel, a single-story wood-frame under the shade of Norfolk pines. Rooms are not numerous, but they are comfortable in an Old West style and get snapped up by budget travelers. The hotel's rotisserie dining room draws visitors from the island's chi-chi hotels, and it's open for lunch.

Across the street is Dole Park, a several-acre lawn planted with Lanai City's trademark pines (the ones with flat boughs are Norfolks; the curly boughs belong to the less-common Cook Pine). Sanford Dole, the canned-fruit king, once owned Lanai and not coincidentally was Hawaii's first governor after the Hawaiian kingdom was annexed by the United States. The town shops, along with quiet residential area, encircle the park. The best thing is to take a spin around the perimeter, wandering to quiet back streets, which are laid out in a grid, as you may be directed by your fancy and the town's humorous signs.

You can't get more folksy than Lanai City. Look for the new Kaupe Cultural Heritage Center that is across the park to your right, on 7th street. A few doors down is Tanigawa's, the choice for island-style plate lunches. Or try the Blue Ginger Café, for its pizza and burgers, and to check out the Heart of Lanai Art Gallery that is behind the café. Across Dole Park, on 8th Street, Richards Shopping Center has been selling groceries and gifts since 1946. Another old-fashioned general store, the International Food and Clothing Center, is down 8th Street—behind the Pine Isle Market. Next door to the market is Pele's Garden, a health food store and juice bar. Schools and churches are at the opposite end of Dole Park from Hotel Lanai; you get a seaward view from behind them. Other business are tucked away on back streets. Many of Lanai City's 2,800 residents have been living in these quiet cottages for 50 years, and to talk to them is a living history lesson.

Hotel Lanai, Dole Park, Tanigawa's

CATCH BUS AT HOTEL LANAI AND VISIT THE LODGE AT KOELE, 2 P.M. TO 3:30 P.M. The lodge is about .5-mile from Hotel Lanai, walking distance if the bus schedule doesn't cooperate with yours. Head up Lanai Avenue, pass 3rd Street, and go right where it becomes Keomuku Highway. This place is hard to anticipate. Stately Norfolks lead to the entrance of the Lodge at Koele, which resides on green slopes like a colonial plantation manor, a ridge of native forest rising above it. It does not evoke Hawaii to the uninitiated, but this site was the center for the Lanai Ranch cattle operations from 1874 to 1951. Inside the elegant 102-room hotel—which is of recent construction—are two-story fireplaces, truss beams, and the feel of an English lodge.

Behind the lodge is an expansive arboretum, perhaps 40 acres, most of it a rolling lawn with large pond, several gazebos, and a glass conservatory full of blossoming orchids. Royal palms, towering kukuis, African tulips and a number of other trees and flowering shrubbery line a path that encircles the grounds. A few structures remain from the ranching days on the perimeter of the gardens, and beyond them a view sweeps toward the red-dirt, wild expanses of north Lanai. Golfing is a prime attraction here, both at the lodge and Manele Bay Hotel, which share the same owner. Each day, you'll need the better part of a grand to pay for a middle-range room and enjoy the lodge's restaurants, which are rated number one in all of Hawaii.

CATCH BUS TO MANELE BAY HOTEL FOR RETURN FERRY TO MAUI, 3:30 P.M. TO 4:30 P.M. Once back at the coast, retrace your path back to Manele Harbor. You can also navigate inland across the point between the two bays. If you have time to spare, a park on the west side of the bay provides grassy slopes to wait, and if you have energy, you can also walk out to the right of the harbor's breakwater, toward Pail Leino Haunui, and to watch for the white ship to round the point. Unless the schedule has changed, the 4:30 ferry is the next-to-last for the day, providing a margin

Hulopoe Bay

Lodge at Koele arboretum

of error in case you miss it, and timing it right for a sunset cruise into Lahaina—a wondrous sight as you approach from the sea.

More Stuff: If you're staying overnight on Lanai, and have a vehicle, you'll want to take Polihua Road north through the Garden of the Gods, red-cinder sculptures on the way to the north shore slopes. The Kanepu'u Nature Preserve is just before reaching this geologic curiosity. Another awesome drive is Keomuku Road, or Highway 430, which snakes down a gulch to the rugged beaches on the east shore. The premier hike on Lanai is the Munro Trail, which follows the 3,700-foot ridgeline from above the bays to near the Lodge at Koele. Mountain biking is a growth industry on Lanai, as four-wheel drive roads fan out on the north slopes of the island.

Manele Bay

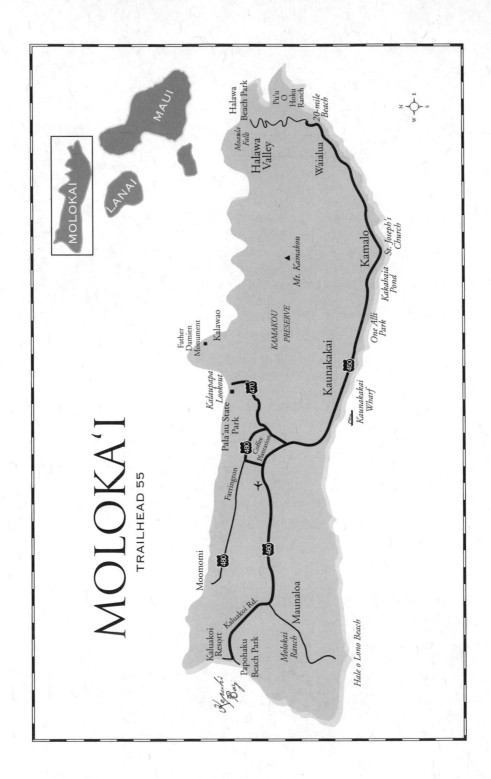

MOLOKA'I
TRAILHEAD 55

MOLOKAI

MAUI

LANAI

Moomomi

Kaluakoi
Resort

Papohaku
Beach Park

Kaluakoi Rd.

Kepuhi Bay

Molokai
Ranch

Maunaloa

Hale o Lono Beach

Farrington

480

460

Coffee
Plantation

470

480

Pala'au State
Park

Kalaupapa
Lookout

Father
Damien
Monument

Kalawao

Kalawao

KAMAKOU
PRESERVE

Mt. Kamakou

Kaunakakai

Kaunakakai
Wharf

One Ali'i
Park

450

Kakahaia
Pond

Kamalo

St. Joseph's
Church

Waialua

20-mile
Beach

Pu'u
O
Hoku
Ranch

Halawa
Beach Park

Moaula
Falls

Halawa
Valley

N E S W

Best For: To know what Maui was like in 1950, take a trip to Molokai tomorrow—quiet towns, serrated green ridges, ancient fishponds, open pastures, and expansive white sand beaches. Select from one of three driving tours, or stay overnight to do them all.

Transportation: *By Boat passage:* Charter boats visit Molokai, but your best bet is an Island Marine Ferry—usually the *Molokai Princess*—which departs Monday, Wednesday, Friday, and Saturday for day trips from Lahaina. Call for current times and ticket prices. Boat travel is recommended because you'll see the island's offshore waters and sight plenty of whales during the early spring migrations. *Note:* Island Marine also offers car rentals and guided tours, in addition to simple round-trip tickets. *By Air:* Several airlines make the short hop to Ho'olehua Airport. See *Resource Links* for all phone numbers.

Parking at Lahaina: On the south end of town, turn toward the ocean off Hwy. 30, on Shaw St., and park at the lot at the corner of Shaw and Front streets. You'll have to walk a few blocks, but this free lot has no time restrictions.

Car rental on Molokai: You'll need your own wheels or a tour taxi to see Molokai. See *Resource Links* for car rentals. If you are taking the ferry, be sure to discuss transportation to and from the airport to pick up your rental car and drop it off. See if your car can be made available at the ferry dock in Kaunakakai. The airport is a 15-minute drive from the harbor. Island Kine Rentals is located near the harbor in Kaunakakai, and they have a shuttle bus that makes the short drive to their office. Their cars may not be as spiffy, but they are convenient and this is definitely a local-style family business, operating out of a home, with a dog likely to be sleeping on the sofa while auntie is in the corner watching TV. If you use Island Kine, or any of the other rental agencies, try to get the paperwork done over the phone when you make reservations to expedite things on the day of arrival.

THREE MOLOKAI DRIVING TOURS

All three tours assume a morning ferry passage with a return trip that same afternoon, making you feel like you've watched an epic movie on fast forward. Of course, you can stay overnight which will allow time to do it all. *Notes:* All tours include a visit to the Kalaupapa Overlook of Father Damien's leper colony, and a walk through Kaunakakai Town. All tours assume a ferry departure back to Maui at 2:30 p.m. Check for most recent ferry schedule. Pack snacks and a few bottles of water before embarking on your drive. Your tour choices:

EAST MOLOKAI TOUR: Begins with mountainous side of the island that has green escarpments, ancient fishponds and heiaus, and churches. Continues to road's end at the rain forest of Halawa Valley and Moaula Falls. Ends with Kalaupapa Overlook and Kaunakakai Town.

WEST MOLOKAI TOUR: Begins with Kalaupapa Overlook, and then continues on the arid west slopes to a coffee plantation, cowboy country, and the long white-sand beaches on the far coast. Ends with Kaunakakai Town.

ALL-ISLAND TOUR: Includes all of the above, with the exception of certain portions that will be noted in the tour descriptions. Excludes Halawa Valley. This is a scouting tour for visitors who might be considering spending an entire vacation on Molokai. You might be the only people in a hurry on the island if embarking on this whirlwind.

FOR ALL TOURS: BOARD ISLAND MARINE FERRY, LAHAINA HARBOR 6:30 A.M. You'll catch sunrise in the Pailolo Channel, which can be choppy when the trade winds are up, but the ride is usually bumpier on the return voyage. The open top deck of the *Princess*, which doubles as a whale-watching dinner cruiser, allows for an experiential voyage. But up there you might be deprived of the intercom reportage by Captain Andy or one of the other skippers who proclaim, "Thar she blows!" and the like. Waters get calmer about two-thirds of the way on the 100-minute journey, when the ferry gets in the lee of Molokai.

Kaunakakai Wharf is midway on the southern coast of Molokai, which is about 38 miles long. Like Maui, Molokai is really two former islands that are joined now by an isthmus. Unlike Maui, the mountainous, green side is the higher, with Kamakou Peak

Moored at Molokai, Docking at Lahina

One Ali'i Beach Park

rising to 4,961 feet, while the red-dirt and grasslands of the west reaches an elevation of less than 1,400 feet. Fewer than 7,000 people live on Molokai, most of them in Kaunakakai.

BEGIN EAST MOLOKAI AND ALL-ISLAND TOURS, KAUNAKAKAI, 9 A.M. (FOR WEST MOLOKAI TOUR, SKIP TO "BEGIN WEST MOLOKAI PARAGRAPH BELOW.)

Head east out of town on Highway 450, the Kamehameha V Highway. A 28-mile barrier coral reef, one of the longest outside of Australia's, extends offshore along the highway. Although shallow waters limit snorkeling opportunities, the reef provided ideal conditions for a series of fishponds that were constructed by the first Polynesian voyagers. The Kalokoeli Pond is offshore the Molokai Beach Cottages before mm2. Just after mm3 are the One Ali'i Beach Parks, two of them, pleasantly decorated with coco palms and fronted by three fish ponds along a mile of coast—Ali'i, Kaoini, and Kanoa. Look for semi-circles of stone that extend into the water.

At mm5, the green relief rises inland, near Kawela. In the late 1700s, this is where Kamehameha the Great's seaborne warriors conquered Molokai on the way to his final battle for Oahu. Near mm6, look inland to the east, as Kamakou, the tallest peak in the island, comes into view. Look also on the right, amid big kiawe trees and coco palms, for Kakahaia Beach Park, which is a National Wildlife Refuge that includes fishpond ruins. Over the next several miles, the straight highway hugs the coast, passing five more ancient fishponds. *More Stuff:* To hike the 2,700-acre Kamakou Preserve, contact The Nature Conservancy of Hawaii or Molokai.

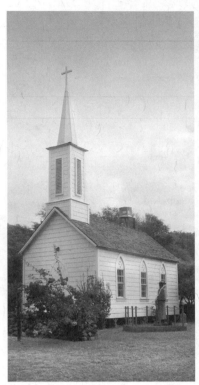

St Joseph's Church, Ualapue Fishpond, Kamakou ridges

At mm10, as you enter a reduced speed zone and the highway curves left inland, turn right at spur road to visit Kamalo Harbor—you'll see the water from the road. The old wharf here symbolizes several centuries of inter-island commerce, since this was the best natural harbor on the coast. In recent times, the barrier reef was excavated to construct the wharf at Kaunakakai. After making the turns through the Kamalo settlement, you'll come to St. Joseph's Church, which was built by Father Damien de Veuster in 1876—the Catholic priest had arrived three years earlier from Maui. A statue of the priest and a small cemetery grace the grounds.

The highway swerves inland for the next several miles, as you pass several intriguing roads that lead toward the east ridge of Kamakou. At mm14 are the portrait quality grounds of Our Lady of Seven Sorrows Church, Father Damien's first effort, dating from 1874. Across the street is Ulalpu'e Fish Pond, on the National Register of Historic Places. The next mile or two is the site of one of the larger settlements of ancient Molokai. Past the bridge at mm15, look for a sign and gate noting the Ili'iliopae Heiau, more than 30,000 square feet, that lies inland less than .5-mile on a trail that transects the island.

By mm17, as the road nears the shore, you'll see breakers that note the waning of the barrier reef. West Maui lies a few miles across the channel. Pockets of sandy beach appear past mm18, and the jagged ridges inland give way to open green slopes, with a pleasing assortment of trees. At mm20 you get to east Molokai's best beach, Murphy Beach Park, a.k.a. 20-Mile Beach, your opportunity to snorkel or take a dip. The park's fishpond and swerving strip of palmy sand are a prime beach walk, with views of Maui and the tiny seabird sanctuary island offshore to the north—Kanaha Rock and Moku Ho'oniki. Camping is available at the Waialua Pavilion, where Kamehameha V spent his formative years.

NOTE: ROAD NARROWS AFTER MM20. FOR ALL-ISLAND TOUR, TURN AROUND AND MAKE THE 40-MINUTE DRIVE BACK TO KAUNAKAKAI. TO CONTINUE ALL-ISLAND TEXT, SKIP TO "BEGIN WEST MOLOKAI TOUR" PARAGRAPH.

Windsurfing off Pauwalu, Waialua Pavilion, Malo'o

East Molokai Tour continued. Sleepy Molokai becomes more so, as Highway 450 narrows after Murphy's Beach. Some areas are definite one-laners. You'll curve inland and climb to a viewpoint at Puhakuloa Point, below which the tiers of waves attract local surfers by the six-pack. This is known locally as Tooth Rock, or Rocky Point. The highway leaves the coast, at Sandy Beach, and climbs into the grassy hills and ironwood forests near mm22.

You'll navigate the toe of east Molokai, reaching an elevation of about 600 feet through the lands of Pu'u o Hoku Ranch. You want horse pics, you got 'em. You'll pass ranch headquarters and a road on the right to Kalanikaula Sacred Kukui Grove, named for Molokai's famous kahuna. Then, near mm26, where the road hairpins left, is a fabulous overlook of Halawa Valley and Bay. Inland to the left is 500-foot Hipuapua Falls and the top part of 250-foot cascade of Moaula Falls. To the north and west is Molokai's roadless north shore, where sea cliffs reach 3,000 feet.

The parklike road then makes a symphonic descent to the Halawa Beach Park, which features two, small sandy beaches, one on either side of the stream—straight at road's end. Snorkeling, body surfing, and board surfing are possibilities. A trail leads inland to both falls, which descend from forks of the stream. This valley was one of Hawaii's earliest settlements, dating from as early as 600 AD, and many archeological sites are to be discovered. Two tidal waves in the mid-1900s did damage, to both ruins and plant life. **Turn around and drive back to Kaunakakai. See next paragraph to continue tour.**

Murphy's Beach, Halawa stream

Kalaupapa Peninsula

BEGIN WEST MOLOKAI TOUR (AND TO CONTINUE ALL-ISLAND AND EAST MOLOKAI TOUR) GO WEST FROM KAUNAKAKAI ON HIGHWAY 460, THE MAUNALOA HIGHWAY.

Just past mm1 is Kioea Beach Park, which has no beach to speak of but is notable for its Kapuaiwa Royal Coconut Grove, planted for Kamehameha V in the 1860s. It's the only accessible royal grove remaining in Hawaii. Heads up for falling coconuts if walking beneath the trees.

AFTER MM4 TURN RIGHT ON HIGHWAY 470, THE KALAE HIGHWAY. The road sweeps over the isthmus, greening up with Norfolk pines, ironwoods, and koa trees. Just before mm4, on the left by a golf course, is the Molokai Museum and Cultural Center, alongside the Meyer Sugar Mill site. Near mm5 you'll reach the north side of the island, where, just past the Molokai Stables, the Kukuiohapu'u Trail switchbacks down to the Kalaupapa Peninsula, a National Historical Park. This is the site of the leper colony overseen by Father Damien in the late 1800s. Some of the colony's residents choose to live there. *More Stuff:* The 3-mile, 1,600-foot hike down is by permit only. Put this on your lifetime to-do list, and call Damien Tours or Molokai Stables.

After the trailhead, the road enters 34-acre Pala'au State Park, passing a picnic pavilion and campground, and comes to a dead end. A short trail to the right of the parking area leads through cypress and eucalyptus about .25-mile to the Kalaupapa Lookout. The squat peninsula far below was formed by a relatively recent wave of lava that created a 2.5-mile nub pointing due north. On the tip you'll see the lighthouse, built in 1909. The Kauhako Crater near the base of the peninsula is now a lake. To look down here is to look back in time. After absorbing the view, head back to the parking lot and, if you have time, go left on another .25-mile trail that leads to Phallic Rock. Few will be able to resist the hike, although those expecting a towering monolith will be disappointed. Partially sculpted by human hands, the rock is an ancient Hawaiian fertility symbol that even today is the locale for the occasional tete-a-tete.

FOR EAST MOLOKAI TOUR, SKIP TO "RETURN TO KAUNAKAKAI" PARA-GRAPH, AND DRIVE THERE. CONTINUE WEST MOLOKAI AND ALL-ISLAND TOURS BELOW.

BACKTRACK ON HIGHWAY 470 AND, AFTER THE GOLF COURSE, TURN RIGHT ON HIGHWAY 480, WHICH IS FARRINGTON AVENUE.

Note: Both tours from here are similar, but All-Island Tour people need to manage time, bearing in mind it takes about 30 minutes to drive back to the harbor from west shore beaches. The West Molokai Tour people can take more time at each stop. At the Farrington junction are the coffee plantation groves, where Coffees of Hawaii offers complimentary pick-me-ups, as well as wagon tours. Coffee has supplanted cane as a cash crop. The Cook House, housed in an old sugar shack, is an institution.

CONTINUE ON HIGHWAY 480. PASS MM2, AND TURN LEFT AS HIGHWAY 480 BECOMES PUʻUPEʻELUA AVENUE. THEN TURN RIGHT, HEADING WEST AT HIGHWAY 460. You'll pass the small airport and head out on a red-dirt straight-away. Just before mm13, you'll be able to see Oahu to the northwest, alight on the sea.

AT MM15, TURN RIGHT ON KALUAKOI ROAD, TOWARD THE RESORT. You'll descend on a grassland road, sparsely lined with ironwoods. After 3 miles, turn right toward the Kaluakoi Villas, and follow the resort's road to its end, near the gift shop. A path leads from the modest, but tasteful condo complex to Kepuhi Beach, which has grass terraces shaded by coco palms and sandy patches interrupted by black-rock reefs— places for good snorkeling. A path leads to the right, past a lava point, to the north end of the beach that is favored by surfers. To the left, a road and path skirts a defunct golf course, past Puʻu o Kaiaka, to Papohaku Beach Park; see next paragraph for driving instructions. Coast hikers will want to make a note of this resort, as you have room to roam both north and south.

BACKTRACK FROM THE RESORT AND TURN RIGHT ON KALUAKOI ROAD. CONTINUE FOR 1 MILE AND TURN RIGHT INTO PAPOHAKU BEACH PARK. This place is a beach camper's fantasy. Large native trees and coco palms decorate its sprawling lawn, which opens up to Papohaku Beach—some 3 miles of open sand, the longest in Maui County. Snorkeling and bodysurfing features are included. *More Stuff:* The road continues for several more miles, passing a short trail to Poʻolau Beach on the

Kepuhi Beach, Papohaku Beach and Park

way. At road's end are several miles of road and trail, fronted by a half-dozen beaches, that end at Molokai's southwest tip.

FOR ALL-ISLAND TOUR, DRIVE BACK TO KAUNAKAKAI; SKIP TO "RETURN TO KAUNAKAKAI" PARAGRAPH. FOR WEST MOLOKAI TOUR, CONTINUE BELOW.

Kaunakakai

Backtrack on Kaluakoi Road—watch out for deer—and turn right at the top of the grade toward Maunaloa. West Molokai's only town, once a camp for pineapple workers, is less than two miles away. Its lazy asphalt track is stained red and lined with a few Norfolk pines and native Hawaiian trees. Horses just about outnumber people here, and the 57,000-acre Molokai Ranch offers horseback rides and a look into century-old lifestyle of the Hawaiian cowboys, the paniolos.

Wind is frequent in Maunaloa, and near the Big Wind Kite Factory, you'll often see colorful creations dancing in the sky. Although not a tropical-vacation-looking town, Maunaloa in ancient times is thought to be the birthplace of hula, the most Hawaiian of dances that enacts history and legend. *More Stuff:* The road continues down to the coast—you can see breakers from town—to Hale o Lono Harbor, which is the start of the yearly outrigger race to Maui. Other dirt roads fan out over southwest Molokai.

RETURN TO KAUNAKAKAI – ALL TOURS

Save time for a stroll around Kaunakakai. The grocery, mercantile, and gift shops along the main street, Ala Malama Avenue, are a throwback to a simpler times. These are not tourist shops. Then stroll out toward Kaunakakai Wharf. Before reaching the water, you'll pass the gardens at Malama Cultural Park. At the water is Wharf Beach, not a great swimming area, but in the afternoon you should see one of the local canoe clubs putting in.

At the end of the wharf, opposite the ferry docking area, is a cruising sailboat harbor. Take a look back at Molokai and get a mental imprint to take home with you. The memory of the place has a way of catching up to the experience a day or two, or a year or two, after your ship has returned to Lahaina.

Kaunakakai Harbor

Free Advice & Opinion

DISCLAIMER

Think of this book as you would any other piece of outdoor gear. It will help you do what you want to do, but its depends upon you to supply responsible judgment and common sense. The publisher and authors are nor responsible for injury, damage, or legal violations that may occur when someone is using this guidebook. Please contact public agencies to familiarize yourself with the most current rules and regulations. Posted signs and changes in trail status determined by public agencies supersede any recommendations in this book. Be careful, have fun.

HIKING

Never walk downhill with your hands in your pockets … A cell phone is safety insurance on remote trails … You see fewer cell phones in Maui because people here see their friends in person … Stay out of stream valleys in the rain … If stranded by a flooding stream, sit and wait it out before crossing … Don't cross if water is above your crotch … Flash-flood threat is greatest the northeast coast and Hana Highway … You often can hear a rumbling flood coming, along with the smell of fresh earth … If the stream rises a little, get to high ground … Backtrack when you get lost … Never try to walk cross-country in Hawaii … Watch your watch: Note when you leave the car, and allow time for your return before sunset, plus an hour insurance time … Ancient roads don't contour, they undulate … Always bring water … Wear bright clothes, other than green colored … Parents: never take your eyes off the kids …

Hunter's are out on weekends and holidays … All beaches are public places to the high-tide line … If you're feet are burning on the surface of hot sand, dig down a few inches … On woodland trails, don't take your eyes off the ground for more than two steps … If you hike in Maui, you will slip … Hiking poles are a third leg … Lawyers' Paradox: Paths with the least amount of danger have the most warning signs … And vice versa … In sunny conditions, try to hike before 10 a.m. and after 2 p.m. … Never climb or walk under cliffs and outcroppings; Hawaiian rocks are unstable … Going down steep hills, you want to fall on your butt, not forward … Wild pigs of 200-pounds or more have right-of-way on trails …

Do not remove or disturb rocks at a heiau or other archeological site; these places are still being discovered and preserved ... Same goes for plants; Hawaii is home to the largest reserves of endangered species ... Hike with a buddy ... Stay on trails ... If you get caught out at night, sit down and wait for morning; don't hike at night ... Always hike with a prepared knapsack; see *Calabash* ... Carry water on all hikes, and drink when you're not thirsty ... Haleakala is high; plan to be short of breath and adjust your pace for the altitude ... Bring warm clothing ... Both hypothermia and heat exhaustion are possible during the same day on Haleakala ...

Never turn your back on the ocean at tide pools and beach walks ... You need a permit to camp on beaches, or anywhere else, on Maui ... Erosion is a big problem here; don't cut switchbacks on trails ... If you must hike alone, always let someone know where you're going ... Assess how long a hike will take before you leave; see *How to Use This Book* ... Forests on Maui are too deep to walk through ... Edges of cliffs might appear solid, when they are only a mat of grasses ... In groups, don't lose sight of the person behind you ... Stay calm if lost or in trouble.

KAYAKING

Kayaking is the easiest way to snorkel the Kinau preserve ... Kayaks with no rudders or freeboards are no good in the wind ... Always call and get weather and marine reports ... Ask local outfitters for trip advice ... File this under unnecessary advice: stay at least 100 yards from a whale ... Wind shifts and sudden choppy water can mean a storm is brewing ... Keep your center of gravity low ... Lash your paddle to the boat ... Wear

a life jacket … Don't go out alone … Maintain your balance: a canoe or kayak won't tip by itself … Make your outbound voyage into the wind, to have the wind with you on the return … Sunscreen your neck … Don't trap sea turtles between boats.

SNORKELING

Rubber booties help with rocky entries … Swim fins are not made for walking forward, except by professional clowns … To enter the water, back in; or, put on your mask, dive in, and put on the flippers while you're bobbing around … Most snorkeling tours take you to places you can get to from shore … Most fish will be around the rocky points between sandy coves … Or in coral beds … Walking on coral reef crushes living things … Only monk seals are allowed to be naked on Hawaiian beaches … Lifeguards generally will place hazard signs on beaches, but don't rely on it … Wave action means more rip currents and danger from shore breaks … Stay away from wave action in rocky areas … Check depth of the water first before diving …

Don't touch a Portuguese man-of-war, a jellyfish with tentacles … MSG helps on man-of-war stings …To test for rip current, lie face-down in the water and observe if you are being carried away … If caught in a rip current, don't swim against it … Swim perpendicular to the current to break free … Lifeguards will be at most county beaches, but not at state beaches … Always swim with a buddy … Good surfing conditions are poor snorkeling conditions … Don't feed the fish; it disturbs the ecological balance of the reef … Presence of other swimmers does not mean conditions are safe … If you snorkel for extended periods, avoid a sunburn by wearing a T-shirt …

Calm water means safer swimming … But watch for boat traffic … Touching a finger to the top of your head is a diver's sign to say you're OK … Incoming waves mean water needs to go back out to sea through a channels; channels can be observed as blue underwater canals, or choppy places where the waves aren't breaking … Sticking your finger or hand in a hole in the reef is a bad idea … Shark attacks are rare, but to make them even more rare, stay out of murky waters near streams, and don't swim at dusk or before dawn … Don't touch sea turtles … Sea urchins will sting if you touch them … Watch the water for several minutes before entering to assess possible hazards … Try to enter at sandy areas … If in doubt, don't go out.

HEALTH

Haole Rot, or sun-splotched skin, is cured by Selsun Blue shampoo … Pump or treat stream water before drinking … Green coconuts are full of water; smash the stem end on a rock … Coconut water helps ailing kidneys . . . Wind evaporates sweat; don't forget to drink water when hiking in breezes … Beware of the white ooze when handling just-picked mangoes; it will burn your skin … Accidents happen; tragedies happen when you're not prepared for accidents …

Tropical sun is fierce; use waterproof sunscreen with SPF 15 or higher, containing zinc oxide and Parsol 1789 … Wear a wide-brim hat … Avoid streams and ponds when you have cuts or abrasions … Treat even small cuts with antibiotics … Leptospirosis, a bacteria in fresh water, causes flu-like symptoms … Dengue fever is, in rare cases, carried by mosquitoes; use repellant in jungle environments … Don't eat strange plants or fruits; some are poisonous … Drinking water helps prevent heat exhaustion … So does wearing loose-fitting clothes … Provide shade and elevate the feet if someone collapses … 1 to 2 liters per person per day, drink it for health and as a liquid safety precaution.

SURFING

Rules one through ten: beginners should hire an instructor ... Outfitters and instructors will happily give advice to novices ... Biggest summer surf: West shore beaches; Biggest Winter surf: east shore beaches ... Eddie would go ... Check *Best of* for beginners' beaches ... See *Resource Links* for instructors ... More waves to surf means Hawaiian surfers are less surly about wave space ... Hawaiians invented surfing; this is the place to learn ... A reasonably good athlete can stand up in one day with a long board on small waves.

DRIVING

Preventing road rage, local-style: park for a while and watch the sea ... Aloha driving: go the speed limit and don't tailgate ... Broken glass at a remote parking spot is a sign of break ins ... Save your driving tours for weekdays ... Be in Paia by dawn to avoid the Hana Highway traffic ... Or leave later, and explore the highway to Nahiku ... One rental car parked attracts others on scenic highways ... Driving in Maui traffic is okay, but getting across traffic is hard ... Always turn right ... See the *Driving Tour* at the start of each trailhead section for specifics of road conditions ...

Take valuables with you when leaving your car ... Check your insurance coverage (including that with your credit card) before leaving home ... Hang bead leis from your rearview mirror to make your car appear more local ... Vandals are only supposed to break into tourist cars ... Your rental car company may advise leaving your car unlocked ... Bring a package of baby wipes to freshen up after a hike or after eating a papaya while driving ... Four-wheel drive doesn't help with Maui's biggest hazard on remote roads: they are narrow ... Drive slowly ... Drive Aloha.

Maui Calabash

LITERALLY, A CALABASH IS A GOURD USED AS A WATER
VESSEL. IN HAWAII, THE CALABASH IS A GROUP OF
FRIENDS, LIKE FAMILY, THOUGH NOT BLOOD RELATED.

TIMELINE

1,750,000 BC: West Maui volcano breaks the surface.

900,000 BC: Haleakala sees daylight.

300: First Polynesians voyage to Hawaii from the Marquesas.

800: Second wave of Polynesian, from Tahiti; round-trip migrations.

1300: Round-trip migrations cease; Hawaiians alone in the islands.

1500-EARLY 1600s: Reign of King Pi'ilanai and his heirs. Major heiaus and the road around Maui (alaloa) constructed.

1736: End of reign of King Kekaulike.

1765: Beginning of reign of King Kahekili.

1776: Kahekili defeats invaders from Big Island at Battle of the Sand Hills.

1777: Queen Ka'ahumanu is born—Kamehameha's favorite wife, and enlightened leader.

1778: British Captain James Cook sights Maui's windward coast, but doesn't land.

1787: French Captain Jean Francois La Perouse becomes the first known Westerner to set foot on Maui, at Makena. Calls it "dismal coast."

1790: Most recent lava flow on Maui, at Cape Kinau (although new charcoal dating suggests the eruption was 300 to 500 years ago). Native population of Hawaii 300,000. Kamehameha the Great defeats Maui's King Kahekili at Iao Valley. American ship *Eleanor*, under Captain Simon Metcalf, slaughters 100 Hawaiians in Olowalu Massacre.

1802: Kamehameha I declares Lahaina capital of Hawaiian kingdom.

1810: Hawaiian Islands united under single rule of Kamehameha the Great, after Kauai capitulates without a battle.

1819: Kamehameha the Great dies. Queen Ka'ahumanu topples old religion of sacrifices and kapus. First whaling ship arrives in Lahaina from Massachusetts.

1823: First New England missionaries arrive, Reverend Richards.

1824: Queen Ka'ahumanu bases code of laws on Ten Commandments. Kamehameha II dies while visiting England.

1825: Conflicts between lawless whalers and missionaries, who have support of the queen, as well as Kamehameha's heirs to the throne.

1826: Mexican ship brings mosquitoes to Maui.

1828: First sugar mill.

1831: Lahainaluna High School, the first west of the Great Divide, is established.

1832: Queen Ka'ahumanu dies.

1835: Missionary Dwight Baldwin arrives.

1842: Some 40 whaling ships visit Lahaina.

1852: Prison erected in Lahaina.

1860: Visiting whaling ships number 325.

1870: Henry P. Baldwin and Samuel Alexander, sons of missionaries, buy their first 12 acres to plant sugar. Their heirs become major land owners.

1850: Capital of Hawaii moved from Lahaina to Honolulu.

1852: First Chinese immigrants arrive to work sugar plantations.

1870: Native population of Hawaii 56,000; mortality due to Western diseases.

1885: First Japanese immigrant workers arrive.

1893: United States Marines enter Pearl Harbor, annex Hawaii as a U.S. Territory. James Dole appointed first governor.

1901: Dole organizes Hawaiian Pineapple Company. Buys Lanai in 1922.

1916: Haleakala made part of national park system; becomes park in 1961.

1926: First Hana Highway, for vehicles, completed.

1934: Inter-island air mail begun.

1936: Pan American Airlines crosses the Pacific. Haleakala Visitors Center built.

1941: Japanese attack Pearl Harbor.

1946: Hotel Hana Maui becomes the island's first resort; tidal wave kills 12 at Hana.

1959: Hawaii becomes the 50th state.

1961: Ka'anapali becomes Hawaii's first master-planned resort.

1969: Kipahulu added to Haleakala National Park.

1970: Maui population 46,000.

1980s: Makena becomes a state park. Haleakala designated as International Biosphere Reserve.

1993: Resolution by United States Congress apologizes to Hawaiians for the overthrow of the Hawaiian Kingdom.

1990s: Wal Mart, Home Depot, Costco.

2000: Maui population 135,000.

2002: Maui Tomorrow, citizens groups, lead efforts to preserve natural resources on Maui. Hawaiian Nation, other groups, strive to restore status of Hawaiian Kingdom.

Keanae Peninsula

THE WORLD'S VACATION HOT SPOT

Only Hawaii can lay claim to being the world's vacation hot spot. Just offshore the Hawaiian Islands, under water that is two-miles deep, molten lava has been roiling up from the mantle of the earth for nearly 100-million years. Volcanic magma from this unique hot spot piles up and eventually bursts the surface, where, to make a long story short, the magic of rainwater, weather, and evolution transform the lava into tropical islands.

The hot spot has remained in the same place. Meanwhile, the earth's crust has been moving northwest, rotating over it like the shell of an egg rotating around its yolk. The rate of movement is about four inches per year. Once at the surface, the lava forms shield volcanoes that rise several miles high, which then move slowly northward on this geologic conveyor belt—only to have wind, waves, and rain slowly erode the peaks and submerge them once again into the sea.

Submerged volcanoes are called seamounts. The Emperor Seamounts that are now some 2,500 miles away off the western tip of Alaska's Aleutian Islands started out at the Hawaiian hot spot. Midway Island, about 1,300 miles distant in the middle of the Pacific, is actually the northwest terminus of the Hawaiian Archipelago, a chain of about 130 islands and sea-washed atolls that comprise the state.

The eight major islands normally associated with Hawaii are the highest mountain range in the world, if measured from their summits to the ocean floor. But they're getting shorter all the time, and they will inevitably be reclaimed by the tides. Kauai, the most-northwesterly among the major islands is several million years older than Maui and, since its birth, has moved about 300 miles and eroded some 5,000 feet in elevation. Maui's Haleakala, still an active volcano, towers 10,000 feet, but was once about 15,000 feet above sea level.

The good news is, new islands continue to emerge. Today, about 20 miles off the southeast coast of the Big Island, magma is boiling into seawater to form the volcano of Loihi, which will one day be the ninth among the primary islands. Time-shares are not yet available.

Volcanoes aren't the only forces of nature that has created Hawaiian real estate. Rising and falling sea levels, caused by waning and waxing ice ages, have created a riddle: What is now four islands, that used to be six islands, that used to be one island? Answer: Maui County. Today, the county consists of Maui, Kahoolawe, Lanai, and Molokai. Way back when, Maui was two islands, West Maui, which is about a million years older than East Maui, or Haleakala. Similarly, Molokai is comprised of two nearby volcanoes of different ages that used to be separated by water. In yet another geologic time, all these islands were combined as one—Maui-nui—when vastly larger polar ice caps resulted in a much lower sea level.

Today, with 728 square miles, Maui is second largest in the major Hawaiian chain— although the Big Island is five times larger. Maui has the most beaches and best swimming among the islands. Its sister islands, less than 10 miles away, provide always changing offshore views. The environs of East and West Maui are vastly different, making a visit like two islands in one. And Haleakala is almost like a third island—a lunar landscape high in the sky. Rain forests, deserts, waterfalls, wildlife ponds, tropical beaches—the list goes on and Maui has it all.

These tumultuous lands of Hawaii have moved about 300 feet north since the prehistoric migration of human beings arrived—the last place on earth to be settled—less than 2,000 years ago. The human race made its way across Asia, then island-hopped down through Indonesia to Fiji, New Zealand, and finally to Tahiti and the other Polynesian islands of the South Pacific. The first Hawaiian voyagers were the legendary Menehunes, the little people, who are thought to have sailed northward some 2,000 miles from the Marquesas. Petroglyphs, irrigation ditches, and fishponds supply archeological evidence to support the mythological origins of these first settlers.

Around 1000 AD, a second wave of Polynesians began to arrive on Hawaiian shores, this one primarily from Tahiti. The second wave is thought to have subjugated the Menehunes, whose numbers were relatively few. Navigating 100-foot long sailing canoes hand-hewn from logs, the Tahitians brought with them most of the plants commonly associated with Hawaii, such as coconut palms, breadfruit, bananas, taro and many others that were to form the cornerstones of their agrarian life.

For several centuries, back-and-forth migrations are thought to have taken place from Tahiti to the nine major Hawaiian Islands, two of which—Maui and Hawaii—were actively spitting lava. The history of these migrations has been preserved over the centuries through hula and chanting. The mythological exploits of gods and demigods, as told in the hula, have their origins is real acts by real people. For instance, the demigod Maui-tikitiki-a-Taranga—from whom the island derives its name—was probably an ancient explorer and warrior. Legends say he captured the sun at Haleakala thereby insuring a longer growing season for the people. This myth may have derived from the man's understanding of the solstice and its relation to crop production.

Around 1300 AD, the migrations from the South Pacific ceased. The Polynesians became Hawaiians, isolated from the rest of the world by several thousands of miles of blue Pacific in all directions—the most-isolated landmass on earth. Effectively, the Hawaiians were as independent as the people of earth are today, alone on a planet in the middle of an ocean of space. This isolation lasted for nearly 500 years, during which time Hawaiian civilization flourished. Learning to live in concert with the abundant land and sea became both religion and science.

Each village was located in an ahupua'a, a triangle-shaped parcel of land that included a seacoast and stream that extended over farmlands and had its origins in the interior woodlands. Expertise in farming, fishing, building, weaving—all crafts—was overseen by a kahuna, who passed knowledge to the next generation. All in nature was preserved and nurtured for future generations.

These several centuries were Hawaii's golden era, as each island prospered independently under ruling chiefs. On Maui during the 1500s, Chief Pi'ilani built huge heiaus and began a roadway system around the island that was furthered through the royal lineage of his sons. On all the islands the ruling chiefs, or ali'i, traced their genealogical heritage to common ancestors, and thus the bloodlines of the ancients, along with their knowledge, was handed from generation to generation.

By the time British Captain James Cook sighted *Mowee* in 1778, the Hawaiian population had grown to an estimated 300,000—and growth pains were evident. During the 100 years prior to Cook's sighting, the islands of Hawaii had been at war. The success of their way of life had brought about population increases that in turn created struggles over finite space and resources. On Maui, Chief Kekaulike and, later, Chief Kahekili, engaged in land and sea battles with the ruling chiefs of the Big Island. The Hana coast of Maui often changed hands between rulers of these two islands.

These skirmishes ended in 1790, when the Big Island's Kamehameha I, defeated the forces of Maui in the Iao Valley. After negotiating a truce with the chief of Kauai, Kamehameha the Great became the first king of Hawaii, ruler of all islands. As smart as he was big and ferocious, he used cannons from a captured American trading vessel to defeat his enemies on Maui once and for all.

Beginning in 1800, new forces converged on Maui, many of them, but not all, for the betterment of the common people. Educational and societal reforms were made by Kamehameha's heirs to the throne, and more significantly by the influence of Queen Ka'ahumanu and Queen Keopuolani. The reforms were aided by the influence of missionaries who arrived during this period, helping to develop the best school system west of the Rockies and a literacy rate superior to the average among Americans at that time.

Also arriving during the 1800s were merchant ships from all points on the compass. British and American ships called in droves, replenishing fresh water and food supplies of trading vessels bound for the Orient. Sandalwood became the island's first export, and forests were denuded. Whaling was huge well into the 1800s, with several hundred lawless vessels dropping anchor in Lahaina during the heyday.

But the real boom came with sugar, as America's sweet tooth was satisfied by Hawaiian cane. Vast tracts of land were altered to become cane fields. Some of the sons of missionary families, like Baldwin and Alexander, went on to become cane growers and rulers of state government. Since the native population decreased to some 50,000 people, due to diseases brought by Europeans, laborers flocked here from throughout the world. Maui's ethnic diversity—Filipinos, Chinese, Japanese, Portuguese, and many others— is a result of labor demands needed to satisfy the sweet tooth.

Eventually, these business interests developed to the point where the United Sates, in 1893, annexed Hawaii as an U.S. Territory. Statehood came in August of 1959. In spite of its American heritage—forever established by the events of World War II—the islands remain distinctly Polynesian.

An effort to restore Hawaiian sovereignty is alive today, and many schools and organizations foster the language, dance, and way of life that developed over the centuries when this island nation was a world apart. Similarly, efforts are underway to re-establish public access to the majority of land that is now in the hands of a half-dozen corporations—and to safeguard from development Maui's natural beauty that was preserved by the ancients, and today is the basis for the island's tourist industry.

HALEAKALA MISCELLANY

Haleakala's oldest rocks are 910,000 years old … the oldest island in the Hawaiian Archipelago, Kure Atoll, is 28-million years ago … Historical maps and interviews suggest the last eruption was in 1790; new charcoal dating by volcanologist peg the date at 1450 to 1600; whichever, current seismic rumblings say it's still an active volcano … The summit is 10,023 feet … When you make the drive up, you pass through as many biological life zones (seven) as you would on a trip from Mexico to Alaska … Haleakala used to be about 15,000 feet: erosion … Measured from the ocean floor, Haleakala is 28,000 feet …

Haleakala crater is technically not a crater, but an eroded valley, pocked with cinder cones … The "crater" is 19 square miles … The National Park is 28, 665 acres … That's about one-tenth acre per visitor, if the yearly total all came on the same day … Rainfall: Summit, 40 inches; Headquarters, 53 inches; Kipahulu, 187 inches … Maximum wind recorded: 128 m.p.h. in 1990, but the wind indicator broke … Temperatures: Average, 53 degrees, High, 80 degrees, Low, 11 degrees … To walk all the trails you need to do 27 miles.

MAUI MAN

If you thought a map of Maui looks like the head and shoulders of a man lifting out of the water, you weren't being silly. Legend says (as recounted in Inez Ashdown's Ke Alaloa O Maui*) that the Goddess Pele agrees with you.*

> "As you study the map of Maui you note that it resembles the head, neck and shoulders of a man. That is how Pele formed the brave land named for the demigod, Maui, whom she loved dearly. His head is West Maui, with Lahaina, Land-of-prophecies, as his mouth and Eke Crater as his ear. Kahakuloa, the Everlasting-master, is his forehead. Ma'alaea is his throat and Kahului is the nape of his neck. His broad shoulders are all of East Maui, with the Haleakala Crater as his heart."

WHALES, SHARKS, DOLPHINS, TURTLES AND OTHER CREATURES

WHALES

Dolphins, porpoises, and whales are all cetaceans—83 species of warm-blooded mammals ... Blue whales, at 100 feet, are the largest ... A whale's tongue can weigh as much as an elephant ... Humpbacks range from 40- to 60-feet in length, with females slightly larger, and can tip the scales at more than 80,000 pounds ... The oldest known humpback was 48 ... A swimming whale's tail goes up and down; fish tails go from side to side ... They can motor up to 20 mph, but cruise around 5 mph ... They can dive for about 15 minutes between breaths ... A month-long cruise gets humpbacks from summer feeding areas in Alaska to winter breeding areas in Hawaii and Mexico ... February and March are the best months to whale watch ...

Newborn calves weigh in at 3,000 pounds ... A whale birth has rarely been documented ... Neither has mating ... Gestation is 10 to 12 months ... Hawaiian population before commercial whaling, 1905: 15,000; by 1966: 1,000; Today, after endangered species status of 1970s: 7,000 ... Humpbacks do not have vocal cords, and how they produce their songs is unknown ... Songs are made up of phrases and last 6 to 18 minutes ... Feeding takes place in Alaska; they use reserves to migrate and do not feed in Hawaii ... They wean their calves here.

SHARKS

Hawaii has 40 species, ranging from the 8-inch pygmy to the 50-foot whale shark ... Maui has had 3 shark attacks over 12 years, including one fatality ... Cars pose a much greater risk to people than do sharks ... About eight species are seen near shore: reef blacktip, Galapagos, reef whitetip, scalloped hammerhead, blacktip, gray reef, sandbar, and tiger ... Tiger sharks are the biggest, reaching 18 feet, and the most dangerous ... Tigers range from island to island in Hawaii ... Sharks can hear and smell over a distance of 2 miles ... They can also detect prey by sensing electromagnetic fields ... Sharks only bite humans by mistake ... oops ...

To avoid sharks: Swim with a buddy ... Stay out of the water at dawn and dusk, when sharks feed near shore ... Don't bleed in the water, or enter with open cuts ... Stay out of murky water ... Don't splash around or wear shiny jewelry ... Stay away from spear fishermen ... And, as if you need this one, do not provoke or harass a shark.

SEA TURTLES

Three species are native to Hawaii: green, hawksbill, and leatherback ... Life-spans are unknown, but they start dating after age 25 ... Turtles are featured in petroglyphs and Hawaiian mythology ... Green turtles are the most common; vegetarians, weighing 200 pounds, they migrate hundreds of miles every several years to mate and nest in the French Frigate Shoals, which are in the northwestern part of the Hawaiian Archipelago ... Hawksbills are endangered, with perhaps only 50 adult females left in Hawaii; one of the few nesting grounds is Maʻalaea Bay ... Directed by starlight and moonlight, hawksbills nest on beaches; efforts are underway to modify coastal electrical lighting that has confused them, causing deaths ... Leatherbacks can be 8-feet long and weigh up to a ton; you'll find them in deep offshore waters feeding on jellyfish.

HAWAIIAN SPINNER DOLPHIN

Spinners swim close to shore during the day ... No one knows for sure why they corkscrew when leaping from the water ... They go out at night to deeper water to feed on squid and small fish ... Their diurnal migrations are opposite those of sharks, their main predator ... Life-span is around 20 years ... Gestation period is 10 to 12 months ... Calves stay with their mothers for 7 months after birth ... Mothers give birth every 2 or 3 years ... Marine debris and boats, along with shoreline development, pose the greatest threat to the spinners ... Other dolphins is Hawaiian waters include, bottlenose and spotted ... Some of the best places to see spinners are Lanai and Little Beach ... Let them come to you, and don't chase after them ... These are wild animals.

NENE

The Hawaiian goose, is the state bird ... It's the rarest goose in the world ... Do not feed them ..., Most likely sightings are at the Halemauʻu Trall and Kolua Cabin, Haleakala ... They'll come to you, don't go after them ... Observe nene crossing signs when driving; they're for real.

MONK SEALS

One of only two native Hawaiian mammals ... The other is the hoary bat; sorry people ... Only 1,300 Hawaiian monk seals remain, and they are endangered ... The Caribbean monk seal became extinct in 1952 ... Most monk seals live in the northwest Hawaiian Archipelago ... If you see a monk seal "hauled-out," it's a local; they live where they are born ... Stay at least 100 feet from a beached seal ... Old monk seals are 25 to 30 years ... Pups are about 3 feet and 30 pounds at birth ... Six weeks later, at 200 pounds, they're on their own ... Sharks are their main predators—but marine debris and habitat destruction historically has been more deadly.

CORAL

Reefs may look like rocks, but coral is actually colonies of tiny animals that are related to sea anemones ... They have cylindrical bodies called polyps that secrete stony cups of limestone around themselves ... Corals have developed over 500 million years ... Tender moment: That oily shimmer sometimes in the water is coral climaxing, as part of its reproductive process... Home for coral: between the 30th latitudes, in saltwater less than 300 feet deep ... Coral comes in many shapes, like cauliflower, lobe, rice, mushroom, and finger ... Called the rain forest of the sea, some old-growth coral is 200 years old ... Thank coral for white-sand beaches ... 80 per cent of reefs in the United States are in Hawaii ... Don't touch the living coral.

ET CETERAS

There are no native Hawaiian reptiles or amphibians ... Used to be 140 native Hawaiian birds; 70 are now extinct, 30 are endangered, and 12 are on the brink of extinction ... Hawaii's landmass is .2% of the United States' total; 75% of the country's plant and bird extinctions have occurred here ... One-quarter of the fish you see snorkeling are found only in Hawaii.

climate

Weather webcam: www.Hawaiiweathertoday.com

Weather phone: *Maui, 808-877-5111, 877-3477*
                    Lanai, 808-565-6063
                    Molokai, 808-522-2477

RAINFALL (PER YEAR)

Kaupo coast 12"
Kihei 15"
Lahaina 17"
Kahului 21"
Kula 23"
Kapalua 31"
Haleakala 57"
Hana 83"
Iao Valley/West Maui Mountains 200"
Hanawi Reserve/East Rain Forests 350"

Mauka, or mountain, showers occur any time of the year, mostly on windward slopes and valleys. In ancient Maui, several dozen different types of rain were identified. Maui's latitude is 20°50', north, which is south of the Tropic of Cancer. The climate is subtropical, with average humidity of 56 to 72 percent.

TEMPERATURES (TYPICAL, DEGREES FAHRENHEIT)

	Summer (hi/lo)	Winter (hi/lo)
Lahaina	87/77	80/70
Kahului	85/75	79/65
Kihei	89/79	82/72
Hana	84/74	78/64
Kula	82/64	66/45
Haleakala	65/45	52/29

Ocean temperature is in the mid- to high-70s—refreshing upon entry, but instantly comfortable.

WINDS

Trade winds blow from the northeast, from 7- to 28-days per month, with the highest frequency coming in June. Kihei and Ka'anapali are the most sheltered from trade winds, and their accompanying storms. The windiest spots are Ma'alaea and Kahului, where the winds are funneled across the isthmus. The Kaupo coast and Hana get direct winds, but are not subject to accelerated winds caused by the funneling effect. Wind speeds average 12 mph, lightest during the winter, but gusts of 25-to-30 mph are common. Winds on Haleakala can reach hurricane force. Kona winds come from the southwest, most often in the winter. *The Hawaiians have some 40 different names for the winds on the various parts of the island.*

SURF

During the winter, surf is largest on the eastern shores, reaching more than 20 feet near Paia. The pattern shifts during the summer, when western shores of Kihei and Lahaina get their seasonally high surf—the Kona surf. North shores and the southern coast have active coastal surf year round. Maui has more than 80 accessible beaches, with more miles of swimming beach than any other island, including the Big Island which is five-times bigger. *When Hawaiians speak of the eight seas, they are referring to the channels that separate all the islands, which all have different characteristics.*

THE GREEN FLASH

In Hawaii, conditions are optimal for observing the green—or emerald—flash, the illusive burst of color that occurs at times just as the sun settles into the horizon. Scientists say green wavelengths of color separate from orange and red wavelengths, as they are bent, prismlike, around the curvature of the earth. Has to be on a hazeless, flat horizon. Whatever, the green flash is rare and fortuitous.

WHAT TO DO IN 'BAD' WEATHER

TOO WINDY ... GO TO:
 Valley Isle, TH11-TH14; or to Sunny South, TH1-TH7.

TO RAINY ...GO TO:
 Sunny South, TH1-TH6; or Valley Isle, TH10-TH12; or Haleakala,
 TH48 through TH52. Or see *Museums and Attractions in Resource Links.*

TOO HOT ... GO TO:
 Valley Isle, TH16-TH20; Windward Coast, TH21-TH24;
 Hana Highway, TH37 to TH41; or Haleakala, TH45-TH47

TOO MUGGY ... GO TO:
 Valley Isle, TH16-TH20; or Haleakala, TH45-TH47

TAKE ADVANTAGE OF CLEAR WEATHER, GO TO:
 Valley Isle, TH15-TH20; or Windward Coast, TH22-TH25; or Hana
 Highway, TH36-TH41; or Haleakala, TH46; or Outer Islands,
 TH53-TH55

PACKLIST

Maui is a shopper's paradise. You may prefer to arrive with just the basics and leave dressed head-to-toe Hawaiian style. Shop Wailea, Kaanapali or Makawao for upscale resortwear or load the cart at WalMart, the Lahina Cannery Mall or Kaahumanu Center, where there's plenty of aloha wear and inexpensive T-shirts to bring home to friends.

ONE-WEEK VACATION

Shoes
> Slippers (a.k.a. zoris, go-aheads, thongs, slappers, flip-flops)
> Plane and hotel shoes (loafers, clean athletic shoes, or boat shoes)
> Hiking shoes (light weight hikers or cross-trainers)
> Surf shoe (optional, Teva or bootie-style)

Dress, or Khakis plus Aloha shirt for plane, hotels
Swimming suit
Two or three pair shorts
4 or 5 short sleeve tops
1 or 2 long sleeve tops (Haleakala hikers bring 2 for layering)
Gore-Tex shell, or equivalent, rain jacket
Fleece vest, lightweight (optional)
Sun hat
Sunglasses
Gloves (optional, for warmth on Haleakala, and to protect hands on lava hikes.)
Retractable hiking pole
Mask, fins, snorkel
Knapsack

> Antibiotic
> Band Aids
> Energy bars, emergency food
> Flashlight
> Handkerchief
> Mosquito repellant
> Small bottle hydrogen peroxide
> Sunscreen, lip balm
> Swiss Army knife
> Water bottles
> Water purification tablets or pump
> Whistle

FARMER'S MARKETS

Ka'ahumanu Shopping Center, Kahului
    Friday, 9:30 a.m. to 5 p.m., 877-3369
Kahului Shopping Center
    Wednesday, 7:30 a.m. to 1 p.m.,
    573-1934
Honokowai Market, Kahana
    M, W, F, 7 a.m. to 1:30 p.m.
Kihei Market
    M, W, F, 1:30 p.m. to 5 p.m.
Maui Swap Meet, Kahului, Pu'uhene Avenue
    Saturday, 7 a.m. to noon, 877-3100
Hana Farmers & Crafter's Market,
    Hasegawa Service Station
    Tu, W, Th, 10 a.m. to 4 p.m.

FREE HULA SHOWS

Whalers Village, Ka'anapali, 661-4567
    Mon., Tu, Wed., F, Sat, 7 p.m. to 8 p.m.
Lahaina Cannery Mall, 661-5304
    Sat and Sun, 1 p.m.(Keiki Hula);
    Tue and Th, 7 p.m. (Polynesian Dance)
Old Lahaina Center, 661-9913
    Tue., Fri., 11:30 a.m.
Ka'anapali Beach Hotel, 661-0011
    Nightly, 6:30 p.m. to 7:30 p.m.
Kapalua Shops, 669-3754
    Thu., 10 a.m. to 11 a.m.
Lahaina Center, 667-9216
    Wed., 2:30 p.m., Fri., 6 p.m.

LUAUS

Auntie Aloha's (breakfast), 800-993-8338,
    661-0813
Feast at Lele, 800-248-5828, 667-5353
Maui Marriott Luau, 800-745-6997, 661-5828
Old Lahaina Luau, 800-248-5828, 667-2998
Outrigger Wailea Luau, 800-367-2960, 879-1922
Royal Lahania Ka'anapali , 800-624-7771,
    667-7777

surfin' da web

INFORMATIONAL LINKS:

www.co.maui.hi.us/ (county government)
www.gohawaii.com
www.lanai.com
www.hawaii.gov
www.hawaiiweathertoday.com (live cams)
www.hookele.com (cultural)
www.infomaui.com
www.knuia900.com (radio)
www.kpoa.com (radio)
www.makena.com (golf)
www.maui.about.com
www.maui.net
www.maui.worldweb.com
www.mauiaccommodations.com
www.mauifishing.com
www.mauimapp.com
www.mauinews.com
www.molokai-hawaii.com
www.nps.gov/hale/ (Haleakala)
www.ohanapages.com
www.spotlighthawaii.com
www.tnc.org/hawaii (Nature Conservancy)
www.visitmaui.com
www.visitmolokai.com
www.windsurfari.com
www.mauigateway.com
www.surfhi.com
www.hawaiitrails.org
www.hawaiistate.hi.us/dlnr
www.hi.sierraclub.org
www.thisweek.com
www.bestplaceshawaii.com
www.hawaii-nation.org/

LINK CALABASH

www.marrymemaui
www.mauimenusonline.com
www.madeinmaui.com
www.hotelmolokai.com
www.mauinokaoi.net
www.mauihi.com
www.muleride.com (Molokai)
www.bikemaui.com
www.guidetotheguides.com
www.hawaiianair.com
www.alohaair.com
www.mauimuseum.com
www.maui.cc.com
www.lanaionline.com
www.mauikayak.com
www.hotellanai.com
www.aloha-hawaii.com
www.pacificwhale.org
www.banana.ifa.hawaii.edu
www.mauidiveshop.com
www.extremesportsmaui.com
www.actionsportsmaui.com
www.mauioceancenter.com
www.mauiprincess.com

Resource Links

PUBLIC AGENCIES

COUNTY OF MAUI

Department of Parks & Recreation
Aquatics Division, 270-6137
Beach Parks, camping, 270-7389
Recreation Program, 270-7979
Office of Economic Development, 270-7710
Reel Maui (Film Commission), 270-7415

STATE OF HAWAII

Department of Land and Natural Resources, 984-8110
Aquatic Resources Division, 243-5294
Boating and Ocean Recreation, 243-5824, 587-1882
Enforcement, 984-8110
Forestry and Wildlife Division, Kanaha Pond, 984-8100
Historic Preservation Division, 243-5169
Land Division, 984-8103
Natural Area Reserves, 873-3506
Parks, Camping, 984-8109
Na Ala Hele Trails, 873-3508 or 3509
Waianapanapa Park caretaker, 248-4843
Volunteer Services, 586-7200

UNITED STATES

Haleakala National Park, 572-4400
Kipahulu District, 248-7375
Weather, 877-5111
Kealia Pond Wildlife Refuge, 875-1582

TRANSPORTATION

See Getting Around Maui *in the front of this book for more travel information.*

AIR FROM THE MAINLAND

Aloha, 800-367-5250, 244-9071
American, 800-433-7300, 244-5522
Hawaiian, 871-6132, 800-367-5320
Delta, 800-325-1999
United, 800-241-6522

MOLOKAI AND LANAI
Commercial Flyer, 888-266-3597
Molokai Air Shuttle, 567-6847
Hawaiian Air, 567-6510
Island Air, 567-6115
Pacific Wings, 567-6814
Paragon, 800-428-1231

CAR RENTALS
Alamo, 800-327-9633, 871-6235
Avis, 800-321-3712, 871-7575
Budget, 800-527-7000, 871-8811
Dollar, 800-800-4000, 877-2731
Hertz, 800-654-3011, 877-5167
Aloha Cars-R-Us, 800-655-7989
Aloha Rent a Car, 877-452-5642
All Kine Cars, 866-986-1700
Good Kar-Ma Car Rentals, 871-2911
Kihei Rent a Car, 800-251-7257
Word of Mouth, 800-533-5929

LANAI
Dollar, 565-7227
Adventure Jeep Rentals, 565-7737

MOLOKAI
Island Kine Auto Rental, 1-866-527-7368, 553-5242
Budget, 567-6877, 871-8811
Dollar, 567-6156

BIKE RENTALS, 874-0068, 661-9005, 877-7744

FERRIES
Also ask for car rentals and tours.
Expeditions (Lanai), 800-695-2624, 661-3756
Island Marine, Princess (Molokai), 800-275-6969, 661-8397, 667-6165

WEST MAUI EXPRESS (SHOPPER SHUTTLE)
Connects all of West Maui, 877-7308

AIRPORT SHUTTLE, 875-8070, 661-6667, 800-977-2605

TAXIS, 244-7278, 874-8294, 665-0003

VISITOR INFORMATION
Also contact Public Organizations.

Maui Visitors Bureau, 800-525-6284, 244-3530
Maui Chamber of Commerce, 871-7711
County Office of Economic Development, 270-7710
Activity Owners Association of Hawaii, 800-398-9698
Destination Lanai, 800-947-4774, 565-7600
Molokai Visitors Association, 800-800-6367, 553-3876
Weather forecast, 877-5111, 877-3477
Lanai, 565-6033; Molokai, 552-2477

SUPPLEMENTAL MAPS
Free maps are widely available in shopping centers, on the plane, and from the visitors bureau. Trailblazer's maps and directions are enough for you to get around the island, but a street map and detailed, all-purpose map is a good idea.

Map of Maui, the Valley Isle, University of Hawaii Press. Full Color Topographic, 2840 Kolowalu Street, Honolulu, HI, 96822. *Best all-purpose map. Indexes place names and shows unpaved roads.*
Maui Recreation Map, Department of Land and Natural Resources, 984-8100. *Available free. Shows hunter's forest reserves, state hiking trails.*
The Ready Mapbook of Maui County, Odyssey Publishing, 888-729-1074, 935-0092. *Best street map. In book form.*
Maui County Bicycle Map, Maui Visitors Bureau, 244-3530
Maui County Shoreline Access Guide, County Parks Department, 270-7389
Map of the Neighbor Islands, Hawaii, Maui & Kauai, Compass Maps, 800-441-6277 *Fold-up street map. Needs update,includes neighbor islands.*
Nelles Maui, Molokai, Lanai;. Nellesl.verlagt-online.de *German company. Good all-purpose map, available in bookstores. Has street details.*
USGS Topos, 800-ASK-USGS.

REFERENCE BOOKS
Also contact public agencies, visitor information, and organizations. They will provide a wealth of information at no cost.

Ashdown, Inez MacPhee, *Ke Alaloa O Maui*, 1970
Bushnell, O. A., and Daws, Gavin *The Illustrated Atlas of Hawaii*, 1970
Judd, Henry P., *The Hawaiian Language*, 1982
Moon, Jan, *Living With Nature In Hawaii*, 1971
Speakman, Cummings E., Jr., *Mowee*, 1978
Sterling, Elspeth P., *Sites of Maui*, 1998
Kyselka, Will, and Lanterman, Ray, *Maui, How It Came to Be*, 1980

Area code is 808 for all numbers, unless otherwise listed.

NEWSPAPERS AND NEWSLETTERS

Maui News (daily), 800-827-0347, 244-3981
Haleakala Times, Cultural & Environmental Awareness, 572-9289
Hawaii's Humpbacks (National Marine Sanctuary), 878-2818
Ho'omalu O Ka Wa'a (Hana Cultural Center) 248-8622
Kahakai (Maui Ocean Center), 270-7000
Ka Waiola (Maui Tomorrow), 877-2462
Keepers of the Coast (Surfrider Foundation), 243-0858
Lahaina News (weekly), 667-7866
Maui Magazine, 661-1155
Maui Outdoor News, (Pacific Whale Foundation), 879-8860
Maui Scene (dining, entertainment), 242-6350
Maui Time (bi-monthly), 661-3786
Maui Weekly, 875-1700
Voice of Haleakala, 572-4400
Lanai Times, (monthly), 565-6538
The Dispatch (Molokai), 552-2781
Molokai Advertiser-News, 558-8253

MUSEUMS, ATTRACTIONS, GARDENS

Alexander & Baldwin Sugar Museum, 871-8058
Bailey House Museum, 244-3326
Baldwin Museum and Courthouse, 661-3262
Carthaginian, 661-8521
Garden of Eden, 572-9899
Hale Pa'ahao prison, 667-1985
Hana Cultural Center, 248-8622
Humpback Whale National Marine Sanctuary, 800-831-4888
Kahanu National Tropical Botanical Garden, 248-8912
Keiki Zoo Maui, 878-2189
Kula Botanical Garden, 878-1715
Ma'alaea Community Garden, 242-9671
Marriott Luau, 661-6887
Maui Nui Botanical Garden, 249-2798
Maui Ocean Center, 270-7070
Maui Swap Meet, 877-3100, 242-0240
Molokai Museum and Cultural Center, 567-6436
Na Kamali'I Te Mea O Te Atua, Keiki Hula, 242-2927
Pi'ilanihale Heiau, 248-8912
Tedeschi Winery, 878-1266
Whale Museum, 661-5992
Wo Hing Museum, 661-4020

PRESERVATION AND CULTURAL GROUPS

Call ahead of your visit to arrange to volunteer.

Association of Fishponds of Maui, 874-5718
Coastal Lands Conservation, 538-6616
Community Work Day Program, 877-2524
Fishpond Ohana Restoration, 879-7926
Friends of Kukuipuka, 242-4931
Friends of Moku'ula, 661-3659
Hawaiian Islands Humpback Whale
    National Marine Sanctuary, 800-831-4888, 879-2818
Hawaiian Nation, 242-6840
Hawaiian Natural History Association, 985-6051
Hui Noeau Visual Arts Center, 572-6560
Lahaina Restoration Foundation, 661-3262
Lahaina Town Action Committee, 667-9175
Malama Kahakai (coastal preservation), 579-9802
Maui Arts & Cultural Center, 242-2787
Maui Coastal Land Trust, 244-5263
Maui Cultural Lands, 572-8085
Maui Flower Growers Association, 800-805-2758
Maui Green Energy, 879-6024
Maui Historical Society, 244-3326
Maui Museums Association, 871-8058
Maui Tomorrow, 877-2462, 572-8331
Maui Zoological Society, 878-2189
The Nature Conservancy, 572-7849
Pacific Whale Foundation, 800-942-5311, 879-8860
Protect Kaho'olawe Ohana, 573-7819
Sierra Club, 579-9802, 573-3454; hikes, 573-4147
Surfrider Foundation, 800-743-7873, 243-0858
Lanai , The Nature Conservancy 565-7430

RECREATIONAL OUTFITTERS, TOURS

BICYCLE

For Haleakala rides, ask if starting point is at the summit or outside the national park.

Aloha Bike Tours, 800-749-1564, 249-0911
Cruiser Phil's, 893-2332
Emerald Island Bicycle Rides, 800-565-6615, 573-1278
Haleakala Bike Company, 888-922-2453, 575-9575
Hawaii Downhill, 893-2332
Maui Downhill, 800-535-2453, 871-2155
Mountain Riders Bike Tours, 800-706-7700, 242-973
Upcountry Cycles, 800-373-1678, 573-2888

HIKES

Private tour companies sometimes go on private lands that are otherwise not lawfully accessible. Ask specifically where hikes take place, and compare information to the hikes available in Maui Trailblazer.

      Sierra Club, 573-4147
      Haleakala National Park, 572-4400
      The Nature Conservancy, 572-7849
      Kapalua Nature Society (Puʻu Kukui hike), 669-0244

HORSES

      Adventures on Horseback, Makawao, 242-7445
      Ironwood Ranch, Kapalua, 669-4991
      Horse Whisperer, Makawao, 572-6211
      Makena Stables, 879-0244
      Mendes Ranch, Kahakuloa, 871-5222
      Oheo Stables, 667-2222
      Pony Express Tours, Kula, 667-2200

KAYAKS, CANOES

      Hana Maui Sea Sports (also snorkel, surf), 248-7711, 264-9566
      Keliʻi's Kayak Tours, 874-7652
      Kihei Canoe Club (visitors welcome), 879-5505
      Makena Kayak, 879-8426
      Maui Eco-Tours (also snorkel, hike), 891-2223
      Maui Ultra Dive (also surf), Kihei, 891-1442
      Ocean Activities, Wailea (also snorkel, surf), 875-1234
      Pacific Coast Kayak, 879-2391
      South Pacific Kayaks, Kihei, 800-776-2326, 875-4848

SURFING

You get a bang for your buck hiring a surfing guide.

      Big Kahuna (also kayaks, snorkel), 875-6395
      Goofy Foot, Lahaina, 244-9283, 229-6737
      Hawaiian Style Surf, Kihei, 874-0110
      Maui Waveriders, Kihei, 875-4761
      Outrageous Adventures, Lahaina, 1-877-339-1400, 669-1400
      Soul Surfing Maui, 870-7873
      Surf Dog Maui, Lahaina, 250-7873

SNORKEL AND SCUBA

Ask about boat size and cancellation policy.

Maui Dive Shop, Kihei, 879-3388, 879-1533; Kahana, 661-6166,
669-3800; Ka'anapali, 661-5117; Lahaina, 661-5388;
Ma'alaea, 244-5514; 661-5388

B&B Scuba, 875-2861

Blue Dolphin, 662-0075

Boss Frogs, Kihei (ask for other locations) 875-4477 x16

Ed Robinson's Diving (scuba), 800-635-1273, 879-3584

Ehukai Catamaran, Lanai (also whale watch), 871-0626

Extended Horizons (scuba), 667-0611

Hawaiian Rafting Adventures, 661-7333

Lahaina Divers (scuba), 800-998-3483, 667-7496

Maui Undersea Adventures, 874-2276

Mike Severns Diving (scuba), 879-6596

Seafire, Kihei, 879-2201

Snorkel Bob, 879-7449, 661-4421

Trilogy, 888-MAUI-800

WINDSURFING

Action Sports Maui, 871-5857

Hawaiian Sailboarding Techniques (HST), 871-5423

Hi-Tech Surf Sports, 871-7766

Maui Sailing Center, 870-2554

Maui Windsurf Company, 877-4696

Second Wind, 877-7467

WHALE WATCHING, CRUISES

Also see Best Of section for places to view whales from land. The ferries to Molokai and Lanai double as whale-watching excursions.

Expeditions, Lahaina, 661-3756

Maui-Lahaina Princess,
Island Marine Institute 800-275-6969, 661-8397

Pacific Whale Foundation, 800-942-5311, 879-8811

Captain Commando, 661-8299

Explorer, Lahaina, 661-5550

Gemini, Lahaina, 669-0508

Pride of Maui (also snorkel), 242-0955

Teralani, Ka'anapali, 661-0365

Ultimate Whale Watch, 667-5678

MOLOKAI

Damien Tours, Kalaupapa, 567-6171
Halawa Falls Cultural Hike, 553-4355
Kalaupapa National Historical Park, 567-6802
Molokai Mule Ride, Kalaupapa, 800-567-7550, 567-6088
The Nature Conservancy 553-5236
Molokai Ranch Hawaii, 877-726-4656, 552-2741
Pu'u O Hoku Ranch, 558-8109
Molokai Bicycle, 553-3931
Snorkeling with Bill Kapuni, 553-9867

LANAI

The Nature Conservancy, 565-7430
Adventure Lanai Ecocentre, 565-7373
Luaiwa Petroglyphs, 565-7600
Munro Trail, 565-7600

Where to stay

Calling is a good way to find out which places have aloha. Inquire about amenities and location specifics, and be sure to ask if you are getting the lowest rate. Almost all listings are oceanfront or ocean view. Prices vary by region, as noted below. Some luxury resort hotels are more than $400 per night; economy-minded travelers should be able to find a place for about $75 per night. Some condominiums have monthly rates. Camping and rustic cabins are available for much less. For island-wide bed & breakfast referrals, try Hawaii Bed & Breakfast, 800-262-9912.

(H) = Hotel, resort, (C) = Condos (B) = Bed & Breakfast, cottages, (A) = Rental agency

SUNNY SOUTH (Makena, Wailea, Kihei, North Kihei)

Best swimming beaches and sunny weather. Arid surroundings. Wailea is a high-end resort strip. Kihei has mid-range condos and resorts, most across the road from beach parks. North Kihei's beaches aren't as popular, and the area is quieter and often more economically priced.

Makena
Makena Landing (B) 879-6286
Maui Prince Hotel (H) 800-321-6248, 874-1111

Wailea
Four Seasons (H) 874-8000
Grand Wailea Resort (H) 800-888-6100
Outrigger Wailea Resort (H) 1-800-688-7444, 874-7981
Polo Beach Club, Wailea Eluua Village (C) 879-1595

Kihei
Condominium Rentals Hawaii (A)
  800-367-5242
Hale Pau Hana (C) 800-367-6036
Kihei Beach Resort (C) 800-367-6034
Kihei Maui Vacations (A) 800-541-6284
Kihei Surfside (C) 800-367-5240
Mana Kai Maui (C) 879-1561

Maui Kamaole (C) 800-367-5242,
  874-5151
Maui Parkshore (C) 879-1600
Maui Vista (H) 879-7966
Royal Mauian Resort (H) 879-1263
What a Wonderful World (B) 879-9103

NORTH KIHEI

Aston Maui Lu (H) 800-321-2558
Kauhale Makai, (C) 879-8888
Kealia Resort (H) 879-0952
Kihei Holiday (C) 879-9228

Koa Resort (C) 800-541-3060, 879-3328
Luana Kai Resort (H) 879-1268
Maui Schooner (H) 879-5247
Waipuilani (C) 879-1458

VALLEY ISLE (LAHAINA, KA'ANAPALI, KAHUNA, KAPALUA)

Excellent swimming beaches. Tropical greenery inland. Lahaina is a quaint but active tourist town, with moderate to high room rates. Ka'anapali is a high-end resort strip. Kahana has mid- to high-end condos and resorts, packed together but with back-door ocean settings. Kapalua has higher-end resorts and nice cove beaches. Weather is sunniest in Lahaina-Ka'anapali.

LAHAINA

Aloha Lani Inn (B) 572-5642
Lahaina Inn (H) 800-669-3444
Lahain Roads, Pu'upana (C) 800-669-6284
Lahaina Shores Resort (H) 800-642-6284, 661-4835
Makai Inn (B) 661-0410
Ohana Maui Islander (C) 800-462-6262
Pioneer Inn (H) 800-457-5457
Plantation Inn (H) 667-9225

KA'ANAPALI

Aston-Maui Ka'anapali Villas (C) 800-922-7866
Hyatt Regency (H) 800-233-1234, 661-1234
Ka'anapali Beach Hotel (H) 800-262-8450
Sheraton Maui (H) 800-782-9488
Westin Maui (H) 888-625-4949, 667-2525

KAHANA-KAPALUA

Hale Kai (C) 800-446-7307
Hale Napili (C) 669-6184
Honokeana (C) 800-237-4948
Kahana Sunset (C) 800-669-1488
Kahana Village (C) 800-824-3065
Mauian Hotel on Napili (H) 800-367-5034
Napili Bay (C) 888-661-7200
Napili Sunset (C) 800-447-9229
Napili Surf Beach Resort (C) 800-541-0638
Polynesian Shores (C) 800-433-6284
Ritz-Carlton (H) 800-262-8440

WINDWARD COAST (MAʻALAEA, WAILUKU, KAHULUI, PAIA)

Yes, it can be windy. Kahului and Wailuku are working towns, with some resorts on the bay; rates are low to moderate. Maʻalaea is a long beach; rates are moderate. All windward coast listings are centrally located, most convenient for trailblazers who plan to spend days exploring. Paia has mostly B&Bs in quiet settings, with moderate rates. Weather is not the sunniest, but beaches are good. Also there's quick access to the Hana Highway and Haleakala.

MAʻALAEA
Kanai A Nalu (C) 244-3911
Maʻalaea Bay Rentals (A) 800-367-6084
Maʻalaea Surf (C) 800-423-7953
Noni Lani Cottages (C) 800-733-2688

KAHULUI-WAILUKU
Banana Bungalow Hostel (B) 244-5090
Maui Seaside Hotel (H) 800-560-5552
Northshore Inn (H) 242-8999
Old Wailuku Inn (H) 244-5897

PAIA
Hoʻokipa Bayview Cottage (B) 800-258-6770
Inn at Mama's Fish House (H) 800-860-4852
Kua Cove Plantation (B) 579-8988
Maui Vacation Properties (A) 800-782-6105
Spyglass House, Beach House (B) 800-475-6695

KULA

Cool country settings are away from beaches and resorts.

Country Garden Cottage (B) 878-2858
Haikuleana (B) 575-2890
Hawaiian Islands B&B (B) 800-258-7895
Kula Lodge (H) 800-233-1535, 878-1535

Kula Lynn Farm (B) 878-6320
Malu Manu (B) 888-878-6161
Peace of Maui (B) 888-475-5045
Silver Cloud Ranch (B) 800-532-1111

HANA

A beautiful non-resort area, away from the rest of Maui. For quiet, outdoor adventures. Not as sunny. Rates range from economy to pricey.

Aloha Cottages (B) 248-8420
Ekena Bed & Breakfast (B) 248-7047
Hamoa Bay Bungalows (B) 248-7884
Hana Aliʻi Holidays (A) 800-548-0478, 248-7742
Hana Hale Malamalama (H) 248-7718
Hana Kai (C) 800-346-2772
Hana Oceanfront Cottages (C) 877-871-2055, 248-7558
Hotel Hana Maui (H) 800-321-4262, 248-8211
Kulani's Hideaway (B) 248-8234
Tradewinds Cottage (B) 248-8980
Tree Houses of Hana (B) 248-7241

LANAI

Hotel Lanai, 800-795-7211, 565-7211 (moderately priced)
Jasmine House, Dreams Come True (B) 566-6961
Lanai City House (B) 565-6071
Manele Bay Hotel, Lodge at Koele (H), 800-321-4666, 565-7300
Yellow House on the Corner (B) 565-7779

MOLOKAI

Hotel Molokai (H) 553-5347
Kahale Mala (B) 553-9001
Kaluakoi Villas (C) 800-525-1470, 800-367-5004, 552-2721
Kamalo Plantation (B) 558-8236
Molokai Friendly Isle Realty (A) 800-600-4158
Molokai Lodge (camp and lodge) 877-726-4656, 660-2710
Molkai Shores Suites (H) 800-535-0085
Pu'umana-Pauwalu Beachfront Cottages (B) 800-673-0520
Sheraton Molokai-Kaupoa Villas (H) 877-726-4656, 660-2725

CAMPING & RUSTIC CABINS

County of Maui Beach Parks, 270-7389
Beach camping won't be a wilderness experience. Kanaha is good. The county parks on Lanai and Molokai are excellent.

Molokai	**Lanai**
County of Maui, 553-3204	Hulopoe Beach Park, 565-3978
Hawaiian Homelands, 567-6104	
Molokai Ranch (private), 877-726-4656	

State Parks and Cabins, 984-8110, 984-8109; Molokai, 558-8150
Waianapanapa, Polipoli, Pala'au, Waialua
Waianapanapa has excellent beach cabins, although rustic, near Hana. Polipoli is a high-elevation cabin, forest location. Pala'au and Waialua are great places on Molokai.

Haleakala National Park, cabins, tents, and backpacking, 572-4400
Hosmer Grove and Oheo campgrounds; Holua, Kapalaoa, Paliku cabins
Hosmer is high-elevation tent camping. Oheo is excellent beachside camping. The cabins, if you can get one, are rustic but set in dramatic locations. Prepare for cold weather backpack on Haleakala.

Camp Pecusa, Olowalu (private), 661-4303; *good location, on the water, but facilities are only fair.*

YMCA Camp Keanae, 248-8355; *rustic cabins, dorms and tent sites available. Memorably beautiful ocean bluff location.*

Where to eat

Cuisine may range from burgers to gourmet, and prices from cheap to swank, but these eateries are all island-style winners. Give them a call before you go to see if they meet your tastes. Not all serve dinner.
(A special mahalo to Sue Kanegai for her tasteful tips.)

(C)   **Cheap or take-out (under $10)**
(M)   **Moderate, family ($10-$20)**
(P)   **Pricey, special occasion (over $20)**

All area codes are 808.

WAILEA-KIHEI

Annie's Deli & Catering, Kihei (C) 875-0128
Bubba's Burgers, Kihei (C) 891-2600
Da Kitchen, Kihei (C) 875-7782
Hapa's Brewhaus, Kihei (M) 879-9001
Hula Moons, Outrigger, Wailea (P) 874-7831
Joe's Bar & Grill, Wailea (M) 667-6636
Roy's Kihei (P) 891-1120
SeaWatch, Wailea (M) 875-8080
Sushi Go!, Kihei (C) 875-8744
Tommy Bahama Café, Wailea (P) 875-9983

MA'ALAEA-LAHAINA-KAPALUA

Aloha Mixed Plate, Lahaina (C) 661-3322
Blue Marlin Grill & Bar, Ma'alaea (M) 244-8844
Chez Paul, Olowalu (P) 661-3843
Down to Earth, Lahaina (C) 667-2855
Erik's Seafood Grotto, Kahana (P) 669-4806
Gerard's, Lahaina (P) 661-8939
Kimo's, Lahaina (P) 661-4811

Lahaina Coolers (M) 661-7082
Ma'alaea Waterfront (P) 244-9028
Mama'a Ribs & Rotisserie, Kahana (C) 665-6262
Plantation House, Kapalua (P) 669-6299
Roy's Kahana Bar & Grill (P) 669-6999
Sanei Seafood Restaurant, Kapalua (P) 669-6286

WAILUKU-KAHALUI

Café O Lei on Main, Wailuku (M) 244-6816
Ichiban Restaurant (C) 871-6977
Koho Grill & Bar, Kahului (M) 877-5588
Manana Garage, Kahului (M) 873-0220
Maui Bake Shop & Deli, Wailuku (C) 242-0064
Maui Mixed Plate, Kahului (C) 877-0706
Mike's Restaurant, Wailuku (C)244-7888
Saigon Café, Wailuku (M) 243-9560
Sam Sato's, Wailuku (M) 244-7124

PAIA-KULA

Anthony's Coffee, Paia (C) 800-882-6509, 579-8340
Café 808, Kula (C) 878-6874
Café O Lei, Makawao (M) 573-9065
Cakewalk Bakery, Paia (C) 579-8770
Hali'imaile General Store (P) 572-2666
Jacques, Paia (M) 579-8844
Kula Lodge (P) 878-1535
Mama's Fish House, Kuau (P) 579-8488
Maui Fresh Fruit Store,
      Hali'imaile (C) 573-5129
Paia Fish Market (M) 579-8030
Pukulani Superette (C) 572-7616
Vegan, The (C) 579-9144

ROAD TO HANA

Pauwela Café (C) 575-9242   Tutu's Snack Shop (C) 248-8224
Picnics (C) 579-8021   Hotel Hana Maui (P) 248-8211

LANAI

Blue Ginger Café (M) 565-6363
Hotel Lanai (P) 565-4700
Pele's Garden (M) 565-9629
Tanigawa's (C) 565-6537

MOLOKAI

Big Daddy's (M) 553-5841
Hotel Molokai (P) 553-5347
Kamuela's Cookhouse
      (M) 567-9655
The Neighborhood Store
      (C) 558-8498

STORES, GIFTS, ART, CRAFTS

Calasa Service, Kula, 878-1818
The Coffee Store, Kahului, 800-327-9661, 871-6860
Ed Lane, Kihei, 875-0828
Hasegawa General Store, Hana, 248-8231, 248-7079
Island Soap and Candleworks, Wailuku, 986-8383
Lahaina Arts Society, 661-0111
Lahaina Cannery Mall, 661-5304
Made in Maui Association, 871-7711
Maui Crafts Guild, Paia, 579-9697
Maui Grown Market (Rent-a-Dog), 579-9345
Maui Hands, Paia, 579-9245; Kahului, 877-0368
Ululani's By the Bay, Kahakuloa, 244-7151
Upcountry Harvest, Kula, 800-575-6470, 878-2824
Whalers Village, Ka'anapali, 661-4567

HAWAIIANOLOGISTS

Hawaiian quilts: Wailani Johanson, 661-0325
Steel guitar: Henry Allen, 669-6189
Hula: Kumu, 553-8348, Tommy and Noa Akima, 242-2927,
     Nina Maxwell, 572-8038
Leis: Gordean Bailey, 878-3828
Carving: Sam Kaai, 572-0076
Hawaiian language: Kiope Raymond, 878-3564
Lauhala weaving: Pohaku Kaho'ohanohano, 572-5626

LANAI

Heart of Lanai Gallery, 565-6678
International Food & Clothing, 565-6433
Petroglyphs of the Square, 565-6587
Richard's, 565-6047

MOLOKAI

Big Wind Kite Factory, 552-2364
Kamakana Fine Arts, 553-8520

HAWAIIAN GLOSSARY

The Hawaiian language was first written by missionaries in the 1820s, who transcribed phonetically. *Hawaiian Grammar*, which is now out of print, was published by Lorrin Andrews in 1854. Only 12 letters were needed—A, E, I, O, U, plus the consonants, H, K, L, M, N, P, and W. Note that there is no B. and S. in Hawaiian.

Hawaiian can be thought of as a dialect of the Polynesian language; others include Samoan, Tahitian, Marquesan, and Maori. The original home of the Polynesians was India, and after a long period of migrations they reached the South Pacific, as their language transformed with their travels. Today, an increasing number of schools in Hawaii are centered around teaching the language, as well as the crafts, dance, and legends. Vowels may follow each other, but consonants stand alone. A "W" is sometimes pronounced as a "V," when in the middle of a word. Words always end in a vowel. The funny apostrophe (') between some vowels is called an okina. It creates a glottal stop in the word; for instance, in "ahupua'a," the ending is pronounced "ah-ah." Among all words, stress is usually placed on the second to the last syllable, unless the word only has two syllables, in which case the last is stressed.

SELECTED WORDS

a'a – sharp, broken lava

ahupua'a – a division of land around
          which a village lived; watershed

aina – land, country

ahi - fire

akaaka – to laugh

akua – God, deity

ale – an ocean wave

ali'i – chief or chiefess descended from
          original chiefs or nobles

aloha – hello or goodbye, welcome or
          farewell, love and best wishes

aumakua – a class of ancient gods;

hale – house

haleakala – house of the sun

hana – work

haole – foreigner, sometimes Caucasian

hau – breeze, dew; a king of tree

heiau – temple, church, worship ground

hoaloha – a friend

hoku – a star

holua – a sled, or sliding place

honi – to touch, taste, kiss

honu – a turtle

ho'okipa – to entertain, to lodge

huhu – angry, offended

hui – group, meeting

hukilau – group net fishing

hula – dance that enacts the stories
          that become myths

Iao needle – Jupiter appearing as the
          moving star

ike – to see, know

iki – small, little

imu – pit or oven used for roasting

ipo – sweetheart, darling

ka'a – cart or car

ka'anapali – rolling precipice

kahului – gathering together

kahuna – teacher, expert, priest

kai – the sea

kama'aina – native born, or
          longtime resident

kamaole - childless

kanaka – the people

kane – man
kapalua – two borders
kapu – forbidden, no trespassing
kaupo – night landing
keanae – the mullet
keawakapu – the sacred harbor
keiki – child, or young banana plant
kihei – a man's garment, cloak
kipahulu – sojourn at forest fringe
kokua – help
kopaʻa – sugar
kukui – a type of tree; lamp or torch
kula – country, field
lahaina – cruel sun
lanai – deck, porch, patio
laulau – fish, pork, sweet potatoes and
          taro leaves in steamed pouch
lei – garland of flowers, vines, or beads
          worn around the neck
lolo – dumb
lomi lomi – a traditional massage
lono – report or news; one of the great
          gods
luau – feast
mahalo – thank you
mahina – lunar month
makai – toward the sea
makahiki – fall celebration of return of
peace and fertility; a year
makena - abundance
malama – solar month; light
mana – spiritual power
mauka – toward the mountain,
          inland
mauna – mountain
Mele Kalikimaka – Merry Christmas
menehune – dwarf person; legendary
          first settlers
moana – ocean
molokini – many ties
moku – island
nahiku – seven districts
nalu – surf breaking on the beach

nani – pretty, beautiful
nene – Hawaiian goose
niu - coconut
ohana – family
ohia – mountain apple
oluolu – please
olowalu – many hills
oʻne – sand
opala - rubbish
pahoehoe – smooth, undulating lava
paia - noisy
pali – cliff
paniolo – Hawaiian cowboy
pele – the goddess of volcanoes
peleleu – a large, double canoe
poi – pasty food made from taro
pono – good, blessed; in balance
          with nature
puka – a hole
puʻu – hill or cinder cone
pupu – snack or hors d'oeuvres
tutu – grandmother
ula - red
ulu – the breadfruit tree
ulupalakua – ripe breadfruit ridge
wahine – woman
waianapanapa – glistening water
wai – fresh water
waiheʻe – slippery water
wailea – water of lea, goddess of
          canoe makers
wailuku – water of breaking waves
wiki – fast, quickly

Index

Notes

END OF TRAIL

For publisher-direct savings to individuals and groups, and for book trade orders, please contact:

DIAMOND VALLEY COMPANY
89 LOWER MANZANITA DRIVE
MARKLEEVILLE, CA 96120

Phone-fax: 530-694-2740
www.trailblazertravelbooks.com
e-mail: trailblazer@gbis.com

All titles are also available through major
book distributors, stores, and websites.
Please contact the publisher
with comments and suggestions.
We value your readership.

DIAMOND VALLEY COMPANY'S TRAILBLAZER TRAVEL BOOK SERIES:

ALPINE TRAILBLAZER
Where to Hike, Ski, Bike, Paddle, Fish
in the Alpine Sierra from Tahoe to Yosemite
ISBN 0-9670072-3-2

KAUAI TRAILBLAZER
Where to Hike, Snorkel, Bike, Paddle, Surf
ISBN 0-9670072-1-6

GOLDEN GATE TRAILBLAZER
Where to Hike, Stroll, Bike, Jog, Roll
in San Francisco and Marin
ISBN 0-9670072-2-4

MAUI TRAILBLAZER
Where to Hike, Snorkel, Paddle, Surf, Drive
ISBN 0-9670072-4-0

*"Help my people.
Help them throw the
opala from the
Garden of their
Hearts and allow
only the golden
blossoms of Aloha to
thrive there. Dear
child, walk with
them in the footsteps
of the Ali'i."*
*—Queen
Liliuokalani to
historian
Inez Ashdown*